D0778849

Lost Time

A volume in the series
Critical Perspectives on Modern Culture

On Remembering
and Forgetting
in Late Modern Culture

David Gross

University of Massachusetts Press
Amherst

Copyright © 2000 by University of Massachusetts Press
All rights reserved
Printed in the United States of America
LC 00-036383
ISBN 1-55849-254-2
Designed by Milenda Nan Ok Lee
Set in Minion and Schablone Label Rough Negative by Graphic Composition, Inc.
Printed and bound by Sheridan Books, Inc.

Library of Congress Cataloging-in-Publication Data

Gross, David, 1940–
Lost time : on remembering and forgetting in late modern culture / David Gross.
p. cm.—(Critical perspectives on modern culture)
Includes bibliographical references and index.
ISBN 1-55849-254-2 (alk. paper)
1. Memory—Social aspects. 2. Memory. I. Title. II. Series.

BF378.S65 G76 2000
128′.3—dc21
00-036383

British Library Cataloguing in Publication data are available.

To Ruthanne,
for things not forgotten.

One who has perfected himself in the twin arts of remembering and forgetting is in a position to play at battledore and shuttlecock with the whole of existence.

Søren Kierkegaard, *Either/Or*

Contents

Preface xi

Introduction: The Past in the Present 1

Part 1   Individual Remembering and Forgetting

    1   Varieties of Memory 11

    2   Memory and Modernity 25

    3   The Vagaries of Forgetting 51

Part 2   Collective Remembering and Forgetting

    4   The Social Frames of Memory 77

    5   Memory in Historical Perspective 87

    6   The Shapes of the Past 116

Conclusion: Memory in Late Modernity 133

Notes 155

Bibliography 181

Index 195

Preface

All that we presently know and value was brought into being through the medium of time. But the same time that ushered everything into existence also ushers it out again.

It is perhaps regrettable but nonetheless true that each present moment and all that it contains is destined to become a moment that is past. Everything now alive and vital eventually passes into a different state where it is in danger of becoming lost to us, for when the present becomes past it all too easily slips out of reach or vanishes altogether.

To be sure, we have memory to recover (in a different form) what might otherwise be lost entirely, but is remembering really what we need to do? Once something is departing or already gone, should we not gracefully let it go? Or is it rather our task to hold on by means of memory to what is disappearing in order to make it present again?

This book arose from a slowly developing awareness on my part of how important these questions are, and how, in answering them, one quickly cuts through to essential matters. I also became interested in how varied the answers to these apparently simple questions have been throughout the ages. Depending on context and circumstance, some individuals have been strong advocates of holding on to the past, while others have been equally strong advocates of letting it go. In noting these many differences of opinion, I endeavored to pose the above questions once again but then answer them in a way that would take into consideration the needs and concerns of the contemporary era. How successful I have been in this effort must be left for the reader to judge.

I particularly want to thank Paul Breines, Will Johnston, and Michael Kammen for their careful reading of this work in manuscript form, and for their sage advice on how to improve it. I am also indebted to Joel Ray, who, with his sharp eye and exacting standards, proved to be an exceptionally astute copy editor. My family provided the moral support I needed to complete this book and for that I am especially grateful.

DAVID GROSS

Boulder, Colorado

Lost Time

INTRODUCTION

The Past in the Present

It would be hard to understate the importance placed upon memory throughout the ages. From archaic times until at least the beginning of the modern period (c. 1600), memory was thought of, almost without exception, as something positive. Forgetting, by contrast, had entirely negative connotations; to forget meant to lose or fail to retain something, resulting in an absence or an emptiness precisely where a memory should be.

Why, historically speaking, has memory been so important? When one calls to mind the many pressing needs experienced by our ancestors over centuries and millennia, the reasons are not hard to discover, for they go to the heart of what was required for individual and social existence. Simply put, remembering was important in the distant past because it made available information needed for survival. Before writing came into use as a kind of *aide-mémoire,* it was the power of individual memory more than anything else that preserved the knowledge of how to make a fire, build a hut, fashion a weapon, or kill game. One learned such information from forebears who had themselves either acquired it from others by word of mouth or picked it up by example from long-standing tribal or communal practices. It was imperative that this vital knowledge be committed to memory, from whence it could later be drawn upon and repeated in emergencies or when the group was not present to remember for the individual. If one subsequently happened to forget what it was essential to remember, death was a very real possibility. Hence, for long stretches of time in early human history, this rough equation seems to have been operative: memory equals life, forgetting equals death. Given what we know about the precariousness of existence for untold generations, this equation was not wrong.

A second reason memory was so important to our remote ancestors has to do with the values it enabled them to preserve inwardly and then call forth when needed. True, traditions and rituals played perhaps the major role in sustaining the key values of social life, but unless the import of these traditions and rituals was actually internalized—that is, unless their meanings were committed to memory and taken seriously on a personal level by each member of the community—they would not have served their deeper social or religious purposes. Through individual memory one remained aware of the moral and spiritual guidelines that were considered indispensable to the group as a whole. To forget these guidelines was the worst of transgressions, for it placed one outside everything the community held dear. One could not be in tune with the gods, with one's family (including those who were no longer living, but who were nevertheless still present in spirit), or with other members of one's group unless one remembered and acted in accordance with the cherished values of the community. It would not be too much to say that in prehistoric and early historic times, memory, especially the memory of essential admonitions, injunctions, and precepts passed down from time immemorial, was the way to truth, while forgetting was the road to untruth.

Third, memory played a crucial role in giving people a consistent sense of identity. By remembering one's own continuity in time, one achieved some degree of ontological security, some sense of who one had been in the past and still was in the present. From at least the time of the Greeks onward, memory was repeatedly praised for the way it made people aware of the temporal dimension of their existence. Despite the physical and mental changes that inevitably occur in the transition from childhood to maturity, or from maturity to old age, remembering, it was said, kept one mindful of the fact that one always remained the same person, and that the responsibilities and obligations incurred at one point in one's life also had to be honored at every other. If this were not so, one's sense of self would be diffuse and chaotic, and it would be impossible to develop anything like a consistent moral character. In fact, without memory, it was argued, one would literally *be* nothing, have no identity, possess no real personhood. Again, a simple but profound equation seemed to go unchallenged for centuries: memory equals being, forgetting equals nonbeing.

Today it is obvious that entirely different ways of thinking about remembering and forgetting have become prominent. Certainly in comparison to the distant past, memory now seems to be greatly played down, while forgetting, at least in some quarters, has been reevaluated as something positive. A case can be made, for example, that in our late modern age[1] people no longer treat memory as a reservoir of vital information for the living of their lives. More common is the assumption that in the fast-paced world of the present much or even most of the data stored in one's memory is outmoded, for the information that may have seemed useful or relevant even a decade or two ago (when it was perhaps first gathered and processed by the mind) has probably in the meantime become obsolete. Similarly, in regard to values or personal identity we are likely to hear that memory deadens rather than enriches experience, or that it leads to frozen modes of perception or habitual forms of behavior. What is needed for a full and free personality, it is often said, is not a self that can remember and repeat but one that can shuck off the past, improvise, and adapt to new situations.

But besides the relatively recent appearance of views such as these, which on the whole treat memory as burdensome or unhealthy, another notion has emerged that might be even more detrimental to the idea of memory as a value. This is the view that memory is not and cannot be as accurate as it was once assumed and thus can be relied upon neither for values, identity, nor any other aim or end in the same way that it had in the past.

Spearheading the assault on the reliability of memory have been the memory researchers, above all the many psychologists, neurobiologists, and brain physiologists who in the last half-century or more have turned their attention to issues of remembering and forgetting. In ways that are difficult if not impossible to dispute, these researchers have drawn on the methods of scientific analysis to call into question the accuracy of memory. The bulk of their work has demonstrated that when we remember something from the past, it comes forth largely constructed on the basis of present needs. Hence, when we think we have remembered a particular event from earlier in our lives, we may not be remembering it as it actually happened but recalling only a recent and highly stylized interpretation of it. Built into our remembering then, or so it is argued, is a strong component of forgetting. The prevailing opinion now seems to be that in most acts of remembering there is as much material from the present that is projected backward as there is material that comes authentically and indisputably from the past itself.

To make such claims about the fallibility or undependability of memory is to contradict three main assumptions that were prevalent from the time of the Greeks until the beginning of the modern period. The first is that the earlier experiences of our lives do as a rule get firmly registered, either as *mnemonic imprints* (of the kind that, according to Plato, signet rings make when pressed into soft wax) or as *iconic images* (of the kind produced, according to Aristotle, when we make mental copies or representations of some original event). Though the actual events of the past fade away and disappeared forever, we can still gain access to them, it was said, by means of these traces or likenesses which persist in our minds.

The second assumption is that these mnemonic traces or images somehow get stored in the mind for long periods of time, even for the rest of one's life. The storage takes place in some vast "inner receptacle," some "large and boundless chamber" of the mind (Augustine), capacious enough to preserve more or less intact countless numbers of imprints or representations until the moment they are retrieved.[2] The comparison of memory to an immense warehouse, a palace with rooms beyond number, or a well-indexed library was common throughout the centuries. These and similar metaphors suggest that memories, safely housed in an invisible mental repository, can usually be recovered with only a minimum amount of difficulty.

The third assumption is that at the instant of recall the stored memory is cued in such a way that it comes forward as something exactly, or almost exactly, identical to what it had been when it was initially deposited. The temporal distance separating the "then" of an earlier experience from the "now" of mental recovery is bridged, and what had long remained latent or unconscious becomes fully conscious again. When the past becomes present, one can be said to have completed an act of memory, or, more simply, remembered something.

Now, with the broad rethinking of the mechanics of memory that has taken place in the twentieth century, these three assumptions have largely been discredited. Today most psychologists dismiss the notion that memory operates by means of mental imprints or iconic likenesses. What is generally argued instead is that memories are registered in the first place as a result of complicated encoding processes which modify the synaptic connections or even the molecular composition of the nerve cells in the cortex of the brain. Likewise, it is now taken for granted that memories are not inertly stored like so many items in a warehouse. On the contrary, contemporary explanations assume that memories are preserved through elaborate mental mappings or schemata which evolve and change over time. These schemata rework and reprocess what the mind retains, thereby shaping memory according to shifting forms, scripts, and patterns which themselves mutate along with changing social circumstances or according to the nature of the information received. Finally, current scientific opinion maintains that there is no such thing as an exact recall of what was initially registered as a memory. Rather our memories are said to get reconfigured in the process of being preserved so that what comes forth in the end as a "memory" is to a great extent a construction— or reconstruction—of what actually happened in the past.[3] Of course, some memories can be more or less accurate, and hence dependable enough for us to accept at face value. But many memories, even though they may have the feel of authenticity, do get significantly distorted because of the particular needs, interests, or desires that happen to be present in the rememberer at the moment of recall.

Taking the foregoing into account, it is easy to conclude that since memory is more imprecise and fallible than previously thought, it is therefore no longer worthy of being considered a value as such, let alone a reliable guide to life. Furthermore, present-day wisdom seems to assume that whenever memory is too strong a force, the individual who remembers tends to become overly committed to a past that it would be better to let fade away as part of the natural course of things. To be too backward-looking today is regarded as insalubrious, and hence something to be avoided. By contrast, the idea is reinforced everywhere that one is more likely to be happy or fulfilled if one is oriented either toward the present or the future.

The same notions also apply to social or collective memory. In the last few decades, not only the historical accuracy but the ultimate worth of many of the West's most venerable memories have been called into question, particularly in light of the calamities of the twentieth century. Doubts about the accuracy of collective memories have been raised because it has now become evident how often the national, class, and religious memories of various groups have been manipulated and falsified for dubious political ends. At the same time, doubts about the worth of collective memories have also been entertained, because it has begun to seem that many such memories are little more than myths or fabrications—carefully cultivated illusions that are either too insubstantial or too dangerous to serve as the basis for communal values.

Thus today we have a perhaps unprecedented sense that both personal and collective memories lack veracity; that they are not only flawed but potentially harmful or damaging; and that, as a consequence, they no longer deserve the place of importance they have held for millennia. But rather than lament the apparent breakdown of former certainties and understandings about memory, I prefer to see the present moment as one that opens up new possibilities for thinking. Though many past notions of remembering have rightly been discredited, there is still much in them that needs to be rescued and reconsidered in our own time. And similarly, though many of the new notions gaining currency often seem convincing at first glance, they sometimes pose more problems than they solve, and hence they too need to be reassessed.

In this book I attempt the kind of rethinking of memory that appears to me to be called for as we enter the twenty-first century. As many readers will know, a spate of works on memory has appeared in the past decade, but the present book stands apart from these works because it sets out to do something different. It does not, for example, focus on the latest psychological research regarding the nature of the memory process (short-term versus long-term memory, modes of encoding, strategies of recall, and the like). Nor is it concerned with the underlying chemical or neurobiological alterations in the brain's cellular membrane that help explain why human memory is able to occur at all. Nor does it deal with the history of mnemotechniques, that is, the varying methods of memory cuing that people have devised throughout the ages to ensure that they remember what they need to know. Nor, finally, does it treat memory exclusively in relation to how or what individuals recall about specific historical events such as World War I, the Great Depression, or the Holocaust. Though several of these matters will be touched upon, it would be inaccurate to say that this book is really *about* any of them.

What it is about first and foremost is the value and meaning of memory for life. Just as Nietzsche, in an important essay written 125 years ago, inquired about the value and meaning of history for life,[4] I want to raise similar issues in our own time with respect to memory. To state my central concern as directly as possible while saving the complexities for later, I intend to address the following question in all of its ramifications: *Which is the better choice as a basic life-orientation, to remember or to forget?* (In actuality, this choice is rarely quite so stark or clear-cut, as we will see. Still, it appears that most if not all of us do in fact opt for one orientation or the other, sometimes in full awareness of what we are doing, sometimes not.) If remembering is judged to be preferable, what ought to be remembered, how intensely, and to what end? If forgetting is thought preferable, what should be forgotten, and why? In answering these pivotal questions, I will be led to raise still others, such as: How exactly should one make use of one's memories? What set of qualities is an individual likely to possess when remembering becomes a primary orientation in life, or when forgetting does? By what measure, if any, can an individual be said to be either remembering too much (even to the point of pathology) or forgetting too much (also to the point of pathology)? And to move to a somewhat different level of analysis, what are the uses to which social or collective memory can be put today, or social or collective forgetting? Finally, to what degree can we speak meaningfully of "cultures of memory" as opposed to "cultures of forgetting," and if such designations prove to be at all helpful, how ought one to characterize our own age at the onset of the twenty-first century?

Throughout this work, even when I make lengthy excursions back to earlier historical eras for purposes of comparison, my main focus will be primarily on the value of remembering and forgetting not so much for the community as for the individual. And my chief concern will not be with the individual understood abstractly, floating apart from any specific time or place, but rather with the individual as he or she exists now, in the West, in late modernity.

I have divided the book into two parts followed by a conclusion. Part I deals mainly with remembering and forgetting at the personal or private level, part II with these same topics at the social or collective level, and the conclusion brings both realms together in a general discussion of remembering and forgetting in the contemporary era. I realize of course that the personal and social spheres cannot be artificially separated in quite the way I separate them in the two main sections of the book, since each overlays and interpenetrates the other to such an extent that it is often difficult to distinguish between them. (I discuss this point at some length in chapter 4.) Nonetheless, for the sake of clarity I have thought it best, at least initially, to treat each sphere independently, beginning with what seems most immediate (personal re-membering and forgetting) and then expanding out to something much broader (collective remembering and forgetting).

PART 1

Individual Remembering and Forgetting

Varieties of Memory

I remember. I forget. We hear such statements every day, or we utter them ourselves, but what do they mean? We cannot answer this question satisfactorily just by explaining the *how* of remembering and forgetting, though this has been the approach of much recent research. For instance, one does not come closer to understanding the statement "I remember" simply by grasping the complicated mental processes of registering, retaining, and retrieving information that constitute the total act of memory. Rather, the real meaning of "I remember" is closely bound up with the *what* that is remembered; only when the content is taken into account does it begin to be clear, at least to the one who remembers, what a memory is really about.

In this chapter I want to explore the meaning of personal (but not yet social) memory by looking at a wide range of things that can be meant or implied when one says one remembers. (I discuss personal forgetting in chapter 3.) For the time being I will avoid addressing the question of the overall accuracy or inaccuracy of memory, though it should be said that I fully accept, as I think one must, that some memories are by their very nature inexact and some may even be erroneous. The issue at hand is what is actually recalled in a typical moment of recollection, for it cannot be doubted that in most memories something from the past does in fact come to mind, whether precisely and in great detail or only faintly and in rough outline. My focus as we get under way, then, is on the nature of this something that we become aware of when we remember.

Since the late nineteenth century, psychologists have sought to delineate the various kinds of memories people can have. Though terms and labels have varied, the following general types of memories have been highlighted as especially important. First, there are *semantic memories,* which make possible the recall of words or the meaning of words, as well as the associational relations that exist between one word and another. Second, there are *propositional memories,* which permit the recollection of specific kinds of information such as the terms of the Pythagorean theorem or the causes of the French

Revolution. And third, there are procedural or *implicit memories,* which enable one to remember how to repeat learned skills such as operating a computer or playing a musical instrument. Though most of what has been written about human memory has dealt with one or another of these three types of memory, none of them will receive detailed attention here, since, for reasons that will become evident later, none has a direct bearing on my primary concern, which is the meaning and value of memory for life.

Another kind of memory which has been written about at some length is *episodic memory,* or the recollection of particular events which an individual has experienced at an earlier point in his or her life. As a singular "now" that stands out from a series of "nows,"[1] each event has its own beginning and end, its own definition and character, and even, at times, its own emotional tone or aura. Every person's life is composed of an inestimable number of these discrete events, some of great personal significance, others relatively unimportant. To a considerable extent, what an individual is or becomes is directly shaped not only by the nature of these autobiographical events, but by how they are interpreted and made use of later in life. We *are* the things that happen to us, or rather we are what we make out of them. Of course, once events occur, they vanish into the past and are gone forever; they can never be exactly reprised as the events they once were, since the past does not circle back and repeat itself. Nevertheless we can still gain access to them through the medium of memory. Thanks to our recollective abilities, happenings from our past can be made present again, even if only as mental representations. No other species is able willfully and intentionally to gather up and keep alive in consciousness such a vast store of information about specific events from the immediate or distant past.

But why is this ability so important? What is it about episodic memory in particular that has led people from the Greeks onward to esteem it so highly? Three answers to this question have continually been stressed. First, events have been considered worth remembering because, when they involve us personally, they contain meanings or messages that it may be essential for us to know. If we forget them we learn nothing from our past; we become unable either to build on what was positive about it or overcome what was negative. Second, remembering earlier events has been said to be important because, when taken altogether, such events become the foundation stones of experience. The larger the number and variety of happenings we can recall, the broader becomes our general fund of knowledge, and, at least in theory, the wiser we are or ought to be. (This premise led earlier ages to regard elders as the wisest members of the community, since the range of their experiences was assumed to be more extensive than anyone else's.) And third, the recollection of events from our personal past has been valued because of the way it allows us to grasp the overall shape and direction of our lives. Memory not only makes it possible for us to revisit, even if only mentally, the things that have happened to us; it also gives us the wherewithal to put these occurrences into some kind of ordered sequence and thereby become aware of the continuities that sustain us through time. Without memory we would simply be what we are at any given moment, and consequently we would possess, in Edmund Burke's apt phrase, as little substance as "flies of a summer." With memory, however, it is a different matter, for memory not only gives us access to another temporal dimension but also provides us with some awareness of how our lives are sedimented, of how we always inherit in the present a residuum of identity from the past.

Of the several kinds of memory mentioned so far, episodic memory is what usually comes to mind when we speak of remembering. But there are other things that can be remembered besides events (or, for that matter, words, skills, or facts), and these are no less relevant for the issues that lie at the heart of this book. Curiously, the sorts of memories I am thinking of have been given little attention by psychologists or memory researchers, largely because they do not lend themselves to description or measurement in the same way that other forms of memory do. Since the pioneering work of Hermann Ebbinghaus over a century ago, most approaches to the study of memory have been based upon rigorous scientific methods. Following Ebbinghaus's example, memory testing has been systematic. Models have been created, experimental data gathered, and variables either eliminated or taken into account. In the reports that summarize research findings, conclusions have been as mathematically exact and quantifiable as possible. As a result, only those memories that are susceptible to scientific measurement and analysis have tended to be studied carefully. But there is a whole domain of memories that by their very nature cannot be approached in such a manner, and it is precisely these other kinds of memories that have the greatest bearing on the value of memory for life.

These neglected or overlooked types of memories are the subject of the rest of this chapter. Rather than merely list what they are I want to introduce them by means of examples, all of which come from within what might be called the Western tradition. Some of these examples concern actual historical figures, while others refer to fictional individuals. For our purposes here, the difference between the memories associated with real people and those of fictional characters is not important, so long as the examples help make clear just how much richness and variety there is in the broad spectrum of memories that exist beyond the kinds I have mentioned thus far.

Odysseus, in his sea journey from Troy back to Ithaca, continually remembers. But, as Homer explains in the *Odyssey,* it is not so much past events that occupy him, but rather the memory of "home" and all that home implies. And when it is not that, it is the memory of commitments made to himself and others, above all to his wife Penelope and his still unseen son Telemachus, to return no matter what to his place of origin.

Odysseus's memory of home is very concrete. It is the memory of the island of Ithaca: its landscape, the smoke that rises from the village hearths, the royal palace he has left behind, the family he misses. But this memory of place also taps something deeper. It calls to mind memories of what the place means to him; for Ithaca is not just a geographic location where he happened to have been born or where he grew up, but is also emblematic of his patrimony, his position as king, and his status in the world, all of which are essential to his identity. In a fundamental sense, in remembering Ithaca he remembers who he is. Thus when he is held more or less against his will by the enchantress Calypso on the isle of Ogygia, Homer tells us that Odysseus's "eyes [are] never dry of tears" longing for home.[2] Even when Calypso promises him a life of perpetual pleasure—and in fact immortality—if he will only stay with her, Odysseus cannot allow himself to forget Ithaca. He cannot because his social and even his human essence is bound up with that and only that place on earth. Without Ithaca he would not be Odysseus, and if he were not Odysseus he would literally be, as he later says to the giant Polyphemus, "nobody."

A second and more complicated kind of memory that grips Odysseus is of his own personal commitment to return regardless of adversity. This memory of a resolution he recalls time and again in the course of his travels, for it is clear that fate alone will not lead him back to Ithaca. To get there he must first *will* his way back, and in addition he must continually remember this resolve to return, or otherwise (as he fully realizes) he runs the risk of being lost forever in his wanderings at sea. This kind of memory—the memory of a commitment one makes to oneself—is evident, for example, when Odysseus and his men land on the island of the Lotus-Eaters. While his men eat of the lotus plant and fall under its narcotic spell, thereby completely "forget-[ting] their homeward journey,"[3] Odysseus refuses the temptation to forget. Instead, he keeps his wits about him by not succumbing to the vegetative state, which in Homer is identified with forgetting. By remembering, Odysseus is able to remain faithful to the project of return *(nostos).* This is what makes him heroic in comparison to his hapless crew. While they, perhaps like most ordinary mortals, too quickly forget and consequently have to be forcibly returned to their ships, Odysseus alone is steadfast in remembering.[4]

Sophocles' Antigone also remembers, and she pays for it with her life. As with Odysseus, it is not particular events that she recalls but something less specific and more important. In attempting to bury her brother Polynices in defiance of an explicit directive issued by Creon, the new king of Thebes, Antigone remembers a sacred duty that she believes has been decreed by both divine and human law since the beginning of time: the duty to respect the dead and properly bury them. What provokes this memory is the death of her two brothers, Eteocles and Polynices. Both had died fighting at the head of opposing armies, Eteocles perishing in defense of Thebes, his native city, and Polynices dying in an effort to seize the city for himself, with the aid of foreign troops from Argos. Into this power vacuum stepped Creon, the uncle of both, to take up the mantle of kingship. But since enemy armies were still in the vicinity, and Thebes had therefore not yet been safely delivered, Creon's position remained shaky at best. In order to assert his authority, he issued a number of commands designed to restore order, one of them being that Eteocles be buried with full military honors as a hero, while the "traitor" Polynices not be buried at all, but rather left on the field where he fell to be ravaged by dogs and carrion birds.

Everyone in Thebes accepts Creon's arbitrary dictates, but in accepting them each at the same time forgets that a higher law exists which forbids desecrating the bodies of the dead. Some forget this higher law out of eagerness for a quick return to normalcy, others out of deference to the new king who needs some leeway in establishing the rules of the polity, and others simply out of an instinct for self-preservation, since Creon has threatened to kill on the spot anyone who defies his commands.

Antigone alone remembers what all the others forget. What she remembers is an obligation that she believes has been ordained by the gods and preserved in "the great unwritten, unshakable traditions," that the dead be given suitable burial.[5] In Antigone's view, anyone desiring to live an ethical life must abide by this unwritten demand. Being moral means, for her, being faithful to just such eternally valid injunctions, not to the whims of political rulers. Moreover, by remembering and honoring what the gods require with respect to the treatment of the dead, one is also remembering and honoring another and equally important duty: to respect the holy bonds that exist within families, above all the bond of loyalty that naturally unites siblings, especially brothers and sisters. In contrast to those around her, including even her sister Ismene, Antigone's life is informed by a kind of deep remembering. The form of remembering she holds highest is not of events or factual information but of the most fundamental, chthonic obligations of which human beings can be aware, such as revering those close to one who have passed away, or remaining true to one's blood and kin no matter what the consequences. From Creon's perspective, this sort of memory is not only irrational but dangerous, for it leads to a disregard for civil authority. Antigone also seems to realize that the primordial duties she recalls and clings to are irrational from the point of view of civil society; she even appears to understand the political logic that leads Creon to impose upon her a sentence of death. Yet she cannot do other than resist what still seems arbitrary authority, for the human or familial responsibilities she remembers are, in her estimation, simply too important to abandon. In one sense at least, Antigone is the victim of her own memories. Had she been able to forget, her life would have been spared and she would have been able, like Ismene and others, to live in conformity with Creon's political order.

Aeneas, as presented in Virgil's *Aeneid*, is also a rememberer, but unlike Odysseus he has no home to which he can return. The Troy he once knew has been utterly destroyed, and everything that had given his life meaning has ceased to exist—not only his country but his parents, wife, and family. Odysseus can recall and long for a still-inhabited Ithaca, but for Aeneas there is no longer any reality corresponding to his memories, so to live merely in recollection of the past seems fruitless. But since remembering backward appears to hold no promise, what Aeneas does throughout most of the *Aeneid* is to remember forward. He remembers the destiny he believes has been charted for him by the gods, a destiny to found a new kingdom, which will be Rome. Yet for Virgil and other Romans, a destiny is not something that happens of its own accord. As Odysseus also knew, it must continually be called to mind and implemented by acts and deeds or else it will never come to pass. In other words, if one forgets the fate the gods intend, that fate will not unfold as it should, since each individual is in the end responsible for actually making happen what is supposed to happen.

When Aeneas is shipwrecked on the North African coast, and soon after meets Dido, the queen of Carthage, he almost forgets his destiny. What induces forgetfulness is *amor,* the allure of love and sexual pleasure. But before love-stricken Aeneas forgets entirely what the gods intend for him, he suddenly comes to his senses and remembers once more the things he previously thought important, the ideals that he believes must be acted upon.[6] Even more than this, he recalls his duty to achieve something momentous, namely to found a new *patria* which will be the greatest the world has ever seen. Memory, for Aeneas, means the recollection of this higher responsibility. In the arms of Dido he very nearly forgets his responsibilities, but when he at last recovers his memory he recalls once again what he is about, and it has nothing to do with living a life of enjoyment in North Africa. In that act of recollection, as Virgil saw it, Aeneas regained an awareness of his own moral worth, which would have withered had he stayed, as one side of him was inclined to do, with Dido in Carthage.

As Aeneas sails away from the Carthaginian shore, he sees behind him the smoke rising from Dido's funeral pyre and knows that her death now puts an end to any further lingering in the realm of *amor*. Dido represented happiness, but also an inglorious life of leisure *(otium)* that comes with forgetting higher things. By leaving Carthage, Aeneas relinquishes the life he might have had with Dido for something that he, and of course his creator Virgil, considered far more important: his world-historical destiny to found the future Roman state.

St. Augustine's *Confessions* is full of remembered events from his earlier life. He remembers, for example, the time when, as a schoolboy, he read the *Aeneid* and wept over the death of Dido. He remembers some of the trials and tribulations he faced as a young teacher in Thagaste and then later in Rome. And he recalls the last poignant conversation he was able to have with his mother before her death, a conversation that took place in a room in Ostia overlooking the Tiber.[7] But events such as these were not primarily what concerned Augustine. More important was remembering a "self" that he had once been but had let slip away.

When, at the age of forty-three, Augustine undertook to write about his previous life, what he found most significant about it was that he appeared to be at different times distinctly different selves. It was from the memory of these different selves (which, he knew, were really different phases of a continuous, evolving self) that he extracted a spiritual message whose elaboration became the very reason for writing the *Confessions*. What Augustine noticed in reflecting upon his life was that as a child he exhibited what might be called an indeterminate self, that is, a self that was a mixture of both good and bad qualities. On the one hand, he repeatedly disobeyed his parents, stalked and killed birds just for the pleasure of the hunt, and stole pears not in order to eat them but simply to throw them at pigs. These acts constituted what might be called his "bad" self, the one applauded by many of his peers. On the other hand, Augustine remembered that even while involved in these indiscretions he felt a sense of guilt about his behavior and longed to be more pious and virtuous. These latter qualities comprised what could be termed his "good" self, which is the one that he remembered his mother, Monica, trying so hard to nurture. Both of these selves, or partial selves, struggled with one another for dominance, but by the time Augustine reached adolescence and early adulthood, the purportedly sinful self had won out over the allegedly virtuous one.

As Augustine recalled, his so-called bad self succumbed to worldliness and a dissolute style of life filled with pride, vanity, and sensual gratification. But as this deterioration was taking place, the seemingly defeated good self never entirely disappeared. Behind his ascendant carnal self Augustine remembered the presence of a phantom spiritual self that continued to haunt the person he had become—and in haunting him this other self reminded him that a better way of being was still a possibility no matter how far he seemed to have strayed from the path of rectitude.

The happy ending that Augustine was able to report in his *Confessions* was that his mislaid virtuous self ultimately did triumph over his temporarily ascendant reprobate one. At the age of thirty-two Augustine underwent a conversion, or rather reconversion, experience, accompanied by a "vast storm . . . of tears."[8] At that specific and decisive moment in his life, the apparently lost self reemerged to displace the false, worldly one. Thus the person that Augustine ultimately became when, some eleven years later, he sat down to write his autobiography, was the outcome of that conversion experience. As a mature man and by then also a highly regarded bishop of the Church, Augustine could finally return to and bring to completion the struggling good self that he remembered being, at least potentially, in his earliest years of life: the self that his mother saw, and loved, and tried to draw out in him from the beginning, with only minimal success until the moment of his conversion.

In the *Confessions,* then, it is evident that Augustine tried to describe a kind of memory that is both unlike and more complex than any I have mentioned so far. It is the memory of an authentic self, or perhaps more accurately an authentic early facet of a single evolving self, seen through the filter of many years of inauthenticity by someone who was at last able to retrieve the initial strains of authenticity and bring them to fruition. Put differently, what Augustine believed he could remember and distinguish were three different stages in his own life history: "what I potentially was," followed by "what I became for a while," leading finally to "what I am now." Augustine was sure that, although almost no one noticed it, his potentially higher or more spiritual self remained implicitly present even during the discreditable middle period of his life, only to burst forth again at last and achieve its own substance and identity after he had returned to the faith he had known as a child.

Dante met Beatrice Portinari only three times, but he never forgot her. The first time he met her was at a social gathering when he was nine years old and she eight. He saw her from a distance several times over the next few years, but did not actually meet her again until he was eighteen. This second encounter happened on a street in Florence in the year 1283. As Beatrice passed him in the company of two older women she greeted him with "sweet salutation."

Later that same year he met her in passing one last time, but on this occasion she declined to greet him. After that, Dante saw his "beauteous lady," his "most gracious Beatrice," just twice more from afar, but he never again exchanged words with her.[9] Beatrice died six years later when Dante was twenty-four.

Despite the fleetingness of these few encounters, Dante made the memory of Beatrice central to his life. At first he remembered her mainly as a creature of flesh and blood (though in his first account of her in the *Vita Nuova* he also gave her symbolic importance). As time went on, however, Dante tended to invest Beatrice with more and more emblematic meaning, and as a result her merely personal characteristics began to fall away. Eventually Dante was really remembering not so much a particular individual as a set of qualities, especially moral perfection, natural dignity, and spiritual beauty. All three of these became important to him as ideals, and precisely because they were ideals he believed he had an obligation to try to live up to them in his moral and creative life. In one respect at least, Beatrice became (especially after her death) a recallable mental image representing notions of excellence which were no doubt present in Dante's mind even before he met her. By remembering Beatrice, then, he was able to recall the qualities or values by which he wanted to measure himself according to his highest expectations.[10] Artistically, this recollection helped provide Dante with the inspiration that led to the writing of *The Divine Comedy*. Morally, it helped keep him on the straight and narrow path and away from "evil desires," for the memory of Beatrice made him want to emulate the perfection she represented.[11] Here, certainly, is a type of memory, but it is not a type that normally comes to mind when one speaks of memory today. If anything, it is the memory of symbols— or in this instance of an individual turned into a symbol—but this sort of memory can, and in the Middle Ages did, have as much legitimacy as the more mundane memory of words, facts, or events.

On Monday evening, November 23, 1654, between 10:30 P.M. and midnight, Blaise Pascal had an experience that was qualitatively different from any other he had known. For him it was an epiphanic event, a breakthrough of the divine into the mundane, of the infinite into the finite. And because of its extraordinary nature, it was also an occurrence, Pascal believed, that carried a message that bore on the one thing that mattered most to him: the salvation of his soul.

For a period of just under an hour and a half Pascal had a vision of God as *fire*. At the same time, and as part of this revelation, he thought he had achieved a direct apprehension of the truth embodied in the figure of Christ and taught by the Gospels. So important was this illumination, and so crucial to his deepest religious convictions, that Pascal vowed never to forget it. To keep alive the memory of his mystical vision, he wrote that same evening:

> God of Abraham, God of Isaac, God of Jacob. . . . Certitude. Certitude. Certitude. Feeling. Joy. Peace. God of Jesus Christ. *Deum meum et Deum vestrum.* My God and Thy God. Your God shall be my God. Forgetfulness of the world and everything in it except God . . . Joy, joy, joy, tears of Joy.[12]

The small piece of paper on which he wrote these words he called his *mémorial.* He sewed it into the lining of his jacket, and later resewed it into every other jacket he wore. In this way his *mémorial* became a kind of memory prompter which allowed him to recall the most profound experience he had ever had or was ever likely to have. By placing his hand on it every day, Pascal was reminded of what he had been privileged to undergo for a brief but remarkable period of time in the thirty-first year of his life. This memory became his link to what he was sure was divinely revealed truth. For Pascal, to forget this truth as it was made known to him, or to fail to remain faithful to the vision he had witnessed, would not only have been an insult to the God who made the vision possible in the first place; it would also have been to put in jeopardy the future of his immortal soul.

In the year 1688, the Swiss physician Johannes Hofer published a study that analyzed a peculiar malaise he found prevalent among Swiss mercenaries fighting in the Netherlands. Most of these soldiers were suffering from what he termed *Heimweh,* meaning an intense longing for "the lost charm of [one's] native land." Being separated for months from their usual surroundings, they could not help but recall with fondness the Swiss valleys and mountain landscapes with which they had been familiar, the popular songs and village settings that had been a part of their everyday lives. These kinds of recollection, Hofer discovered, produced feelings of deep sadness, despondency, and depression in the mercenaries he queried, and this assessment led him to diagnose *Heimweh* as a disease of "homesickness." Its cause lay, he said, in the persistence of mnemonic images that cling to the "fibers of the middle brain."[13] According to Hofer, these images were usually representations of trivial, almost inconsequential things such as "small external objects" from one's homeland, "pleasant breeze[s]" from the mountains, or the "morning broth" one could remember sipping. It was not, however, the recollection of these things per se that aroused homesickness; rather homesickness was produced by the *sense of loss* that followed when one was deprived of daily contact with them. But for Hofer even this was not the whole story. In themselves the small objects, breezes, and broth which the soldiers missed did not matter as much as what they signaled in a larger sense. What they signaled was not status or patrimony as with an *aristos* like Odysseus. Instead, for Hofer's lowborn mercenaries these trifling things evoked something much simpler and yet harder to define, namely a sense of belonging, a feeling of being situated within a particular way of life, a certainty that one had some kind of rooted identity within a larger social whole. Without such feelings and certainties, Hofer implied, one would fall all too easily into a depressive or melancholic state. Noting all this, he suggested that the best remedy for *Heimweh* was not to try to forget what one yearned for, and in this way somehow accommodate oneself to absence, but rather to return to Switzerland as quickly as possible. "The patient," Hofer concluded in his treatise, "should be taken [home], however weak and feeble, without delay, whether by a traveling carriage with four wheels, or by sedan chair, or by any other means."[14]

Finally, numerous examples of neglected types of memory within the Western tradition occur in Marcel Proust's classic novel of memory, *Remembrance of Things Past.* There is the famous memory triggered by the taste of a madeleine dipped in tea; the memory evoked by a sensation of unevenness in two paving stones in the courtyard of the Guermantes' mansion; the memory sparked by the sight of a favorite childhood book, *François le Champi,* on a library shelf; and the memory of Marcel's deceased grandmother which suddenly overwhelms him as he stoops to unbutton his boots in a hotel room in Balbec. All of these are certainly memories, but memories of what? In part they are memories of earlier moments in time, some of them happy ones (*moments bienheureux*), others unhappy (*moments malheureux*). In part they are also memories of Marcel's former selves, which he mistakenly thinks he has outgrown and left behind. (As will be seen in more detail in the next chapter, Proust, unlike Augustine, believed that we have not one continuous self but many successive selves, which supersede one another over time and which can be resurrected through the operations of memory.) But most important, Marcel's memories are of previous *states of mind* which appear to have been forgotten but have only been deposited in what Proust called an "unknown region" of the psyche where they still remain available to be recalled at some later point.

In *Remembrance,* Proust was less interested in remembered facts or events than in remembered feelings, moods, and emotions. These mental states, Proust believed, survive in the unconscious like lost islands in the midst of "vast stretches of oblivion."[15] They persist in their original form and intensity "enclosed, as it were, in a thousand sealed jars, each filled with things of an absolutely different colour, odour, and temperature."[16] This being so, what a memory, particularly an involuntary memory, can recover is precisely that past state of feeling or emotion which would normally remain inaccessible to the rational mind. The taste of the madeleine brings back a feeling of "exquisite pleasure"—not a feeling that merely resembles the one Marcel had known in the past, but the very same feeling. The two uneven paving stones remind Marcel of an identical sensation he felt when he stood on the flagstones in the baptistry of St. Mark's in Venice. This single recollection in turn triggers a cluster of additional memories, including all the other sensations and emotions he felt on that particular day in Venice many years before.[17] The same is true of his other memories, such as that of his grandmother, or of *François le Champi.* In Proust's presentation, then, the interesting and important characteristic of memory is that it can retrieve past and seemingly lost moods, feelings, and sensations along with past events. In this respect, Proust helped broaden our understanding of what sorts of memories it is possible to have. Yet in the end what concerned him most of all were not the kinds of memories that simply report *that* an emotion or sensation was once experienced in the past. This, according to Proust, is one of the least valuable types of memory, because it merely turns remembered emotions into facts, or says in effect "'you were [or felt] such,' without allowing us to become [or feel] such again."[18] Rather, the memories that most interested Proust were those that could bring forth past feelings or moods in their original state, thereby permitting us to reexperience them as they actually were with their initial charge intact.

The above examples should make it clear that the range of human memory is far wider than is usually indicated by psychologists or memory researchers. Besides the memory of words, factual information, skills, or events, which perhaps by now have been studied to excess, we can also have memories of more elusive things such as ideals, goals, intentions, commitments, symbols, emotions, promises, states of mind, desires, earlier selves, and much more. Because memories like these are hard to study with control groups in experimental situations, they have not, as a rule, been given the attention they deserve. But it is just these nebulous or difficult-to-pinpoint memories that may have the greatest bearing on questions relating to the value of memory for life.

A further point needs to be made in this regard. Though certainly all people except those suffering from the most extreme forms of amnesia do remember the kinds of things I have been discussing in this chapter, some have made memory more central to their lives than have others. How does one account for this variation in the importance placed on memory? The answer may ultimately be determinable only on a case-by-case basis, but speaking generally there are likely to be both personal and social reasons for such differences.

Some individuals are by temperament or disposition more reflective than others, and hence are more inclined to look to the past rather than to the present for their basic orientation in life. On the social level too there may be built-in inducements that foster memory as a value. One may, for instance, be born into a family that happens to stress the importance of genealogical roots or the accomplishments of forebears and thereby be led to look backward for some sense of identity; or one might be socialized into a particular class outlook—for example, that of the European peasantry in the early modern period—and, by internalizing such an outlook, esteem or even cling to a thoroughly traditional mode of life. Whatever the reasons, it is evident that some people do indeed come to cherish and hold on to memory more than others. Those who in some manner or other put remembering at the center of their lives I want to call, very simply, *rememberers.* Those who see little or no value in memory, but instead point to the gains that accrue when memory is expunged, I want to call *forgetters.*

At this early point in our discussion, neither the term "rememberer" nor the term "forgetter" can have any real content; both extremes in this rudimentary typology will need to be filled out in considerable detail as we go along. For now, however, one ought not decide too quickly that either the rememberer or the forgetter is a type worthy of emulation. How one ultimately comes to think about either should be determined only after one first understands what and how a rememberer remembers, and what and how a forgetter forgets. One might, for instance, want to believe it a good thing that the rememberer's attention is directed to the past, yet this attentiveness to what is now gone could take many forms, not all of which would have salutary effects. At the most innocuous level remembering the past might amount to little more than a momentary orientation backward in time, where one is firmly anchored in the present but is nevertheless emotionally or intellectually influenced by some small aspect of what is temporally distant. At a more extreme level it could mean being dominated by the past in some respects; here one might lose one's contemporary footing, and "go over" to the past in significant ways, at least with regard to some though perhaps not all matters affecting the living of one's life.[19] And finally, at the most extreme level, remembering could mean something like an obsession with what is over and done with—an obsession that, as in the famous Ellen West case diagnosed by Ludwig Binswanger, could become so all-consuming that the past literally gains supremacy over and blots out the actuality of the present.[20] It is possible that only the first of these three modes of remembering would be considered acceptable to most people, while the third, or even the second, might be judged completely unacceptable. Thus keeping such distinctions in mind is essential for anyone trying to evaluate the rememberer or the forgetter as types.

In the next chapter I will deal mainly with the rememberer, first by locating this particular type of individual within a broad historical context and then by raising questions about the place or status of the rememberer at the present time. In chapter 3 I will turn to the forgetter.

Memory and Modernity

From the prehistoric period until at least the seventeenth century, the dominant image of the rememberer in the West had been a positive one. Despite their great differences in outlook, all the ages of the past—archaic, Greek, Roman, medieval—were rooted in custom and tradition; all greatly valued the social, political, and religious legacies of the past, to which they looked for guidance and direction. In historical settings such as these, it should be no surprise that the individual who remembered well was held up as an ideal. What made the rememberer an ideal was not just his or her ability to store and retrieve a large amount of information; that mattered to some extent, but it was not the decisive thing. Much more important was the kind of information recalled and the effect that recollection had on behavior. The true rememberers not only remembered better than others the events and experiences of their own lives but repeatedly called to mind the highest goals and values of the culture, not simply as a feat of skill, but in order to take them to heart and incorporate them into the fabric of their lives. The ideal rememberer, in other words, internalized what was recalled. Even when one's memory was extensive, it had also to be intensive. Just having the capacity to recall cognitively a large number of disparate things was not enough to make one a genuine rememberer; one also had to go beyond rote memory and imprint what was recalled into the core of one's being, thereby making it an essential part of who one was.

Those individuals through the centuries who deeply interiorized what they remembered, especially when it included the kinds of values and ideals I gave instances of in chapter 1, were what I am here calling true rememberers. Almost without exception, these individuals received high praise from the societies or cultures in which they lived, because it was assumed that an orientation toward the past was something good and healthy in itself, and therefore any conduct that flowed from such an orientation also had to be good and healthy.

What, generally speaking, were the positive attributes rememberers were said to possess?

Piety. Above all, the rememberer was said to be pious. In both the ancient and medieval worlds, piety meant dutiful respect for what had been passed down by forebears. Because it was taken for granted that values were not something one could create *ex nihilo,* but only something one could receive from others, all of premodernity felt a great sense of indebtedness to the heritage of the past. Piety was, simply put, an awareness of this indebtedness. The pious individual not only acknowledged what he inherited from ancestors, but assumed a reverential attitude toward it. The person who remembered most thoroughly and scrupulously what he had received from predecessors—and even more, performed the obligations that went along with such memories as a matter of course—was thought to be the most pious. For the Romans, *pietas* was the preeminent quality an individual could possess, the highest virtue in the pantheon of virtues. But *pietas* was unthinkable without *memoria.* As important as reverence, veneration, and deep respect for the past were, they were no more than abstractions unless they became integral aspects of one's self, and for this integration to happen there had first to be a memory of what was worth revering or venerating. The same intimate link between piety and memory persisted into the Middle Ages. The pious Christian had not only a duty to recall with devotion the religious and spiritual legacies from the past, but the obligation, as Hegel later put it, to "keep faith with the dead." Here piety meant remembering and honoring deceased relatives or benefactors through prayers, votive offerings, necrologies, commemorative Masses, names inserted in liturgies, and the like. For medieval Christians, the dead were not necessarily to be thought of as gone or departed. They could, in a manner of speaking, be kept alive through the memory of devout believers, in which case they continued to live on as bona fide members of the community long after they had ceased to exist as corporeal entities.[1]

Ethics. Ethical behavior was understood as strict adherence to prescribed social and religious standards of conduct. As with values in general, fixed ethical or moral standards were presumed to have been established at some (often mythical) point in the distant past; they came from a god or gods, founders, lawgivers, prophets, or holy men who made it clear what was expected in terms of the rights or wrongs of conduct. The task of the moral individual was not to question the validity of what had been passed down but rather to internalize the commands and injunctions of the culture, and then, once they had become components of the self, to act on them as inner imperatives. The person who not only remembered more conscientiously than others the social or religious "oughts" and "ought nots" but also acted in accordance with them was deemed to be the highest type of ethical individual, and therefore a model for others to follow.

In this respect, memory was as essential an ingredient in ethics as it was in piety. One sees evidence that this was a widely accepted view from the ancient period onward, though the theologians of the Middle Ages may have gone somewhat further than their Greek or Roman predecessors in tying memory to ethics. As Aquinas saw it, for example, ethical behavior was possible at all only because human beings possess the unique quality of *prudentia,* that is, "the capacity to make moral judgments."[2] Only where there are moral judgments, he argued, could there be right as opposed to wrong choices, and only where there are right choices can there be ethical conduct. In Aquinas's words, "[Prudence is] a virtue of the utmost necessity for human life. To live well means acting well. In order to perform an act well, it is not merely what a man does that matters, but also how he does it, namely that he acts from right choice. . . . Consequently, an intellectual virtue is needed [and that] virtue is prudence. . . . Prudence is necessary [for ethical behavior] not merely [so] that a man may become good, but so that he may lead a good life."[3] Yet as Aquinas and others insisted, without a strong memory prudence would be impossible. In order for *prudentia* to enable the performance of the tasks God intended, there must first be an accumulation of stored knowledge and experience with which to work. Only where there is a "well-furnished memory"— and for medieval thinkers the greater and more disciplined the memory the better—can there be sufficient information to deliberate over in coming to some moral decision. By contrast, the person whose memory is weak or undeveloped would have a difficult time being ethical at all, since he or she would have nothing substantive to reflect upon in trying to arrive at a moral judgment. In premodern times, then, it was generally taken for granted that those individuals who had the best mental "habit[s] of retention," who were most adept at tapping the information they had accumulated, and who knew how to make their memories "integral and enabling" would manifest the highest moral and ethical qualities of the culture.[4]

Character. A person of character forged a fixed identity based on probity and rectitude, and then remained loyal to it throughout his or her life. But since it was commonly understood that character was built upon good habits, that is, on remembering and repeating traits acquired since childhood, it was also supposed that those most proficient at turning the ideals they had learned into forms of behavior would also be the ones most likely to possess character.

In the classical and medieval past, character was not viewed as the spontaneous expression of personality, as many nineteenth-century Romantics came to believe. Instead it was something that had to be achieved as a result of long years of rigorous self-formation. Once one had developed character, the task was then to remain steadfast and never deviate from the self one had become. The best way to ensure this kind of constancy, or so it was thought, was to develop a dependable and predictable set of "right habits." Habits were seen as contributing to the natural perfection of the self, for they permitted the values one had acquired to become embodied in behavior. In this sense, habitude was the key element that defined a "person of character." Only with good and regular habits could one be guaranteed that one's character is not merely something to be exhibited now and then or when it is convenient (which would not be character at all), but rather something to be maintained and manifested in a steady and determined way over the course of a lifetime. And if character was founded on habit, habit was in turn founded on memory, since at bottom habit was said to be nothing more than congealed memory, that is, memory exercised over and over again until it had become second nature. Thinkers from Aristotle to Aquinas and beyond had continually made this point.[5] They were certain that there were natural links fusing each of the three elements I have been discussing: memory, habit, and character. And since, for philosophers and theologians alike, there was never any doubt that character is a value, there was also no doubt that memory and habit are values as well, for without their informing presence character itself was considered impossible to attain.

Spirituality. The connection between memory and spirituality may not seem evident to most people today, but it was rarely questioned in the ancient or medieval eras. In those times it was assumed that remembering was not something that happened accidentally; rather it was thought to require a great deal of disciplined effort. Discipline, however, implied rigor and singlemindedness, both of which were seen as qualities constitutive of spirituality; only if an individual possessed a high degree of will and focus could he raise himself out of the physical and into a spiritual realm of existence. A propensity to forget, on the other hand, all but erased one's chances of becoming a spiritual person. For centuries in Western history forgetting was associated with laziness, softness, and laxity, and these attributes were said to lead to a low or merely pleasure-seeking mode of life the Greeks called *hédonè*.[6]

Though the presumed connection between memory and spirituality probably extends back to a time before recorded history, some early indications of this linkage are clearly evident in ancient Greece. Pythagoras, for instance, instructed his disciples to practice demanding memory exercises in order to deepen their "quality of soul." For him, memory was a means of "purification which transfigures the individual and promotes him to the ranks of the gods."[7] The same notion was just as central to Plato; in fact, Plato's entire theory of recollection (*anamnesis*) was premised on the supposition that memory is a *via regia* leading to the highest spiritual truths a human being could know. According to Plato, those who could recall through the "eye of the soul" the knowledge of the "holy visions" they had experienced before birth would be able to reclaim what was divine in their natures. By contrast, those who could not recollect what they had known prior to drinking of the waters of Lēthē (forgetfulness) in the course of wending their way toward a merely earthly existence were condemned to live out their lives in the shadowy world of the mundane. Christianity also joined together memory and spirituality. In Christian hagiography there are numerous examples of holy men and women whose spiritual qualities were directly related to their exceptional recollective capacities. St. Francis, for one, was reputedly able to recall virtually everything he had learned or experienced since early childhood. St. Aquinas's memory was allegedly so prodigious that no detail of what he saw or read ever escaped him ("He never forgot," wrote his contemporary Bernardo Gui).[8] St. Anthony was said to have learned by heart the entire Bible simply by hearing it read aloud. Apocryphal or not, such feats of recollection were thought to be manifestations of an especially "soulful" disposition. The spiritual individual, above all the saint, not only remembered Scripture well but recalled and took seriously exactly those things that ordinary people were inclined to forget as unimportant, namely *Idealfaktoren* ("symbolic formations," or things religiously important but temporally remote) as opposed to merely practical and immediate *Realfaktoren.* And of course for a person in the Middle Ages in quest of spiritual perfection, there was something even more important that needed to be remembered and imitated, and that was the model of spiritual excellence represented by Christ, and after him by the many saints and martyrs who lived in "imitation of Christ."[9]

Creativity. In premodern times, as opposed to the present, creativity was not associated with the idea of producing something absolutely new. Rather, the creative person was one who first of all accepted and then built upon, extended, or reworked—with variations of his own, to be sure—the great intellectual and cultural achievements of the past. A superior memory was therefore assumed to be an indispensable ingredient for any kind of creative activity. This assumption made sense not only because it seemed clear that the more information an individual possessed, the more he or she had to draw on in the act of creation, but also because the more knowledge one retained, the more complex, differentiated, and inwardly rich a person's mind or intellect would necessarily have to be.[10] Generally speaking, it was thought that two different types of things needed to be remembered if one was to be creatively productive: first, the various perceptions, impressions, feelings, and associations gathered from one's own earlier life experiences, and second, the ideas and forms developed by predecessors and passed down as an essential part of the cultural heritage. The latter, especially, were seen as important sources of inspiration. If one had no effective memory of the intellectual legacies of the past, there would be nothing to create from, no material for the imagination to work with. It was no accident, then, that for the Greeks the mother of the Muses was Mnemosyne, the goddess of memory. Without the benefit of memory as a starting point—and for the Greeks and others after them Mnemosyne meant not just "recollection" loosely understood, but also and more strongly "memorization"[11]—any notable accomplishment in poetry, painting, music, or the other arts would have been impossible to achieve.

Thus the characterization of memory in premodernity was almost always positive while that of forgetting was almost always negative. But from roughly the seventeenth century on, and especially since the late nineteenth century, this favorable view of memory has undergone a fundamental revaluation. In some instances, qualities once closely linked to memory simply lost their status as values. Piety, for example, gradually ceased being considered a personal attribute worth striving for. New virtues such as self-assertion or self-determination began to usurp the place once held by *pietas* in the hierarchy of values, and as they did so, the standing of memory noticeably declined. In other instances, qualities such as creativity were maintained or even accentuated as values, but only after the centuries-old connection between memory and creativity had been severed. As we know, it is still considered highly desirable to be a creative person; but now the key ingredient producing creativity is said to be not memory but insight or imagination, two qualities that seem to exist apart from and independent of memory.

There are many reasons for this radical reassessment of memory. To some extent it was a by-product of deeper, more profound changes that had been underway in the West since the Middle Ages. I will discuss some of these changes at greater length in chapter 5, but it would be helpful here to make at least passing mention of them. They include, among other things, the advent and spread of capitalism and capitalist relations of production and consumption; the successful outcome of political revolutions in Europe and America between the eighteenth and early twentieth centuries; the gradual breakup of traditional society and traditional ways of life which had provided the cultural milieus of memory for generations; and the accelerating processes of urbanism, industrialism, mobility, and migration, especially in the nineteenth and twentieth centuries. All these social, political, and economic transformations, acting on and reinforcing one another, ushered in what is now called modernity, and one of the most important consequences of modernity has been the precipitous decline of memory as a value.

In the new world that had come into being, memory lost its importance in part because grounding in the past did not seem as essential as it once had. In stable societies, where the circumstances and experiences of any one generation are not greatly different from those of any other, remembering the "wisdom of the past" usually seems appropriate; what one's ancestors developed and passed on is likely to remain applicable for decades if not for centuries. But when one's world has been significantly transformed, the past does not appear to have much to say to the present. To many it ceases either to shed light on contemporary experience or to offer useful guidelines for contemporary thought or conduct. In situations such as this, remembering and repeating what has been inherited from forebears can often lead to something maladaptive or dysfunctional. Hence, under the circumstances it may appear advisable to let go of the past as much as possible in order to develop new attitudes that are more in tune with the times. Those who, despite the rapidity of change, choose to cling to the past like Don Quixote would seem to risk becoming, like him, absurd or risible figures. For once the past is superseded by new forces and developments, so the argument goes, its meaning and value change fundamentally. At the very minimum the past stops being a source of wisdom and becomes a burden, a dead weight, an impediment to further growth. And once a climate of opinion hostile to the past takes hold, it is not surprising to find that forgetting is revalued as a good.

Such revaluation began to happen in the West during the seventeenth century. Not only did collective or historical forgetting start to make more sense, but so did forgetting on a personal level. Thinkers in the early modern period and after began to point out that when one forgets the "old lumber" of one's past, one becomes freer to loosen up, improvise, even start over afresh. The qualities of freedom, improvisation, and innovation seemed especially needed if one were to cope successfully with emerging realities.

The loss of the value placed on memory was a slow process stretching from the post-Reformation era to the twentieth century. In the mid- to late nineteenth century, however, a new factor made its appearance. Now, in addition to the natural ebbing of memory's importance due to the social, economic, and political forces of modernity mentioned above, there also emerged a more focused attack both on memory as a value and on the rememberer as a particular type of individual. This attack came in the form of three claims, none of which had been previously well articulated.

The first was that individual memory is far more unreliable than had been thought. Thanks to studies by Théodule Ribot and Pierre Janet in France, Hermann Ebbinghaus and Hermann Helmholtz in Germany, Henry Maudsley in England, and William James and others in the United States, it became evident that memory was not always the dependable instrument for recovering information from the past that many in premodern times assumed it to be. Rather, it appeared incapable of accurately reproducing past events, emotions, or perceptions as they existed in their original state. In their work these psychologists tried to indicate scientifically that the processes of memory involve so much selecting, editing, revising, interpreting, embellishing, configuring, and reconfiguring of mnemonic traces from the moment they are first registered in the mind until the moment of retrieval that it is impossible to think of memory as a trustworthy preserver of the past. What is remembered is usually more distorted than people realize, since it is derived, the psychologists maintained, from a more or less accidental combination of impressions.[12] In fact, much late-nineteenth-century research was intent on showing how often purported memories were actually "confabulations," that is, memories of occurrences that never happened at all.[13] Much of Freud's early work was very much in the mainstream in this respect. In the 1890s, for example, he and several others pointed out that memories which seemed to be of actual events were often only memories of desires or fantasies. If so many of our memories were flawed or distorted, or only rough approximations of the past, or even fabrications, how reliable could memory be? And to the degree that memory lost its veracity, it also lost much of its value, and in losing value it ceased to be the certain guide to life it had been in earlier eras.

The second nineteenth-century claim, also made especially by psychologists and psychiatrists, was that a powerful memory is not necessarily a good thing, even aside from the issue of how accurate it might be. For instance, an individual may accumulate and retain such an excess of information from that past that he becomes unable to coordinate it or bring it to bear on a particular situation. In such cases, memory actually harms the individual by overwhelming and weakening his decision-making capacities with a superabundance of trivia. Hence, far from promoting spiritual or ethical behavior, memory may turn out to have the reverse effect: it may make one inert and listless, thereby undermining one's will.[14] To be a vital and engaged individual, one might need to forget a great number of past perceptions so that the mind can be cleared to receive new, more important, more up-to-date information. A certain amount of tabula rasa, in other words, came to be seen as beneficial, for if the mind does not continually open itself to fresh impressions leading to new associations, the individual unavoidably becomes confined within his own past and thus incapable of successfully coping with the demands of modern life. And perhaps just as troubling, as a consequence of an overabundance of information the rememberer was said to lose both a capacity for "spontaneous reasoning" and an ability to use his imagination in novel or creative ways.[15] In sum, to the many commentators on memory around 1900 who adopted this point of view, the person of prodigious memory was not the exemplary individual he was earlier thought to be. Indeed, the person inundated by "multiple recollections spring[ing] up on every side" (Ribot) was labeled a "disturbed" individual. And the same label was attached to those who remembered not too many things but one single thing with such intensity that it became an *idée fixe* that oppressively ruled their lives. Whether the issue was extensive or intensive memory, the argument began to be put forth that too much focus on memory in an individual leads to "hypermnesia," a newly coined mental disorder.[16] Once remembering came to be seen as a real or potential disorder, it became possible to talk about it in completely new ways—as an "impediment" or even a "monstrosity" (to cite one early twentieth-century psychologist).[17]

The third and last claim worth mentioning here is partly related to the second. It was that the rememberer sometimes recollects not out of the highest or purest motives of loyalty to the past but out of some pressing inner fear, based on an incapacity to fully engage life as it presents itself in immediacy. To many people in the late nineteenth and early twentieth centuries, the best measure of an individual's psychological health and well-being was his or her willingness to face up to or "test" reality. This being so, it was hard to understand why any sound, robust person would want to opt out of the present. The suspicion was that those who preferred retrospection or reverie over an active involvement in life-as-it-actually-is were likely to be suffering from a form of cowardice attributable to a fear of failure, or a fear of the vicissitudes of existence, or even a fear of owning up to or dealing with the *moi haïssable* one had become. Whatever the cause, the urge to remember began to be seen as rooted in something discreditable, something that drives one to escape into an imagined "better time" or to a "better self" believed to have existed in the near or distant past. Especially for many vitalists, Nietzscheans, and advocates of *Lebensphilosophie* around 1900, the motives that would propel a person to remember rather than to seek after "life and more life" in the present always seemed questionable. To such present-minded individuals remembering represented a kind of running away—a withdrawal into nostalgic reflection that was suitable only for timid or fainthearted souls more interested in searching for solace in the past than in bravely confronting the world around them. Viewed in this way, it seemed clear that personal weakness, not strength, was the main factor leading individuals to remember and hold onto what was best left behind.

These three claims amounted to an "epistemological deflation" of the value of memory, a rethinking of the once positive qualities associated with the rememberer, and a new suspiciousness regarding the motivations behind the urge to recollect. At least in some quarters, the picture of the rememberer which began to emerge carried forward none of the traces of spirituality, creativity, or rectitude that were to be found in nearly all premodern descriptions. Rather, as widely depicted from roughly the 1870s on, the rememberer was a person who had gotten locked into habitual patterns of behavior and was therefore dull and routinized; had become haunted by the losses of the past and consequently tended to be morbidly melancholic; or had become obsessed by certain alleged hurts or injustices suffered in the past and hence was rancorous and vengeful about what had wrongly befallen him. Each of these attributes now said to mark the rememberer deserves brief elaboration.

From the time of ancient Greece until at least the seventeenth or eighteenth centuries, habits were seen as memories that had hardened into practices. Where habit existed, there too was regularity, predictability, constancy—all qualities that were vigorously applauded throughout the centuries. If one acquired and repeated the right habits, one became not just a dependable but also a good person, for as Aristotle and others maintained, "moral virtues come about *as a result* of habit."[18]

This view persisted even into the nineteenth century. One can find it expressed, for example, in the numerous self-help books and manuals that proliferated in Europe and America between the 1840s and the 1880s;[19] and one can find it as well in works of a higher intellectual pitch such as Herbert Spencer's *Data of Ethics* (1884) or William James's *Principles of Psychology* (1890).[20] But in the late nineteenth and early twentieth century this favorable assessment of habit shifted dramatically. What came to the fore instead was a massive, if uncoordinated, assault on the person of habit as a particular type of rememberer. This assault was carried forth in psychiatric and psychological literature, novels, guide-to-life books, popular magazine articles, and even eventually newspaper advice columns. The thrust of the attack was that the person of habit, far from being a model to imitate, is actually someone who lacks imagination and therefore tends to flatten his experience by reducing it to what Walter Benjamin later called the "Always-the-Same" *(das Immergleiche)*. By operating only within a range of behavior dictated by the past, the person of habit was said to close himself off to the rich and teeming life around him. Instead, he imprisons himself within mechanical and repetitive modes of behavior which, though they might offer some protection from the shocks of modernity, nevertheless produce in the long run a person who is pinched, cramped, and in the last analysis irredeemably banal.

Perhaps even more disturbing than this, the person of habit was alleged to fear freedom and to hide this fear behind routines. By putting everything "on automatic" so to speak, such a person does not have to be concerned with either choosing or willing, since the inertia of the past is given the power to choose or will for him. Moreover, in the new language of psychology that began to achieve popularity around 1900, the person of habit was presumed to be "inhibited" or "repressed" because, in the process of holding firmly to routines, he or she could not help but deny expression to a supposed "true self" thought to lie buried deep within each person. As has already been suggested, it was simply taken for granted in earlier times that one becomes who one is *through* the habits one adopts, since habits actualize rather than constrict the self. But by the early twentieth century, the opposite point of view was becoming more common, for it now seemed that when one straitjackets oneself with habits, one blocks or suppresses the person one "really" is. Though habitude may produce something that might generously be called a self, it was believed to be artificial. Underneath the false, role-playing self, however, there was assumed to be another one that was natural, spontaneous, and "authentic." Only by breaking habits could this truer, more genuine self be set free and real personal fulfillment be attained. Otherwise one could look forward to little except a life of stagnation and sterility—at best a kind of death-in-life.

Even those few individuals who, around the turn of the century, mounted a rearguard defense of memory (I will turn to this defense shortly) had virtually nothing good to say about the person of habit. Relatively suddenly, then, this type of rememberer seemed to have few or no redeemable qualities. The French philosopher Henri Bergson, for instance, described the person of habit as a dreary individual who chooses to follow conventions rather than liberate the purportedly hidden self within that is always clamoring to be actualized. "Obedience to duty [that is, habit]," he wrote in a typical formulation, "means resistance to self."[21] For Bergson, habits deaden the soul and obliterate personality; where they gain the upper hand, they produce a petrified, spiritless form of life deserted by the *élan vital*. Similarly, Freud often treated the person of habit as someone who falls back on routinized patterns of behavior as a way of hiding from rather than coming to terms with anxiety. For all too many people, Freud warned, habits become fixations, repetition compulsions, or flights from reality. Instead of being signs of virtue as they once were, they may, he proposed, be symptoms of personality disturbance. Marcel Proust likewise denigrated the person of habit. Though he admitted that such a person does indeed create an orderly world for himself—at once predictable, familiar, and comfortable—the costs of this achievement seemed exorbitantly high, for by turning some memories into "inveterate habits," the person necessarily excludes from consciousness other, more important ones.[22] The most crucial of these occluded memories are the *mémoires involuntaires* which for Proust contained valuable, even indispensable, messages from one's personal past. But if one ensconces oneself in habit as a kind of second nature, the memories that stem from one's prior and more profound first nature are never received, and consequently one never gains access to the vital meanings concealed within them.[23] For Proust, everything that it is truly important to know comes not from a reliance on the "colorless routines" of everyday life but from epiphanies or breakthroughs of awareness, many of which are available to us only through the medium of involuntary memory. The person of habit, however, just because he remains incarcerated within a frozen world of his own creation, never connects with the deepest layers of his own past, and hence never becomes acquainted with those insights or illuminations that he must come to know if he is to know himself.

Thus, according to many psychologists, philosophers, and novelists of the late nineteenth and early twentieth centuries, one's psychological well-being required the breaking of habits, not a thoughtless adherence to them. Behind this notion lay the growing assumption that both physical and psychological health meant being as fluid and plastic as possible, holding oneself open to change or reconfiguring oneself as conditions dictated. The person ruled by habit appeared to be a disappointingly staid and spiritless individual, and hardly a model for imitation.

Another assault that began around 1900 was directed against the morbid or pathological rememberer. A rememberer was viewed as pathological if his or her urge to recollect was due either to some psychogenic disorder or to some physiological impairment of the brain itself.

In earlier centuries no one had attempted to discredit the rememberer as an ideal by raising questions about why one would want to recall the past in the first place; since remembering was by definition a good thing, it was simply assumed that the reasons for remembering must also be creditable. But by the late nineteenth century this assumption began to be undermined, and as it was, a new concern with the so-called disturbances of memory emerged.

Memory was said to be disturbed when it drove the individual toward an excessive or neurotic interest in his or her own past. What would cause such an interest? Why would a person be drawn so intently toward a past that is over and done with when the visible, present world cried out for attention and involvement? According to some, the propensity to remember or abnormally dwell on the past was due to a fear of the present, a fear prompting one to turn to already lived life out of a need to escape the confusion, uncertainty, or feelings of apprehension induced by the pressures of the moment. According to others, the reason had to do with an irrational terror of the future; if one came to believe that what was yet to come would likely be calamitous, then one might think it preferable to retreat to the past, since there at least everything was known. According to still others, the rememberer turned to the past because he or she was obsessed with some loss or alleged "wrong turn" that had happened. In this case, the rememberer recalled what he or she *almost* had, or what he or she *might* have been, since reflecting backward was the only way that one could recover the lost possibilities of a life, even if the recovery was only arrived at in reverie. Finally, the rememberer might be driven to recollect not because the past contained missed opportunities but because it contained everything valuable or meaningful in his or her life. In this instance the rememberer would feel compelled to cling resolutely to the past in order to maintain his or her very being.

These kinds of analyses of the pathological rememberer began to appear in the late 1890s and early 1900s, first in the psychiatric journals and later in more popular works.[24] Almost without exception, the pathological rememberer was described as a person suffering from "arrested development," "mental derangement," or, even worse, madness. One especially pronounced tendency in these discussions was to link these and similar "disorders of memory" with clinical melancholia. Because this particular diagnosis was so typical of the time, it deserves a few words of comment here.

For centuries the term "melancholia" carried almost exclusively negative connotations. From the time of the Greeks through the Middle Ages, the melancholic was an individual whose liver secreted an inordinate amount of black bile. As this bile entered the internal organs, it affected a person's temperament; one became a victim of *humor melancholicus,* making him or her not only cold and sluggish but also depressed, misanthropic, solitary, mournful, petulant, and subject to unwholesome fantasies and forebodings. During the Renaissance, however, melancholia underwent a kind of reinterpretation, in part because of a rethinking of some relatively obscure ancient texts assembled by Aristotle's pupils (the *Problemata physica*). Writers such as Marsilio Ficino argued that although certain forms of melancholia do indeed lead to depression or even madness, other forms can produce the highest imaginative and even visionary states of mind. Especially among artists, melancholia began to be taken as a sign of exceptional ability, surpassing insights, or, most desirable of all, genius.[25] In the seventeenth century some religious thinkers continued this line of thought, seeing in the melancholic disposition an indication of deep spiritual anguish, or evidence that one had been specially marked by God for salvation.[26] The Romantics of the early nineteenth century also treated melancholia as something positive; to them it was an unmistakable sign that one felt more acutely than others the *pathos* of the human condition. But by 1900, when melancholia began to be redefined clinically by the emerging psychiatric community which had by then largely taken over the

discourse of mental illness, the term once again became overwhelmingly negative. And perhaps just as significantly, melancholia was seen as bound up
with, though not necessarily always caused by, some kind of memory disorder. The melancholic, it was said, had developed "an exclusive attachment to
his past."[27] He was the sort of person who could not get over what once had
been but was no more, and as a result he became neurotically imprisoned in
the very past that was destroying him. This longing for what would never
return, this dwelling on past losses real or imagined, not only manifested itself
in the typical symptoms of melancholia (relentless self-reproach, despondency, morbid brooding, and so on); it also manifested itself in a horror of
time as such, since for the melancholic time was not, as it was for most people,
a medium of fulfillment but a medium through which life became more and
more depleted, more and more emptied of significance the further it carried
one away from certain moments in the past that were perceived as the locus
of everything worthwhile.

The last attack on the rememberer as a type focused on the characteristics of
anger and enmity. To the question "What, at bottom, is it that a rememberer
remembers best?" the new answer was not ideals, ethical injunctions, or the
wisdom of ancestors, but slights, insults, indignities, and humiliations. According to the psychologists and psychiatrists who attempted to describe or
explain the psyche of the rememberer, what such individuals recalled more
exactly than anything else, it seemed, was the *pain* of past moments. In his
Lived Time of 1933 the French psychiatrist Eugène Minkowski wrote that
memories of the hurts and offenses of the past register deeper and persist
longer than "memory of the good." The mind simply retains a more intense
and vivid impression of the harm done to us than of joys formerly experienced, and consequently it "obliges [the pain of the past] to remain with [us]
longer."[28] To the extent that the rememberer is held in the grip of hurtful
recollections, he or she is susceptible to feelings of bitterness and resentment;
and when these feelings linger or fester for any length of time they produce
an all-consuming urge to strike back. Too much focus on remembered pain,
especially pain inflicted by others, creates a wounded individual who does not
simply endure his or her sufferings passively but wants to retaliate by making
someone pay for them.

This peculiar mental disposition, at least according to Nietzsche, Max
Scheler, and others who claimed to understand the psychology of it, is reputedly the chief source of the urge for revenge. For those who continually recall
real or imagined injuries but are too weak to do anything about them, the
consequences can be seething resentment leading to impotent rage.[29] In this
state one merely fantasizes revenge, nothing more. The rancor one feels smol-

ders in what Nietzsche called a "tremulous [subterranean] realm," and eventually it poisons the individual inwardly, making him or her both emotionally and spiritually "sick."[30] For those who are strong and willful enough to turn their yearnings for revenge into actual deeds, the result is an externalization of *ressentiment* that can have equally destructive consequences in terms of cruel or aggressive behavior directed against others or against the world in general.

The discussion of the so-called man of *ressentiment* put the rememberer in an entirely negative light. By comparison, the forgetter seemed to be a model of robust good health. Nietzsche in particular pointed out that the forgetter, because he happily lets go of all the pain or hurt of the past, feels no need for vengeance or retribution. (In this respect the French revolutionary figure Mirabeau was, according to Nietzsche, an exemplary forgetter; he "had no memory for insults or vile actions done him and was unable to forgive simply because he—forgot.")[31] Moreover, the forgetter ceases being the sort of reactive individual that the rememberer, condemned always to harbor and then respond to things that have already happened, is by his very nature. Instead, the forgetter gives himself the right to be active rather than reactive, and hence to create a new future free of the burdens of the past. The resentful rememberer, on the other hand, owing to the noxious recollections weighing him down and enervating his spirit, cannot help but sink deeper and deeper into anger, vindictiveness, and self-pity. Thus there appeared to be little that was good about the past-dominated or even the past-oriented individual.[32] Far from an ideal, the rememberer was seen, at least by those who adopted the interpretation just described, as disturbed if not potentially dangerous.

Of course, not everyone writing around the turn of the century joined in the assault on memory. Between the 1880s and the 1930s numerous works appeared which upheld remembering as a value. Much of this literature focused on the importance of memory training or memory improvement for what was termed "successful living." The assumption on which this popular literature was based was that if one had a good memory for names, faces, or the details of one's surroundings, one did better in personal relationships and had a better chance for career advancement. Other pro-memory books and articles recycled premodern views that memory is an important ingredient in character development or an essential factor in establishing a continuous and reliable personal identity.[33]

For the most part, the authors of these various works formulated apologias for memory that were intellectually unimpressive. However, there were others writing during this same fifty-year period who extolled the value of memory in more sophisticated terms.

Four such writers were Sigmund Freud, Henri Bergson, Marcel Proust, and Walter Benjamin. Each generally wrote favorably of memory and of the person who remembers, but each also qualified his pro-memory position with a number of conditions and reservations. Despite their overall affirmation of memory, none of the four could completely escape the dominant anti-memory mood of the age, which may partly explain why in the writings of each there is a certain ambiguity regarding the ultimate value of remembering and forgetting for the modern individual.

At first glance Freud appears to embrace the "disorders of memory" approach to mental disturbances so common within the psychiatric profession around 1900. As already noted, he regarded the structuring of one's life around fixed habits as a form of memory dysfunction; one who unthinkingly remembers and repeats old behavioral patterns is, according to Freud, using memory as a way of fleeing from the kind of engagement with present circumstances that would provide the best chance of restoring health. Melancholia, too, was viewed by Freud as a pathological mode of remembering based on a refusal or inability to disconnect from the past. In Freud's opinion—and that of many others of his time—melancholic remembering was an indication of mental illness. As Freud summarized it in his "Mourning and Melancholia" (1917), the melancholic was sick not just because he remembered too well but because he identified with and then introjected what he remembered, thereby inwardly prolonging the existence of exactly those people or events that it would be better either to push to the margins of consciousness or let go of altogether.[34]

At first, then, Freud gives the impression that forgetting the past is a good thing. (Repressing the past, however, was not. As I will point out in more detail in the next chapter, Freud, at least from the early 1900s, saw forgetting and repression as distinct and even opposed mental phenomena, though in popular accounts of Freudian theory the differences separating them have often been blurred.) For example, in an early case study dealing with the hysterical symptoms of a certain Frau Emmy von N. (1895), Freud seemed to suggest that some patients could be restored to mental health simply by inducing them to forget painful memories that have lingered in the mind too long, perhaps by means of hypnosis if all else fails.[35] Similarly, in his *Five Lectures on Psycho-Analysis* (1910), Freud appeared to doubt the value of remembering and to uphold the value of forgetting. "What should we think," Freud asked, "of a Londoner who paused today before the memorial of Queen Eleanor's funeral [dating from the thirteenth century] instead of going about his business? . . . Or again, what should we think of a Londoner who shed tears before the Monument that commemorates the reduction of his beloved metropolis to ashes [in the Great Fire of 1666], although it has long since risen again in far greater brilliance? Yet every single hysteric and neurotic behaves like these two unpractical Londoners. Not only do they remember painful experiences of the remote past, but they still cling to them emotionally; they cannot get free of the past and for its sake they neglect what is real and immediate."[36] The sentiments Freud expressed in this revealing passage seem to place him solidly among those who had begun to speak out against the virtues of memory around the turn of the century. And apparently even more hostile to memory was Freud's famous statement in *Studies in Hysteria* (1895) that *"hysterics suffer mainly from reminiscences."*[37] If this was what Freud believed, then memory would have to be considered the problem and forgetting the solution, for his words suggest that it is only after the root causes of suffering (namely, "reminiscences") are dispelled from the mind that a hysterical patient has a chance of being restored to health. Remembering, in other words, simply prolongs the sickness of his patients; forgetting presumably sets them on the road to recovery.

On closer examination, however, it becomes evident that Freud's message is exactly the opposite. It is because people unconsciously retain what they consciously forget that they suffer from a variety of mental disturbances. Accordingly, the way toward health for Freud's neurotic and hysterical patients was not more forgetting, but just the reverse: more and better remembering. Only when this apparent paradox is understood can one begin to grasp the central notion informing Freud's entire psychoanalytic project.

Freud believed that many if not most people experience traumatic events early in their lives. These events produce emotional affects, often very painful ones. The best way to handle affects of this sort is to discharge them the moment they occur, or soon thereafter. Freud called such discharges "abreactions." When, according to him, abreactions are successful, the emotional intensity associated with traumatic events is dissipated, thereby preventing the events themselves from becoming pathogenic. In time, both the event and its affects are as a rule forgotten, and this is as it should be. But in many instances something very different happens. An affect can at times be not merely let go of and forgotten; it can instead—especially if it is highly charged—be suppressed (*unterdrückt*) or repressed (*verdrängt*), which is to say, forcibly pushed out of consciousness. Such suppression or denial does not cause an affect to dissipate or fade away in the normal manner. Rather, the affect is frequently retained unconsciously. It survives below the surface of awareness, often becoming (because it is dammed up) even stronger and more disturbing than it was initially. Eventually, in Freud's view, the undischarged affect may come to manifest itself outwardly in precisely the kinds of symptoms, phobias, and compulsions that were incapacitating those individuals who had come to him for help. Though at the beginning of his practice as an analyst Freud entertained the idea that a more complete or more cathartic forgetting of the past might provide the answer to his patients' problems, it gradually became clear to him that the solution lay in more adequate modes of remembering. What needed to be recalled, Freud concluded in his mature work, was both the original traumatic event and the affect attached to it. Each (but especially the second) had to be retrieved from the dark realm of the unconscious and brought back once again into the light of consciousness. This retrieval, ideally, is what the psychoanalytic method was designed to achieve. As Freud conceived of it, psychoanalysis's primary goal was to help patients remember and then work through traumatic occurrences from the past that continued to disturb them in the present. Thanks to the medium of memory, Freud hoped finally to induce in his patients the very abreaction that they badly needed but which they had not been able to achieve earlier on, when such a response was appropriate and should have occurred.

Seen from this perspective, Freud was a defender, not a detractor, of memory. Though reminiscences, when operating unconsciously, were for Freud one of the chief sources of human suffering and unhappiness, they could also be, when brought fully into consciousness, the means by which people were able to overcome suffering and unhappiness. In the last analysis, memory for Freud held the key to an individual's mental well-being. When properly exercised, it opened up possibilities for personal freedom and fulfillment that could never be realized so long as a person's life was unconsciously shaped or determined by the harmful affects of "forgotten" events.

Henri Bergson also had favorable things to say about memory, along with much that was unfavorable. In his important early work, *Matter and Memory* (1896), Bergson distinguished between two kinds of memory. The first he called "motor mechanisms," and the second "independent recollections." Motor mechanisms, according to Bergson, are memories that evolve into habits. When something is recalled and repeated often enough, it ceases being a memory as such and becomes instead a "habitual bodily exercise," an "intelligently constructed mechanism" of behavior.[38] Along with others of his era, Bergson acknowledged that habit memories have some value—for example, they help one develop dependable physical skills and ensure consistency of conduct—but also like others of his generation, he generally stressed their shortcomings more than their benefits.

Bergson maintained that whenever habitude shapes the life of an individual, the result is flatness and dullness. The person of habit is stifled by the "closed system of automatic movements" in which he or she is ensconced. Since the habits that most people enact tend to be those that are most socially approved, such a person is not only unfree but likely to be conformist in his or her behavior. Bergson sharply criticized those individuals who develop what he called "habits of obedience," thereby becoming "closed souls" who subordinate themselves to regnant social norms without really thinking for themselves.[39] Bergson even suggested that, appearances to the contrary not-withstanding, the rememberer types who build their lives around habits can-not truly be moral, even though their acts often create the illusion of morality. Genuine morality, Bergson claimed, must be founded on free choice, that is, on the freedom to decide and do what is right rather than what is wrong; it cannot be based on automatic responses which virtually bypass conscious-ness. If, in other words, people are good merely because of the routines they develop, their morality can never be ethical in the highest sense. In order for the highest kind of ethics to exist, something more must be present than forms of behavior that seem almost neurologically repetitive. For Bergson, that something more, which he called "authentic" morality, always comes from the heart. It springs from an "affective stirring of the soul," and hence it is a quality possessed only by those individuals who operate from within outward, instead of the other way around. A life centered on memories that have turned into mechanical habits might be called ethical if the conduct that results is socially acceptable or socially integrative, but for Bergson such conduct can never be ethical in the strongest sense of the word if it is the outcome of something merely automatic rather than something free, heart-felt, and entirely volitional.

Besides motor mechanisms, Bergson also spoke of "independent recollec-tions"—that is, images of past experiences that can be lodged either in the conscious or unconscious mind, the latter of which he referred to, without much elaboration, as the realm of "pure memory" (*mémoire pure*). These im-ages are representations of former occurrences that remain distinct and in-tact. They do not blur, or run together, or lose their "affective coloring" as happens when particular memories are repeated so often that they become habits. Instead, they preserve specific and often very detailed bits of informa-tion, datable in time and locatable in space, about an individual's personal past. Independent recollections come closest to fitting the picture of what most people understand memories to be, namely the recovery, in the form of mental representations, of experiences that are otherwise over and done with.

But here Bergson made a further distinction. In *Matter and Memory* he differentiated between those independent recollections that seem to rise up of their own accord and those that come forth because one intentionally seeks them out. Bergson had little good to say about the first type of independent recollection, but he very much approved of the second.

What bothered Bergson about "spontaneous" independent recollections is that they cannot be adequately harnessed and utilized for practical ends. They come and go, seemingly without causation and independent of one's will. When they flash up unpredictably from out of an "immense zone of obscurity," they often throw one off balance, because they bring forth remembered material that appears strange and unrelated to one's present situation. Put differently, for Bergson spontaneous recollections tend to disorient or undermine rather than "consolidate [an individual's] present equilibrium."[40] If one became especially susceptible to many such memories—memories, that is, from which one cannot "profit," or memories from which one can gain no "advantage"[41]—the consequences could be disastrous. At the very least, an overabundance of spontaneous recollections could cause one to lose contact with reality and thereby become "unfitted" for the demands of daily life. (Here one finds in Bergson the warning that was typical of his age but not of premodernity—that too much of any kind of memory is always harmful and destabilizing). Beyond losing touch with reality, which was serious enough, two other dangers lurked. One was that the person inundated by spontaneous recollections would become nothing but a "dreamer," a ne'er-do-well, an individual who is unable to bring himself to act because he simply watches his own memories appear and vanish almost as if they were aesthetic experiences.[42] The second, even graver, danger was that one would become insane. In Bergson's view, it was conceivable that an individual could become so overwhelmed by the flood of images coming from his own past that he would not be able to assimilate or integrate them in a satisfactory manner. The result would be mental incapacitation bordering on madness,[43] which would obviously make one incapable of dealing successfully with the practical tasks of ordinary life.

Independent recollections that are brought to mind consciously and in a controlled fashion are, according to Bergson, an entirely different matter. These he called "voluntary recollections," and without exception he treated them as salutary rather than dangerous. Voluntary recollections were said to be like spontaneous recollections in nearly every respect, except that they come forth because they are directly summoned by the conscious mind, not because they flare up of their own accord. In Bergson's view, what leads the mind to summon them is always some immediate situation that calls out for attention and action. In responding to such situations, the mind instantaneously scans the reservoir of images retained from past experiences in order to search out those that might be useful for interpreting or reacting to a present moment. When one or more memory images are found, the mind seizes upon them, brings them forward, and applies them to existing circumstances. The memories that are "projected toward" or "sent out to meet" those circumstances are the ones most likely to be efficacious in illuminating some pressing issue or clarifying some anticipated course of action. The key here is that in a voluntary recollection the conscious mind always directs and orients the memory; it is always in control, always steering memories into new combinations to help one better interpret, and thus better cope with, some matter of concern. In this regard, voluntary recollections do two things that spontaneous recollections cannot do: they clarify perception and understanding by bringing forward those images from the past that are "analogous to" or "contiguous with" a present reality that needs to be addressed, and they stabilize one's mental equilibrium instead of fundamentally subverting it, as can and often does happen with spontaneous memories.[44]

In sum, Bergson was fully in tune with the late-nineteenth-century assault on habit memories and spontaneous recollections. But unlike many other philosophers and psychologists writing around 1900, he enthusiastically affirmed those forms of memory he called voluntary recollections so long as they accentuated one's "attention to life" or strengthened one's practical orientation to *la vie quotidienne*.

On just this issue of the practical uses of memory, the German critic Walter Benjamin, writing more than three decades after the appearance of *Matter and Memory*, represents an interesting dissent from Bergson's point of view. Benjamin agreed with Bergson on the importance of bringing the past to bear on the present, but he disagreed about how memories ought to be treated when the mind brings them forward, and about what should happen to them after they have been "launch[ed] in the direction of a perception." According to Bergson, those memories that are not directly serviceable with respect to an immediate situation should be left in obscurity, since they can have no value for the individual trying to cope with some present reality. Furthermore, he held that when a memory is summoned and then applied, it is natural and acceptable that it lose some of its original vividness and singularity. Such a loss is to be expected when memories are instrumentalized into useful perceptions or practical actions, for in the process of being materialized, the sharpness that memories can have becomes diminished. For Bergson, however, this diminution was no great matter, since what memories lose in color and vivacity they can more than make up for in efficacy.

Benjamin was unable to embrace such a pragmatic notion of memory. It was unacceptable that memory be approached with only utilitarian considerations in mind and that memories lose their integrity, or "distinct individualit[y]," once they are drawn into the sphere of immediacy. Were either or both of these things to happen, memory would be prevented from achieving the full effect Benjamin wanted it to have, which was to enrich experience in other than the merely practical or pedestrian way Bergson seemed to suggest.

At the heart of Benjamin's concern with memory was the sense that in the twentieth century individual experience was beginning to be stripped of its temporal dimension. As he saw it, the dominant mode of experience within modernity was a type he termed *Erlebnis,* meaning experience focused on each isolated instant with little or no awareness of how that instant might be shot through with duration or sedimented by the weight of the past that preceded it. To the extent that *Erlebnis* was becoming the norm in the West, experience was becoming increasingly fleeting, episodic, and fragmentary, since it had no real ballast, no firm grounding, in what had gone before. Lacking memory, *Erlebnis* could not help but be empty and superficial, for it existed outside of any context except that of pure immediacy, which for Benjamin was no viable context at all. At first sight, Bergson (with whose work Benjamin was intimately familiar) seemed to represent an advance beyond this vacuous form of experience, since he wanted to fuse memories into perceptions so as to make the past relevant to the present. But because of the way Bergson operationalized the past in the process of bringing it forward, he tended to reduce it to something merely functional. Everything in one's memory that was not directly useful to some matter at hand was, for Bergson, hardly worth bringing to mind.

What Benjamin valued far more than Bergson's practical memory was another kind of experience which he called *Erfahrung.* As Benjamin used this term it meant a type of experience in which images from the past (along with "accumulated . . . unconscious data") do not vanish once they combine with perception but continue to be present in the mind, giving experience a layered, multifaceted quality.[45] For Benjamin the memories that may be most valuable for enriching everyday life are not necessarily those attuned to present-day needs but those that keep alive something different or divergent that may in fact be entirely incompatible with a present situation. What was this incompatible material that so attracted Benjamin's interest? Sometimes he spoke of it as the cumulative and consciously recallable "lived experience" of one's own personal past, which could often appear strange when set against the self one might prefer, ahistorically, to imagine oneself to have been. At other times, he spoke of it as that which had never "been consciously and explicitly experienced" but which had managed to get lodged in the mind nonetheless (in the form of buried images that became recognized only in the act of remembering them).[46] And at yet other times, and most intriguing of all, he spoke of this incompatible material as composed of "certain contents of the individual past combine[d] with material of the collective past."[47] Were this last type of memory to come forth, experience *(Erfahrung)* would be informed by something supra-individual and perhaps even primordial, achieving a depth impossible to attain in the relatively more impoverished and delimited kinds of experience associated with *Erlebnis.*

From Bergson's perspective none of this would have made any sense. If memories were not efficacious—if they did not, as he put it, have "practical application"—they were superfluous. Benjamin's unique defense of personal memory came by means of a radical rethinking of just this category of superfluous recollection, which allowed him to find value in those impractical or discordant memories that Bergson and others considered worthless.

Marcel Proust's discussion of memory largely centered on what the artist or writer needed in order to produce his or her best work. In *Remembrance of Things Past* Proust expressed the view that memory was essential both for inspiration and for providing access to the material that can give content to a work of art. But in stressing the importance of memory Proust emphatically did not mean habit memory. Throughout *Remembrance* as well as in his other writings Proust took the position that habit is an "anaesthetic." It is, as he put it, a "second nature [which] prevents us from knowing our original nature"; it causes a stale repetition of the same, making life banal and cliché-ridden; it "weakens every impression," thereby deadening the quality of our experiences; it shields us from the very suffering which is necessary for growth; it renders the strange familiar and kills a sense of mystery; it "cuts the tap root" which gives depth and significance to our encounters with people and things.[48]

In comparison to habit memory, Proust wrote more positively about what he called *mémoire volontaire* (though to be sure even this was not espoused with anywhere near the enthusiasm that Freud showed toward conscious remembering, or Bergson toward independent recollections). While admitting that voluntary memory could be useful for recalling factual information from the past, Proust did not think it was of much value for artistic types whose inspiration had to come from something other than what he termed their "practical intelligence." It was precisely those memories which Bergson had labeled "spontaneous recollections" and had rejected out of hand that Proust, after renaming them *mémoires involontaires,* wanted especially to explore and affirm.

For Proust, an involuntary memory comes unsolicited, often with explosive force, to unsettle the individual in the present. When an involuntary memory appears, it takes the form of an *ek-stasis* of the past in the present. Since the conscious mind plays little or no role in drawing it out, nothing in ordinary awareness is able to meliorate the shock effect of the memory. Paradoxically, the disturbing power of an involuntary memory rests on the fact that it has been completely forgotten, whereas voluntary memories, for Proust and for Bergson too, can always build upon established ties of contiguity, similarity, and logical association between the mind that remembers and the material that is remembered. This is another reason why, when involuntary memories occur, they bring with them jarring differences and discontinuities unlike anything known to voluntary memory. (Benjamin noted the same thing, which was one reason he was so drawn to Proust and in fact undertook to translate *Remembrance* into German.) What makes involuntary memories jarring, according to Proust, is that they represent "fragment[s] of time in [their] pure state," which is to say, memories that are fresh and vivid just because they have not been reworked or interpreted by the conscious mind.[49] With *mémoires involontaires* it is as if certain "luminous moments" from the past were enclosed and preserved in "sealed jars" *(vases clos)*. Such moments would appear to exist outside the confines of time itself and thus to be impervious to its corroding effects. But if such memories should somehow break into consciousness—if the sealed jars should suddenly be opened—something entirely strange and unfamiliar would get released. As Proust put it in a passage cited earlier, it would be as if the "absolutely different colour, odour, and temperature" within each jar from "bygone years" were unexpectedly dispersed into the completely different atmosphere of the present.[50] The result would be the same kind of shock to the senses, the same momentary disorientation, that one would experience when overtaken by an involuntary memory. Because of the dissonant nature of such memories, it seemed to Proust all but impossible to assimilate them either into normal categories of perception or into normal patterns of habitual behavior.

What, according to Proust, triggers an involuntary memory? Never a practical action or deed which needs the aid of memory to be interpreted, but always some incidental sensation, some unanticipated impression in the present. A sensation, for Proust, is any intense but seemingly insignificant experience which happens without the "attention to life" that Bergson considered so essential. Because such sensations stand outside the realm of utility, they are able to evoke a swarm of long-forgotten and literally useless memories (such as the taste of a madeleine dipped in tea) which have nevertheless been retained in the unconscious. It was an important point for Proust that the deepest, most profound memories really need to have been "lost" by being gradually covered over by other memories which are more bland and superficial and thus misrepresent the true emotional tone of the past. In Proust's view, these superficial recollections are the only ones voluntary memory can tap and utilize. By contrast, an individual's more distant and powerful memories remain "in an unknown region where they are of no service to us." But if, as Proust put it, "the setting of sensations in which [such memories] are preserved [should] be recaptured, they acquire in turn the same power of expelling everything that is incompatible with them, of installing alone in us the self that originally lived them."[51] Under the right conditions, then, a sensation can activate what appear to be long-forgotten memories. It can help one recall not only an antecedent sensation but, more importantly, the entire ambiance surrounding that sensation: the feelings, thoughts, impressions, and moods of the self that experienced such things years or decades earlier.

It is critical to mention here that Proust's whole concept of memory was founded on the notion that we are not continuous but altogether discontinuous selves. (This, too, was foreign to Bergson, who mainly emphasized the continuity of the self in time.) The person we happen to be now, Proust thought, is entirely discrepant from the one we were years ago. In reality we are composed of numerous successive selves, in fact a multiplicity of selves spread over time, each one apparently excluding the self preceding it, and each in turn virtually lost to the one that follows. This being the case, when an involuntary memory occurs it brings in its train a revived awareness of one of the previous selves we had formerly been. It also resuscitates all the emotions and sensibilities that enveloped that earlier self, which a merely voluntary memory would be unable to do.

For Proust, then, only involuntary memories are able to capture the aura and richness of those singular, unrepeatable moments of the past. Far from adapting recollections to a set of existing practices and thereby instrumentalizing them, involuntary memories produce exactly the opposite effect: they overwhelm, confound, and disorient an individual, preventing successful adaptation to quotidian existence. In every instance in *Remembrance* when an involuntary memory sweeps over the character Marcel, it makes him uncertain of who he is, or creates a feeling of "dizziness" or "oscillation" between the past and the present.[52] This was not at all what Freud or Bergson wanted memories to do. They hoped that memory would implant an individual more firmly in the present, not innundate him with a flood of seemingly disconnected images from the past. For Proust, all that is really important about life comes as a result of these eruptions from within. The most essential truths are those contained in the depths of memory and obtainable only by reflectively repossessing the material that emerges involuntarily. The creative individual's primary task, therefore, is not, as it was for so many of his generation, active engagement in the world; it is contemplative self-understanding. The insights that arise from the reading of what Proust referred to as one's unique "interior text" *(livre interieur)* are fundamentally impractical by their very nature; they lead invariably to a greater disequilibrium with the world, not toward a better accommodation to it. Still, in bringing his novel to its conclusion, Proust felt compelled to add one last thing. It is not enough, he insisted, merely to receive involuntary memories or passively ruminate on them. One needs to treat each remembered moment from the past as a unique invitation or appeal which, as Georges Poulet summarized it, is "addressed to all [one's] being, and to which all [one's] being ought to respond."[53] For Proust, the "artistic personality" had an obligation above all to turn the raw material brought forth by involuntary memory into its "spiritual equivalent," which is to say, into a work of art.

This point is one of the central messages of *Remembrance of Things Past.* It leads the narrator of the story to decide in the end to convert the memories that had been inwardly resurrected into a literary work, which is the novel itself. The implication is that every individual has the responsibility, though apparently few live up to it, to seize upon his or her profoundest memories and transform them into aesthetic objects. Only by artistically reworking the images arising from involuntary memory could one finally create something beautiful, something that could then take up a separate existence outside and beyond the self. In the last analysis, this, for Proust, became the only, or at any rate the most satisfactory, way for an individual to justify the accident of his or her appearance in the world.

The positive assessment of personal memory of the kind found in the work of the four individuals just discussed hardly extended beyond the 1930s. By the following decade all four had passed from the scene—Proust in 1924, Freud in 1939, Benjamin in 1940, and Bergson in 1941—and since that time the climate of opinion in the West seems to have grown increasingly doubtful about the value of memory as such. Though apologias for memory continued to appear in the second half of the twentieth century, only one or two were particularly original.[54] Most, especially those written in a popular vein, were little more than reworkings of older arguments, many of them dating back to the premodern period. What appears to have become more prominent at the present time is a defense of forgetting. This reversal of positions, if that is what it can be called, did not happen suddenly. As we have already seen in part, the way for it had already been prepared long before, and hence the reversal itself has a history which it would now be helpful to recount in some detail. In the next chapter, the reevaluation of forgetting as the other side of the denigration of remembering will be the main focus of attention. Two matters will be of special concern: first, how a favorable view of forgetting gradually took shape, particularly after the late nineteenth century, and second, what the chief arguments in support of forgetting have come to be in our late modern age.

The Vagaries of Forgetting

In premodern times, forgetting was viewed almost entirely negatively, for where there was forgetting there was, by definition, occlusion, absence, deprivation.[1] Similarly, the forgetter as a type did not appear to possess any redeeming qualities. Whereas the rememberer was generally thought to be creative, dependable, responsible, and ethical, the forgetter was seen as mentally dull, inconstant, untrustworthy, and unethical. In the medieval world, as Mary Carruthers has rightly pointed out, "[a] person without a memory . . . would be a person without moral character, and, in a basic sense, without humanity."[2] The same held true in ancient times as well. Since at least the classical age of Greece the only occasions in which forgetting was credited were those in which it was presumed to lead to a profound remembering. Plato, for example, called for a forgetting of the mundane so that the memory of the Forms which the soul possessed before birth could be brought to awareness. By mentally letting go of banal or commonplace memories based on mere sense impressions, one could recover and reactivate the mnemonic traces of the "higher truths" that allegedly still lay buried in the soul, and that were yet retrievable through *anamnesis*. For Plato, ordinary memory, meaning the memory of acquired information, past events, or community opinion *(doxa)*, simply cluttered up the mind, thereby preventing one from recollecting the deepest spiritual and philosophical truths of existence, including the "vision of everything that is."[3]

Likewise, neo-Platonic and gnostic thinkers throughout the centuries stressed the need to forget everything gathered from the material or "fallen" plane of being in order to recover the spiritual memory of one's sacred origin and destiny. By erasing as much as possible what one had learned through the senses, these thinkers claimed, it becomes possible to get back in contact with the "divine spark" that resides in one's innermost spirit *(pneuma)*, and in this way to find one's way back to God. Plotinus's statement from the *Enneads* typified this point of view: "The more the soul strives after the intelligible [i.e., the holy], the more it forgets. . . . In this sense, therefore, we may say that the good soul is forgetful."[4]

Medieval monasticism, to mention one final example, exhibited a similar attitude toward forgetting. Under the guidelines laid down by St. Benedict and Pope Gregory I in the sixth century A.D., monks were asked to forget not only all the trivial things of the world, since these were fated to disappear anyway, but also everything pertaining to the self including the biographical details of one's life, which, from a soteriological point of view, amounted to nothing very important. Within this frame of near total forgetting of the world and the self, the greater requirement was to remember a small number of significant things, among them the magnificence of God and the future rewards he had promised his faithful servants. Paradoxically, then, the monastic emphasis on the most extreme forms of quotidian forgetting went hand in hand with the most focused forms of spiritual remembering; as Benedict's Rule expressed it, there must be both *oblivio* and *semper memor,* that is, one must forget the ephemeral in order to achieve a more intense and all-consuming remembrance of the eternal.[5]

By the early modern period many of these attitudes toward forgetting had begun to change. The disruption and discontinuity that modernity brought in its wake undermined the premise that remembering the past was the right thing to do. Why, the question began to be asked, should one want to remember the historical past when it appears to be quite unlike the present? Why should one want to remember even one's own past when the lessons to be learned there would likely no longer be applicable to the altered realities of one's present? Especially for those eager to stay abreast of the times, there was a growing disinclination to place much value on memory, since "what was" no longer seemed to have a bearing on "what is."

There is no need at this point to chart these changes in attitude over decades or centuries. (I discuss this matter in some detail in a later chapter.) Suffice it to say for now that by the nineteenth and early twentieth centuries in the West, both a new social and economic reality and a new outlook favorable to forgetting had become clearly discernible. At the heart of this outlook was the assumption that remembering by its very nature tends to be more constraining, and at times more destructive, than previously thought. For, as many began to argue, when one lives with too much awareness of his or her own past, that past can easily become oppressive. Not only can it overburden and deform the self, but, by constantly drawing one back to the times in one's life that have little or no affinity with the present, it can take away the freedom and spontaneity every individual needs to respond successfully to issues immediately at hand. Hence, whereas remembering was increasingly said to lead to a reduction or narrowing of the self, forgetting began to be regarded as the path that leads to "wholeness"—with wholeness now redefined to mean not a complete and successful integration of the past into the present but something very nearly the opposite: an expansive unfolding of all one's suppressed or denied possibilities once the dead weight of the past has been, in Marx's words, "sprung into the air."

To express this point somewhat differently, one thing that many in the nineteenth and twentieth centuries came to abhor above all else was any kind of outside determination. Anything originating from beyond the individual and yet imposing itself physically or psychologically against one's will began to be considered anathema, since it both delimited freedom and undermined the newly important values of autonomy and independence.[6] But the past itself came to be seen as just such an outside determination; it too appeared to be coercive, to weigh one down, or to unduly and restrictively circumscribe the range of one's thoughts and actions. As many commentators of the last two centuries have suggested, the past is a burden to "modern" individuals for two primary reasons: first, because of the way in which it constricts people on the social level (through "inhibiting" traditions, antiquated value hierarchies, and the like), and second, because of the way it smothers people on the personal level (by means of oppressive habits, impossible ideals that one nonetheless feels compelled to live up to, and so on). When viewed in this light, it might be better to dispense with the past altogether, for, at least theoretically, the more dead lumber one could clear away, the more free and undetermined one would become. Of course, such a view never favored total forgetting, not even for the most implacable enemies of memory, since those who have extolled forgetting have never proposed that amnesia represents some arcadian state of bliss. On the contrary, it was obvious that without some memory the normal functioning of everyday life would be practically impossible. Still, a radically new idea had emerged: that forgetting could be good rather than bad, and that the forgetter might be someone to emulate rather than censure.

Exactly what were the claims regarding the benefits of forgetting that began to be advanced in the modern period, and more particularly in our own late modern era? In regard to personal memory, the main ones were the following.

First, our personal pasts are more filled with anxiety and suffering than we are usually willing to acknowledge. This being so, no useful purpose is served by remembering the wounds of the past extending back to early childhood. Nor does it do us any good to cast a false veil of sentiment over the remembered past, for this only disguises but does not dispel the real pain and hurt that existed there. We would do better simply to forget those things that cannot be reversed and concentrate instead on the more important issues of the present and the future.

A second claim was that action—any action at all—requires forgetting. Without "active foregetfulness," as Nietzsche termed it,[7] nothing new would ever be initiated, since without a canceling out of the past there would be no room for fresh beginnings and one would be left with little choice but to repeat again and again what had already been done.

A third claim was that we cannot successfully adapt to the rapidly changing conditions of modern existence unless we let go of what we learned in the past, most of which is outmoded in any case. The supposition here was that whereas remembering draws us into the inertia of a predictable life history, forgetting opens the door to "potentiall[y] new ways of being and acting"[8] out of which a full emancipation of the self may at last become attainable.

A fourth and last claim was that forgetting is not only a liberatory but a regenerative force; by clearing away the debris of the past, it sets us on the path toward what the French philosopher Louis Lavelle referred to as "purification and rebirth."[9] In this view, forgetting, far from being a condition of corruption and defilement as the Greeks had supposed, actually renews and revitalizes us in ways that remembering and repeating are wholly incapable of doing.

On the basis of these several claims, the idea began to be put forward that the forgetter has a number of qualities that were either overlooked for too long or wrongly considered liabilities instead of assets. For example, because he is not interested in looking back or dwelling upon what has already happened, the forgetter is better able to experience the present more intensely. Unlike the rememberer, who tends to be excessively cautious and deliberative (weighed down as he often is by the spirit of gravity that accompanies reflection), the forgetter is naturally lighter, more buoyant, even more cheerful. Furthermore, because he is not haunted by the ghosts of the past (all such ghosts having been dispelled), the forgetter is willing to strike out in new directions, to experiment and improvise, even, if he so chooses, to make every instant a new point of origin, which is something that rememberers seem constitutionally unable to do. And the forgetter appears to have a greater receptivity to life, for, being generally more tolerant of the world as it is, he is not only more generous toward others but less likely to hold grudges, since the memory of past hurts or offenses does not last long enough to issue in vengeful behavior.

All in all, it has seemed to many in the modern and late-modern eras that the forgetter as a type comes much closer than the rememberer to approximating the Nietzschean ideal of the "free spirit." As a roaming non-identity, the forgetter travels lightly. He is versatile and flexible, recalling only what he needs to know and happily shedding the past when it becomes a burden. Also, because he is inclined to assume that values are made or "constructed," not inherited, the forgetter feels few obligations to anything that has lost its *raison d'être.* This detachment, many have argued, makes it possible for the forgetter to experience a kind of exhilaration that the rememberer can never know: the exhilaration of being liberated from, and hence seemingly undetermined by, the often crushing weight of the past.

Certainly many today continue to point out the forgetter's shortcomings. The notion that the forgetter is shallow, directionless, undisciplined, or lacking in convictions has not by any means faded from modern discourse. But even allowing that there are many voices of dissent, it would be hard to deny that in our own time the forgetter has been elevated to a new and much more favorable status than the one he held in the premodern era.

During the past four or five decades especially, the same revolution in attitudes that led to a reappraisal of the forgetter has also led to a reconsideration of other matters that have a bearing on our theme of remembering and forgetting in the contemporary age. I have selected three such matters for discussion here: creativity and what stimulates it, happiness and what engenders it, and wholeness and what produces it. As I hope to show below, in the distant past there was no doubt that memory in some form held the key to creativity, happiness, and wholeness. Now, however, a strong case has been made that it is rather the quality of forgetfulness that is the central and perhaps even indispensable element in all three kinds of experiences.

Mircea Eliade has pointed out that in the prehistoric and early historical periods no creative act of any kind was thought possible without memory, especially without a memory of the "beginnings," a primordial time before time when the most fully creative act that had ever been performed—the founding of the world and everything in it—was carried out by supernatural beings. For archaic peoples, this founding act represented the most "prodigious outpouring of energy, life, and fecundity" imaginable.[10] Compared to it, no human act could ever be thought of as even remotely creative unless an individual or a community were somehow able to tap into the inexhaustible energy of that one absolutely unique primordial event. The prevailing assumption at the dawn of history was that human beings, by simply following their own devices, could create nothing significant. Only by remembering and then ritually repeating the act of the beginnings could an individual or a group acquire the wherewithal to construct or "give form to" anything worthwhile.[11]

In ancient Greece the relation between memory and creativity changed somewhat. From the perspective of the Greeks, the creative individual was not the one who simply repeated, in everyday life, some exemplary prototype derived from the gods; he was instead the one who fashioned some new object or artifact—for example, a poem, a sculpture, or a painting—by reworking previous ideas or forms already known and present in his memory. The reworking could be mimetic, and hence roughly faithful to the original, or it could be more experimental, with a greater element of artistic license. Either way, there first had to be memory—not supernatural memory, but the memory of the "forms laid down by tradition"—or else there could be nothing to imitate or experiment with, and consequently no creative or productive activity.[12] Beyond providing the material with which to work, memory also provided inspiration. In order to write a poem, for instance, the poet needed to be touched by the spirit of the goddess Mnemosyne, who, the Greeks believed, gave the poet vision, allowing him or her to see more clearly the nature of reality (including the reality of the distant past to which Mnemosyne had direct access) than would ever be possible for an ordinary mortal acting on his own initiative. Without Mnemosyne's aid, there could be no inspired "second sight" and ultimately no creative espression.[13]

In Roman and medieval times, memory was seen as equally indispensable for creativity. The creative individual was believed to have an exceptional capacity for retaining mental images *(phantasmata)* collected from previous experience or acquired by means of rigorous study. The greater the number and variety of images one had to draw on, the greater would be one's potential for making creative associations among them. If these associations were then given proper form, new or innovative work would likely result. But everything began with and depended on *memoria,* since only after it was firmly in place could some shaping principal then be applied to it. (In this regard, the bee was often mentioned as a model of creative activity. Just as the bee gathers nectar from flowers and transforms the nectar into honey, so the creative individual gathers fragments of knowledge and experience from the "fields of memory" and converts them into something new.)[14]

Notions such as these continued on into the early modern period and were still common in the late eighteenth century. When Edward Gibbon, for example, wrote in *The Decline and Fall of the Roman Empire* (1776) that "memory must be exercised before the powers of reason or fancy can be expanded," or Wordsworth suggested in the Preface to his *Lyrical Ballads* (1800) that all fine poetry is "emotion recollected in tranquility," neither writer was out of step with his age.[15] But by the early nineteenth century, the existence of a close connection between memory and creativity began to be challenged. Instead came the notion that forgetting is more conducive to creative expression than remembering. As this new view increasingly gained acceptance, the old one by no means disappeared; variations of it have survived into our own time and remain highly credible. Nonetheless, the idea that forgetting is the necessary, though not sufficient, condition for creativity is now more in tune with the temper of the age than the idea it replaced; it seems to have acquired wide currency both at the level of popular culture and among psychologists who have made the study of creativity their particular area of expertise.

Simply put, the new view maintains that freshness of perception or immediacy of vision is the essential element in creativity. Thus to be creative one would be advised to jettison old modes of thinking or old forms and frameworks in order to achieve a kind of "second naïveté" out of which creative expressions might come. From this perspective, the true source of creativity is direct, sensuous engagement with reality, which enables one to see, grasp, and surrender to what is unique in the present moment, and to do so unimpeded by memories or memory frames left over from the past.[16]

For those who have accepted this position, a sure sign that someone is authentically creative is that he or she produces something original. But in order to produce something original, or so it has been assumed, there could be no retreat to the storehouse of memory. Rather, one had to break with the past entirely, for nothing original—now redefined to mean absolutely novel and unprecedented—could ever be brought forth by looking backward.[17] By the late nineteenth and early twentieth centuries, the drive to create things that did not repeat or imitate other things had, for many, become almost obsessive. The novelist Remy de Gourmont, for instance, claimed that, due to the pressures of the market and modernity in general, the writer's "sole *raison d'être*" had become, by the 1890s, simply "to be original" no matter what the cost.[18] At about the same time the artist Georges Seurat complained that he and his fellow painters felt compelled to turn out unique or idiosyncratic paintings that had never been done before just in order to be noticed—and by being noticed to lessen the risk of getting lost in a crowd of nonentities. "The more of us there are," he wrote in 1888, "the less original we will be, and when the day comes that everybody begins using [my] technique, it will have no further value and people will look for something new—which is already happening."[19] In the case of both of these individuals and others like them, one sees something not found in earlier centuries, namely the urge to be original simply for originality's sake.

Still, if by the early twentieth century originality had become a new goal, and if it necessitated a forgetting of the past, then precisely what qualities did one have to possess in order to be original? Not a good memory, obviously, and not just vividness of perception or acuity of vision either. These in and of themselves could not ensure that something genuinely original would issue forth. Instead, the new quality said to be needed for the creation of something singular or unprecedented was imagination.

In premodern times, imagination did not figure much as a factor in creativity, let alone in originality. For Plato, imagination was simply an undeveloped form of perception which yielded not insight but pseudo-knowledge. For Aristotle, it was little more than a mediator between perception and cognition. For Francis Bacon in the seventeenth century, imagination hindered rather than advanced creativity because the useless flights of fancy it evoked actually prevented new ideas from coming to the fore. By the following century, especially because of the influence of Kant's discussion of *Einbildungskraft* in his *Critique of Judgment* (1790), the concept of imagination began to undergo a profound reappraisal, and this to such an extent that it came to rival and then surpass memory as both the main ingredient in creativity and the chief source of originality. This revolution in thinking made it possible for Coleridge to argue in the early nineteenth century that imagination is, in effect, the wellspring of all creative expression. Other Romantics supported Coleridge on this point by claiming that the greatest geniuses of any age are those who, because of their exceptional imaginations, can form mental images of *things they never experienced,* while those who are merely talented are fated to work with the more pedestrian images of things that have already happened and merely been retained in memory. Later, some of the early European psychologists also weighed in on this issue. Though none dismissed memory altogether as a factor in creativity, most nonetheless placed it far behind imagination as a source of creative insight or achievement. No doubt typical in this regard was the position staked out by the popular and prolific Henri Piéron. In his *L'évolution de la mémoire* (1910), Piéron captured the view of the majority of his colleagues when he argued that "all creation is impossible to the one who constantly submits himself to the imprint of past events . . . [since] a surcharge of memory makes new [mental] acquisitions more and more difficult."[20]

Though the views articulated by people like Coleridge and Piéron were often contested, their position seems ultimately to have triumphed. Not only do many contemporary writers and artists now extol imagination with the same enthusiasm that their predecessors extolled memory, but many present-day psychologists have similarly come to play down memory as a relatively insignificant factor in creative production.[21] The two things that have generally replaced memory in importance today are immediacy or intensity of vision and a powerful imagination, which are presumed to work together and complement one another. This shift away from an emphasis on memory has been evident not only in recent theorizing in the arts and humanities but also in the sciences, where creativity has been increasingly understood to mean breaking with or "disaffiliating from" old paradigms and striking out in directions undetermined by the constructs of the past.[22]

In the latest discussions of creativity, the higher valuation now being placed on forgetting over remembering is something relatively new in Western culture. In previous historical periods it was inconceivable that creativity could be associated in any way with forgetting. Today, however, it is not unusual to see forgetting treated not so much as an obstacle to creative achievement but as one of its essential components.[23]

Just as the supposedly natural bond joining memory and creativity has now been broken, so too has the one joining memory and happiness. In earlier times the assumption had been that memory as a rule produces happiness. Thanks to memory, it was often said, the best of what happened in the past gets preserved and carried forward to brighten one's present, while, by means of processes not fully understood, the worst seems to fall away into oblivion, or at least to lose its sting with the passage of time. If we do indeed possess an inborn tendency to suppress the negative in order to foreground the positive, then it is hardly surprising that memory was believed to engender an overall sense of contentment and well-being while forgetting was thought to lead to feelings of emptiness and nullity.

This view of the connection between memory and happiness has undergone serious questioning in the twentieth century. Again, according to many contemporary psychologists, the happy pasts people think they remember were almost never as rosy as they imagine, for most people tend to misrepresent their pasts by unwittingly bathing them in the glow of nostalgia and sentiment. Nearly everyone's childhood, adolescence, and early adulthood were, in actuality, filled with far more pain, grief, loss, humiliation, failure, depression, psychic injury, and unresolved conflicts than most individuals would like to acknowledge.[24] Generally speaking, we misremember the acute suffering of our past; we tidy up what we lived through or falsely interpret it and thus place it in the best possible light. If we were to remember our personal past as it really was, many now insist, we would recall levels and intensities of pain no reasonable person could want to recapture. Remembering this pain would not produce the contented, satisfied life most individuals appear to seek, but rather a troubled and unhappy one.

Freud, of course, addressed just this problem; as we have seen, many of the patients he treated early in his career suffered from what he called "painful reminiscences." It is no wonder then, given the disturbed psychological state of those who sought his help, that Freud at first tended to regard his patient's memories as extremely distressing if not traumatic mental experiences. Hence at the start of his career (though this changed somewhat later) Freud saw remembering as something that by and large brings unhappiness to those who cling to it. This being so, the rememberer had essentially two options when faced with hurtful memories: he or she could either repress them or work through them. Freud strongly opposed repression because it did not relieve remembered pain but only drove it deeper into the unconscious, thereby making it more diffuse and harder to deal with. "Working through" was naturally the option Freud preferred; in fact, it was on the basis of this approach to memory that he built his entire psychoanalytic project. As he later formulated them, the key tasks of the analyst are to help patients consciously recall harmful events from their past, to assist them in contextualizing those events both emotionally and "rationally," and to aid them in integrating the remembered material into their present lives.[25] When a patient learned how to do these three things successfully, he or she was said to have finally worked through the debilitating memories of the past.

Still, it is not often noticed that Freud suggested yet another way to handle hurtful memories, and that was simply to forget, or "deactivate," them. According to Freud, most of the memories that cause unhappiness are of events that are painful to recall for the simple reason that the events themselves were painful experiences. As a rule, such memories carry no deeper symbolic meanings, nor are they attached to repressed material in the unconscious. They are merely unhappy memories, or what Freud called "disagreeable impressions," which any individual would be better off forgetting, since holding on to them would only do damage to the psyche in the long run.[26] It was difficult enough, after all, to deal with contemporary problems without being burdened by memories of personal sufferings or misfortunes. Thus, for the sake of even a minimal notion of happiness, it seemed best to let go of "unpleasant recollections" when such recollections "awaken . . . pain" without providing any benefits.[27]

If one accepts what Freud says here, it would seem that forgetting can be and often is an entirely appropriate response to past suffering.[28] The experiences of many Jewish survivors of the Holocaust appear to support this point. Though conventional wisdom says that remembering the Holocaust is a good thing (because it makes succeeding generations aware of the human capacity for evil and teaches important lessons that may prevent similar catastrophes in the future), for many of the survivors of the camps it does not seem to have been personally a good thing at all. For those who, in recalling the Holocaust, recollect their own camp experiences, memory always brings back unspeakable pain; indeed, it brings back a type and intensity of pain that for many becomes all but impossible to incorporate into the normal routines of everyday life. If a reasonably happy or contented life is what one craves, then for Holocaust survivors forgetting might arguably be an imperative, since by recalling what happened to them and their families they only prolong the grief and hurt of the past.

One might legitimately reach such a conclusion in reading Lawrence L. Langer's recent *Holocaust Testimonies,* a study based on extensive interviews with over fourteen hundred survivors.[29] According to Langer, most of those who survived the camps felt two contradictory impulses, the first being to remember and the second to forget. The first impulse stemmed from a social or cultural sense of responsibility to bear witness to the crimes they had experienced firsthand lest those crimes be entirely lost to posterity. (Many survivors revealed to Langer that it was only the urge to convey to others what they had seen that sustained them through the months and years of their ordeal.) The second and often stronger impulse, however, was not so much social as deeply personal, based on the understandable desire to keep the worst of the past at bay—especially if, by remembering it, one risked undermining the very stability or integrity of the self. Every survivor undoubtedly experienced both of these contradictory impulses, but each handled them differently. The few who chose to become memorialists of the events they witnessed endured the sorrow memory brought for the "higher end" of documenting the atrocities they observed. But most survivors, almost as soon as they were liberated from the camps, tried to forget the horrors they had experienced there, since remembering them would have made it more difficult to get on with the new lives they would now have to lead.

When one looks at exactly what remembering the Holocaust meant for the survivors Langer interviewed, it becomes obvious why blocking out their experience seemed to make sense. For the most part, remembering meant not only recalling incidents of deprivation, exhaustion, starvation, degradation, and dehumanization that were beyond one's ability to control. It also meant recalling incidents that one *could* have controlled—for example, incidents of perceived moral failure in one's treatment of other inmates—particularly when one's acts of commission or omission led to unnecessary suffering or death. Memories of these latter acts seemed to have been especially hurtful for survivors to recall, even when they were able to acknowledge that in the camps it was nearly impossible to abide by the normal rules of ethical behavior. A great many of the survivors who spoke to Langer mentioned specific deeds that seemed in retrospect to be unpardonable acts of betrayal. Victor C., for instance, spoke of the unassuageable sorrow that yet seizes him when he remembers how he abandoned his sick brother when he should have stayed and attended to him. Hannah F. recalled the time when, in desperation, she stole the shoes of a camp inmate, knowing that to leave the other without shoes was virtually to sentence her to death. Another survivor remembered how she surreptitiously took part of her sister's bread ration because at that moment she was more concerned with satisfying her own pangs of hunger than with whether her sister lived or died. And still another survivor recalled that, against all established notions of parental love, she refused to accompany her own pleading children when, on the railway ramp at Auschwitz, they were to be sent "to the left" (which is to say, to certain death) while she was sent "to the right." It would be practically impossible for anyone to entertain such memories without experiencing feelings of shame or self-loathing, even if one did in fact keep in mind—though this often proved difficult to do—the completely different moral climate that obtained in the camps.

When the acts or events one remembers are this distressing, memory, it would seem, cannot lead to happiness, for the memory of either pain received or pain inflicted is likely only to deepen one's overall feelings of anguish or wretchedness. Yet the case against memory, or more specifically against the presumed link between memory and happiness, has not been made only with Holocaust survivors in mind. It is also true that memory brings forth in all of us similar, though surely less overpowering, recollections of particular acts from our past for which we feel shame, guilt, or regret. To keep, by means of memory, such acts in the forefront of consciousness would be to live under constant self-reproach.

In earlier times such remembering was not necessarily thought of as a bad thing, especially if it led to acts of repentance, expiation, or atonement. Today, however, terms such as these seem jarringly anachronistic, since in the therapeutic culture of late modernity the idea that remembering transgressions or failures might in some way be desirable has largely been discredited. A host of popular psychologists, newspaper advice columnists, and mental health professionals now remind us daily that remembering incidents from the past that produce guilt feelings or their equivalents can only have deleterious consequences. The reason this is so, they say, is that guilt, like shame or even remorse, poisons the psyche by engendering a sense of individual unworthiness. For those inclined to remember mainly regrettable things from the past, the result is likely to be not just "low self-esteem" but neurosis, depression, or other forms of deep unhappiness. And to follow this same line of thought in the reverse direction, in order to be happy and life-affirming it would be essential to free oneself from negative feelings as quickly as possible—not by means of various forms of ritualized self-punishment as was frequently suggested in the past, but simply by putting them out of mind. Since memory is the main conduit of shame or guilt, if we were discouraged from remembering so much or so often the hurtful past would not linger in our consciousness, and we would not be subject to damaging feelings of dejection or self-disgust. In this respect, the recommendation to let the past go (or in the current parlance, to "get over it!") makes good sense. Of course, no contemporary therapist or psychologist has claimed that forgetting is in and of itself a guarantee of happiness. The claim is merely that happiness can never become a real or lasting possibility until there is first a considerable amount of forgetting.[30]

The same premodern outlook which assumed that memory produces happiness also assumed that memory is necessary for wholeness. But in recent decades this assumption too has been overturned.

In earlier centuries in the West, to be whole or well-rounded generally meant to be *one self,* but with many facets, many dimensions. An individual achieved wholeness or well-roundedness by bringing together into a single identity the sum total of the experiences, ideas, and values he or she had accumulated over a lifetime. Even as late as the nineteenth century a figure such as Goethe still served as a classic model of many-faceted individuality, because, as Nietzsche put it, he knew how to "put himself in the middle of life" in such a way as to take "as much as possible upon himself, over himself, into himself," and by doing so, to become a "*totality.*"[31] It was never doubted that a powerful retentive memory was essential to achieve this sort of many-sidedness. For if the accumulated experiences and impressions of one's past were not at hand there would be very little personal material to draw upon beyond what is afforded by the raw immediacy of the present, and as a result one would lack the substance needed to become a whole personality.

In more recent times, however, the importance of memory for wholeness has begun to be questioned. This questioning has come about, in part, because many modernists (and later, postmodernists) over the past century have redefined the meaning of the term "wholeness," taking it to refer not to the presence of some core identity with various sides or facets to it but rather to the presence of *many selves,* each more or less autonomous, more or less unconnected to the others. If this is what "being whole" means, then one would arrive at it not by means of a centering but a decentering of the self. The whole person would be one who is able to be at different times and in different ways all the selves he or she potentially is without ever being delimited by any one of them. Seen from this perspective, memory becomes detrimental to the notion of wholeness or totality, at least if remembering is understood to mean a continual recollection of, and faithfulness to, the one and only core self one had been from nearly the beginning of one's existence. And to the same extent that the connection between memory and the older, premodern concept of wholeness is weakened, that between forgetting and wholeness is strengthened. From this new point of view, it is primarily by forgetting the alleged rigidities of the centered ego that a variety of other hitherto unacknowledged or undeveloped selves or potential selves can finally acquire the breathing room needed to "become who they are."

This new conception of wholeness uncoupled from memory became possible only in the wake of a rejection of the two predominant notions of the self in the Western, and especially the Judeo-Christian, tradition. The first notion maintained that there is one and only one essential self, and that this self is present and fully formed from the earliest years of one's life. If one stays true to this fixed self, one not only becomes whole but also develops a firm and solid character. To "have character" in this sense meant to remember and remain loyal to the self one inherently is. By contrast, to lack character, or to be "out of character," was synonymous with forgetting; it meant not keeping in mind, or not living up to, the qualities that one's quintessential self comprised.[32]

The second rejected notion of the self was less static but equally dependent on memory. It contended that although everyone has only one self, this self evolves over time. At different stages along the continuum of one's life it might appear as if there is more than one self, but only because every individual, in the course of his or her development, normally experienced twists, turns, and reversals, each of which could seem to produce different personae as one moved from infancy to adulthood. St. Augustine, for example, in recalling his early life in the *Confessions,* initially gives the impression that he thought he had literally been a different person, or even a succession of different people, at various points in the past. As mentioned earlier, he saw himself first as a young boy who possessed a mixture of good and bad qualities, then as a bright but arrogant adult in whom the bad qualities came to predominate, and then finally as a middle-aged bishop of the Church who, with God's help, was able to recover the good qualities he had as a youth. On closer examination, however, it became apparent to Augustine that he was in fact not a concatenation of disparate selves, but rather only one self struggling to find and unfold his innermost spiritual identity. What at the outset appeared to be prior selves were in retrospect discovered to be anticipatory aspects of a later, integrated self. Or put differently, these putative earlier selves represented only developmental phases of a single continuous identity which turned out to be the very one Augustine had managed to bring together into a totality when he wrote his *Confessions.* Thus, according to this more complicated notion, the self is not fixed for once and all but unfolds over time on the basis of its own *potentia.* The unfolding involves occasional rapid advances followed by temporary retreats, which is why it takes years or even decades for a self to become in actuality what in its origins it was only potentially. A recent variant of this concept has reappeared in Erik Erikson's so-called *epigenetic principle,* which states that "anything that grows has a ground plan, and that out of this ground plan the parts arise, each part having its time of special ascendancy, until all parts have arisen to form a functioning whole."[33] For Erikson, one becomes a distinct and whole individual by means of this "inner law of development." But for a law like this to work, all the parts that go into making the whole, many-faceted person must be inwardly retained, otherwise there would be nothing available to be gathered in, or integrated into, some final entity worthy of being called a self.

In the nineteenth and twentieth centuries in the West, the two memory-grounded notions of the self I have just described were challenged by a number of quite different conceptions. In important ways, these new conceptions, forged in response to what were seen as uniquely modern conditions, made forgetting far more central than remembering for the constitution of a viable, well-rounded self. Though for present purposes it is not necessary to describe these new views in detail, it would nevertheless be helpful to mention a few examples of how the self has come to be thought of in ways that share little or nothing with the memory-based notions mentioned above.

First, the idea began to appear in late-nineteenth-century psychology that there is not simply one self, fixed *or* evolving, but rather two: a true and a false self. According to this view, a false self is acquired when one adapts to or internalizes the conventional habits, roles, and expectations of social life, and hence becomes merely what the social norms induce one to be. Underneath this false or artificial self there was presumed to be another one crying out for attention or realization, and this one was said to be natural, genuine, and "authentic." It was widely argued, particularly in the new genre of popular psychology books that began to gain a broad readership around 1900, that every individual's task—indeed, obligation—was to liberate the true but suppressed self from the constraints imposed by the false but dominant one. For many, it seemed that there was no other way to become the free and healthy self one potentially was without first setting aside, shattering, or in some other manner "forgetting" the stultifying and deadening self that most people were thought to have developed in response to social pressures to conform.

Those who adopted this rudimentary framework manifested increased interest in the nature of the authentic, uncontaminated self that would supposedly be able to come into its own once the superficial, role-playing self had been dismantled. What exactly did this purportedly true but hidden self look like? Since it still remained vague and undefined, it seemed to represent only *pure possibility*—a concept perhaps not specific enough to be very appealing. For this reason, commentators at the beginning of the twentieth century worried that many people would lack the patience to draw this concealed self out into the open; they might instead be more inclined to deny their own possibilities by retreating to the safer but narrower self endorsed by custom and convention. To a great extent, this worry was understandable, for if one really could become, say, a dozen different selves, then an awareness of this fact might create an excess of apprehension about whether or not one was becoming the full personality one was capable of being. The vertiginous sense of freedom either to realize or fail to realize the self one could be might in all probability increase, not reduce, anxiety.

One way to handle such anxiety was to create a strong, controlling, rationalizing ego that would shape the self in *one and only one* direction, thereby excluding the self's other actual or apparent possibilities. Choosing this option would mean reducing the latent self's allegedly unlimited capacities in the interest of order, regularity, and organization, and for probably the majority of commentators from the turn of the nineteenth century to the present day that has not been an acceptable plan at all. Hence it began to be suggested that, for the sake of realizing the self's rich potential, one ought to remain as unstructured or decentered as possible. The difference between this point of view and the premodern one discussed earlier could not be more pronounced. In ancient and medieval times what is now called "centeredness" would have been seen as an essential aspect of wholeness. Today, for many postmodernists in particular, the reverse seems more true, as centeredness—especially when too intently sought or too rigorously embraced—has become increasingly associated with the qualities of rigidity, inflexibility, and immobility.

A decentered self, briefly put, is one that shuns, as one contemporary writer put it, any "thralldom to a particular stance."[34] Precisely this thralldom is what many observers now think discredits older, character-based notions of the self. Rather than remaining locked into only one identity, the self, some have contended, needs to become more mobile, fluid, porous; it needs to develop the ability to be "polymorphously versatile," to be comfortable with a diffuse identity, and to be open to a broad spectrum of possibilities that would have been almost unimaginable to our forebears. But for all this to happen, there would first have to be a forgetting, not only of the false, role-playing self upheld by society at large, but also even of the ordered self one might create on one's own initiative, since both tend to restrict the person one could be by confinement within the straitjacket of a single, fixed identity.

This new view of the self permeates modern humanistic psychology, and through it popular psychology in general. The widely read works of Carl Rogers, for example, have enthusiastically endorsed the "person of tomorrow"—a term which for him refers to the individual who has managed to free himself or herself from the prison-house of past identities in order to adjust more successfully to the new world coming into being. According to Rogers, the full, well-rounded personality of the future will be one who rejects "memories and previous learnings" which only serve to hinder the unfolding of an individual's "continually changing constellations and potentialities."[35] In contrast to old-fashioned character types, the so-called person of tomorrow will be more open to experience, more capable of seeing and appreciating each moment's freshness, and therefore also more adept at dealing with the rapidly changing configurations of modern existence. Robert J. Lifton has echoed Rogers in lauding what he has termed "protean man." Just as the Greek god Proteus became at different times a sea god, a leopard, a wild boar, and a tall green tree, all the while still remaining Proteus, so too, Lifton argues, the modern individual should strive to be mutable and decentered. In the world of late modernity a person can best fulfill himself or herself not by firming up one permanent identity, but by continually transforming, reconstituting, and reconstructing the self in such a way as to allow, at different times and in different settings, all of the self's many facets and dimensions to come to the fore. For this to be achieved much forgetting is necessary, since protean man must always be ready to discard one aspect of the self in order to take up another. Whereas for Lifton memory is generally identified with the dubious qualities of consistency, predictability, and what he calls "stuckness," forgetting is by contrast associated with heterogeneity, plasticity, and the ability to improvise. In reading Lifton one is never in doubt as to which of these two sets of qualities he believes to be the more important for late modern individuals to cultivate.[36]

Yet a third notion of the self to gain some prominence in the twentieth century maintains that each individual is not a single self, centered or decentered, but a succession of discontinuous selves, each of which displaces the previous one over the course of a lifetime. In this view, each earlier self needs to be erased and forgotten, since only thus can the empty space necessary for something new to come into being ever be created. Rimbaud had hinted at something along these lines already in the late nineteenth century.[37] Later Proust similarly suggested that every individual is only a collection of "intermittent" selves, each possessing its own uniqueness, and each subsisting independent of and separate from all the others, so that when one self comes into being and "achieve[s] sufficient consistency," the others "vanish."[38] According to Proust, the disappearance of past selves is nothing to be lamented, for there is no other way for a new self to take hold except by abolishing former ones.[39]

Notions such as these have survived in some form or other down to the present day,[40] but recently they have themselves been adumbrated by yet another conception of the self which has gained popularity in many circles. This conception postulates that individuals contain not so much consecutive as simultaneous selves. For one self to come into being, a previous one does not necessarily have to vanish but can remain alive and intact and continue to coexist within the same person. From this point of view, that entity traditionally referred to as a "person" or an "individual" is actually little more than an assemblage of autonomous or semiautonomous selves, each with its own attitudes and preferences, its own "energy," its own "voice," and even its own "soul."[41] These selves purportedly come into being as a result of different processes. Some are the products of congealed desires, with different desires producing different selves. Others supposedly originate as effects of internalized images, again with different images of what or how to "be" engendering different selves. And still others are said to come about through various forms of social interaction, with one set of relations producing one kind of self, and another set producing another kind. In all of this, the presumption is that people do not simply possess one self with many different facets, as proponents of the decentered self such as Rogers or Lifton have averred. Rather, the presumption is that they possess many separate selves, or even whole ensembles of selves, all of them inhabiting the same bodily space.

For example, according to James Hillman, a much-acclaimed champion of this position, being a mother, daughter, wife, nurse, and muse—or a father, son, husband, worker, or colleague—is not simply playing different roles; it is literally enacting different selves.[42] And because all of these selves exist simultaneously, apparently without subverting or negating one another, each individual has the opportunity to experiment with a plethora of available identities. This being so, wholeness or multidimensionality is perforce reinterpreted to mean honoring one's plurality of selves by giving each a chance to express itself in its own fashion. It may happen that one self is inconsistent with another, but for the defenders of this position, inconsistency is not a matter of particular concern (as it always is for advocates of the centered self). Since each self is merely contiguous and not continuous with every other, no one self need feel responsible for the promises or commitments made by the others. When one self is put on hold, whatever obligations it may have incurred can be bracketed or even temporarily nullified. To abide by the commitments made by one self while at the same time trying to give attention to another self clamoring for expression would only have a narrowing, constrictive effect on one's personality. Consequently, for Hillman and others who have followed him on this point, it would seem best to let each self live its own life, "coming and going" as it pleases, independent of the inclinations of all the other selves that may happen to reside within the same person.[43] Still, the ideal here would not be, as would appear to be the case with the notion of successive selves, a complete forgetting but rather only a partial or momentary forgetting. For if, in actualizing one self, a person were to forget all the others, it would be impossible later to recuperate the remaining selves that go into the makeup of his or her total personality. Or, to use Hillman's terminology, if there is to be a healthy polytheism (meaning an assemblage of multiple, simultaneous selves) instead of an oppressive monotheism (the restrictive ego-centered self) there must be at least enough forgetting to allow each self freely to speak its own voice without continually being interfered with by a cacophony of other voices.

In sum, all of the views of the self that I have been describing here have emphasized to one degree or another the link not between remembering and wholeness but between forgetting and wholeness. The assumption underlying all the theorists just discussed is that when one constructs an identity based on memory, the result is a self that is too past-oriented and consequently too rigid or calcified. To forget, on the other hand—which means to let go of continuity, consistency, linearity, and repetition *as values*—is to make possible a looser, more open-ended self, or even a multiplicity of selves. By forgetting, so the argument goes, one becomes freer, more elastic, and more indeterminate, and these qualities in turn help produce the kind of many-sided personality that is increasingly being put forward as a model to imitate, both by contemporary psychologists and by promoters of present-day commercial culture.

In these last several pages I have tried to indicate the extent to which forgetting has moved into the center of modern notions of creativity, happiness, and wholeness. This vindication of forgetting, though a relatively new development, had gained a fairly wide hearing by the late twentieth century, but this is not to say that those who have been concerned to defend the value of memory have been silenced or defeated. Before bringing this chapter to a close, I want to return to the three themes I have been discussing in order briefly to present the pro-memory side of each issue. Though the arguments in favor of forgetting have much to recommend them, they also overlook a great deal, as the following remarks should demonstrate.

Memory and Creativity. It is hard to deny that too much allegiance to remembered ideas, concepts, and methods could serve to block the new perspectives or novel ways of thinking that one generally associates with creative minds. But this view itself forgets that most creative expression draws on a repertoire of forms and meanings passed down from one generation to the next. In creative work as in much else, one almost never starts *de novo.* Even the most radical innovators in every field of endeavor have been aware of and have learned from what went before; every one of them has been cognizant of how his or her work "fits" in relation to the accomplishments of the past. More than this, virtually all creative achievement is the result of some form of agonistic struggle with strong or weak predecessors. If these predecessors are forgotten, one has no reference point for one's own work and therefore no adequate means of defining the project one wants to undertake. To be sure, once a project is underway a creator may offer completely different solutions to inherited problems, or may even reject entirely the very way a problem had been posed in the past. But in either case one usually needs a *point d'appui* of some kind, or nothing will be initiated.[44] Memory, in the form of some clear and even detailed knowledge of what has already been done, most often provides that point of support, and to the degree that it does, it underlies and informs nearly every creative act.

Similarly, the notion that forgetting stimulates creativity seems to assume that freshness of perception unclouded by the interpretive frames of the past is one of the primary, if not *the* primary, factor in engendering a creative state of mind. But this may be a mistaken notion of what actually makes an individual creative. It might not be "pure perception," or the unfiltered experience of sheer immediacy, that most encourages a creative condition, but rather the opposite: a sense that every instant and every experience is rich with reverberations from the past. By bringing the past associatively into the present with the aid of memory, one makes the world more multilayered than it would appear to be if simply taken at face value. Experience without memory runs the risk of being little more than empty, durationless sensation—something that one would hardly think of as a stimulus to creative expression. Experience informed by memory, on the other hand, is likely to carry resonances that evoke a wide range of personal and symbolic meanings out of which higher levels of creative achievement might well be expected.

There is yet another point to be made in this regard. A spontaneous insight or novel impression may make one *feel* creative, but in fact one is not truly creative unless such insights or impression are given form. Properly speaking, the term "creative" should describe an act, not a feeling or mood. After all, when we speak of creators we mean individuals who are able to transmute perceptions, emotions, or experiences into objectifications of some kind. To turn a perception or an emotion into a painting, novel, or musical composition requires a knowledge of techniques, even a long training in method, which in turn requires a disciplined memory. Without such memory one would not know how to give shape to what would otherwise be merely fleeting sentiments or intuitions. Thus it seems misguided to think of the creative individual as a "genius of forgetting." Rather, it appears more correct to view him or her as a rememberer, that is, as someone who can take in and then imaginatively work through, reconfigure, and literally "re-member" ideas, forms, and materials handed down from the past.

Perhaps all significant creation is, in some manner or other, re-creation. Certainly the new does come forth in a creative work, but usually when the latent or unnoticed potential of already existing forms and ideas is drawn out and made manifest. Our contemporary age may not like to think so, but it still appears that the new mainly comes into being through a *completion* of what has been left incomplete, or by bringing to awareness implications hinted at but never quite grasped or expressed before. Hence creation as re-creation means not merely repeating what is, but inventively reinterpreting and reconceptualizing that which has been received from the past. Kierkegaard called this particular understanding "remembering poetically," by which he meant making something novel and unfamiliar out of what is old and familiar.[45] A careful look at even the most innovative achievements of modern times would, I think, reveal that far more poetic remembering informs them than the innovators themselves probably realized.

Memory and Unhappiness. Undeniably, memory often brings unhappiness in its train, for where there is memory there is bound to be remembered pain or guilt. Hegel implied as much when he portrayed the rememberer as someone with especially strong ties to an interior world of suffering. In his view, memory cannot help but lead to reflection, and reflection to some amount of Unhappy Consciousness. By contrast, the individual who can easily and unproblematically forget the past has that much less burden of hurt to deal with. This may be why, as already noted, forgetters seem to be happier and more lighthearted than rememberers; it is because they do not linger at length over the harm they once did to others or the harm others did to them.

But to relate memory too facilely with unhappiness fails to delve deeply enough into the matter. The choice of remembering and then working through the hurt or guilt dredged up from the past opens the door to potentially greater levels of satisfaction and well-being than would be possible if one simply dispensed with the past altogether. The highest forms of happiness may well come about when one willingly enters the "nocturnal pit" (Hegel) of the past and then transforms the negative that one finds there into something positive. Sometimes happiness, if it is to have any quality or depth to it at all, has to be achieved by means of a struggle with, among other things, one's memories. Often the elation one feels at the end of a long and difficult process of self-overcoming is far greater than the comparatively thinner and more superficial joy experienced when one merely forgets the painful aspects of one's past in order to delight in as undisturbed a fashion as possible in what is immediately at hand.

If it is true that remembered pain or sorrow can, if worked through and transformed, produce a measure of satisfaction unknown to the forgetter, the same does not at first sight appear to be so with respect to remembered guilt. The persistence of guilt feelings, whatever their origin, would seem to have little to do with happiness, for the bite of conscience cuts deeper into the psyche and produces more mental anguish than anything else we know. Yet even here no simple, one-to-one relationship can be established between guilt and unhappiness. Instead of wearing one down with regret or remorse, guilt can, when it leads to behaviors that overcome it, produce exultant states of mind which, to express it in the language of religion, are often associated with the "release" that comes with feelings of purification or redemption. As premodern societies certainly knew, when individuals follow the protocols of repentance and reparation they can reestablish a oneness not only with an injured or aggrieved party, but through that individual with the community as a whole. The same feelings of harmony and serenity are also possible when one comes to terms with and forgives oneself for various faults or failures and then proceeds to make amends for them. The feeling of happiness one experiences as a result of such cleansings and renewals is not, on the whole, available to modern-day forgetters, who are quick to put their past behind them and consequently feel no pressing need to reflect upon their forgotten shortcomings. Yet in the absence of any reprising and repairing of what one has already done, there can be no "labor of the negative," and without that no higher positivity either.

Seen in this light, then, it would be wrong to assume, as many now do, that a direct link exists between memory and unhappiness. But there is another side to this as well, for it is often overlooked that memory can connect us with past instances of love and generosity no less than of pain and hurt. Remembering, for example, the warmth or kindness that others have shown us can lead to the deeply satisfying feeling of gratitude. Gratitude comes when we appreciatively recall "how much of what we are and what we have depends upon the gifts [and the love] of others."[46] Without a sense of gratitude informing our lives, we are more depleted as human beings. The person who too quickly forgets what was bestowed upon him in the past, especially through acts of caring or selflessness on the part of others, loses awareness of much for which he should be thankful. Forgetting such gifts can actually eliminate one of the deepest wellsprings of happiness, while remembering can keep those wellsprings open and flowing. Remembering what we have to be grateful for can also be an inducement to ethical behavior if we try to replicate the good shown to us by being similarly generous and giving toward others.[47] In this regard, the German sociologist Georg Simmel was not off the mark when he called gratitude the "moral memory of mankind."[48]

Memory and Wholeness. If remembering does in fact reinforce and stabilize the ordered, structured self, as many have argued, then forgetting would open up possibilities for a decentered or disseminated self—or indeed, even for the emergence of consecutive or multiple selves. To the extent that wholeness now appears to be associated with the fluid, protean personality, the propensity to forget would seem to be an especially valued quality, since forgetting is what helps disaffiliate one from the controlling ego, thereby making it difficult for an individual to hold fast to any single, fixed identity even if he or she wanted to.

But is it really true that forgetting leads to wholeness? In order to understand why there is reason to be skeptical of the connection between forgetting and wholeness, it would first be helpful to distinguish between "wholeness" and "well-roundedness." Earlier I used these two terms more or less interchangeably, but it may be that they refer to quite different things.

Wholeness, it might be said, means the attainment, on a personal level, of unity and integration; it is achieved when one gathers together into a totality all that one has learned and experienced. Well-roundedness, on the other hand, might best be defined as the sum of characteristics one acquires through experimentation with a variety of roles or personae, none of which needs to be organically related to any other. While the first implies something centripetal, where all one's qualities and experiences are drawn together into a center, the second suggests something centrifugal, where one seeks, in a quantitative more than a qualitative sense, to think, feel, or experience as many different things as possible within the framework of a single lifetime.

If this distinction is valid, then wholeness would require memory, for in order to achieve integration, the past would have to be not only retained and drawn upon, but, as Goethe expressed it, "woven into the fabric of [the] inmost self," or otherwise there would be no substantial content out of which to fashion a unified identity.[49] Well-roundedness, by contrast, would seem not to be harmed and may even be aided by forgetting, that is, by letting go of centeredness as a desideratum in order to try out as many different and even contradictory lifestyles as might attract one's attention.[50]

What appears to have happened in late modern culture, partly no doubt because of the influence of media and marketing images, is that wellroundedness has become the new ideal. Today people are encouraged to be, and seem also genuinely to want to be, what are now called "dispersed" or "multifaceted" personalities. Yet despite the apparently wide appeal of wellroundedness as a value, the urge to be whole still appears to be fully present, and, at least for a small number of people, still remains the higher, more worthy goal. Even a thinker like Nietzsche, who has lately been transformed by some postmodernist interpreters into an advocate of well-roundedness,[51] was in his strongest and most characteristic statements a defender of the idea that wholeness grounded in memory is, or ought to be, the true aim of life. In *On the Advantage and Disadvantage of History for Life*, for instance, Nietzsche wrote that the greatness of an individual depends strictly upon his capacity to "grow out of [himself], transforming and assimilating everything past and alien, . . . replac[ing] what is lost and reshap[ing] broken forms. . . . The stronger the roots of the inmost nature of a man are, the more of the past he will appropriate or master; and were one to conceive the most powerful and colossal nature, it would be known by [the way it] draw[s] its own as well as every alien past wholly into itself and thereby transform[s] it into blood, as it were."[52] If Nietzsche is correct here, it would seem that for one to be whole rather than merely well-rounded one would have to remember, build from, and grow out of one's personal as well as one's collective past.

In sum, if our posttraditional definitions of the self as fluid, mobile, and heterogeneous truly express the kinds of identities people want or need today, then forgetting the past would be in order, since for each individual's new identity to thrive there would have to be some clearing away of those residual memories that bolster the interest of the centered ego. If, however, it is not many-sidedness that one is seeking, but rather something that used to be called totality or wholeness, then forgetting would be ill-advised, for it would push out of consciousness exactly those things that would have to be retained and gathered together into a unity.

Ultimately what one thinks of either forgetting itself or of the forgetter as a particular type of individual may come down to the criteria one uses to assess them, and these have varied from one historical era to another. In the ancient world or in the Middle Ages, as we have seen, remembering was considered centrally important, while in the twentieth century forgetting seems to have usurped memory's privileged place—or at least now a forgetter is more apt to feel in tune with rather than opposed to the tenor of the age. What has caused this shift in attitude, and what are its implications? Is it legitimate to say that today we simply no longer need to remember as much or as well as our ancestors did? Or can it yet be claimed that we still do need memory, but perhaps now memory of entirely different things than were emphasized in the past?

In order to address these and similar questions adequately, it is important first to take a closer look at the broader social and cultural context in which acts of remembering or forgetting take place at the present time. Without a better sense of this context, it is difficult to know how to judge the relative merits of remembering or forgetting, since how each is valorized is never decided in a vacuum but always under the shaping influence of particular historical conditions. Once these conditions have been described, it will be possible to return to and answer more specifically the question I posed at the outset and have tried to keep in mind ever since: What, in the contemporary era, are the values we want to assign to remembering and forgetting in our lives?

PART 2

Collective Remembering and Forgetting

The Social Frames of Memory

Obviously many other things can be remembered besides the events, feelings, or experiences of one's personal past. Society, for example, wants each of its members to recall certain supra-individual things, and it often goes to great lengths not only to encourage but to compel such memories for the sake of social or cultural cohesion.

There are essentially three ways in which society, operating through its dominant institutions, involves itself in issues of memory. First, it plays a powerful role in determining which values, facts, or historical events are worth being recalled and which are not; second, it has a hand in shaping how information from the past is to be recalled; and third, it has a say in deciding the degree of emotional intensity to be attached to memories.

With regard to the first point, every society in every historical era preserves a specific stock of information which it then makes generally available for recall. Of the nearly infinite number of things that any collectivity could designate as memorable, comparatively few are actually retained and made accessible as social knowledge. In earlier ages, much information was preserved through formal rites and rituals, but much was also kept in circulation informally, through traditions, customs, and folkways. As societies became more complex and highly differentiated, specialized institutions came into being (conservatories, archives, libraries, museums, and the like) which sought to preserve particular values, practices, or forms of knowledge that were believed to be in danger of disappearing. Whether in ancient or more recent times, those who possessed the authority to speak for the social order had a decisive voice in determining which aspects of the past ought to be stored and passed on, and which need not be. In this respect, it seems that very little information of real social or cultural import is remembered automatically or unthinkingly. When something is retained over time, there is usually a good reason for it; the retention is not accidental, but purposeful, intentional, and institutionally supported. Thus it would be hard to give much credence to theories of social memory that assume the presence of some unseen collective mind. In my view, no such collective "psychical unit" exists beyond the individual—neither a Durkheimian *conscience collective* (which has a life of its own separate and apart from individuals), nor a Jungian group unconscious (which is supposedly lodged in the mind at birth and "outlast[s] all generations").[1] If social memories are preserved and remain active over a long period of time, it is because particular traditions or particular institutional carriers have made it possible, not because there is some alleged collective psyche at work recalling by its own agency what individuals would otherwise forget.

Second, and beyond the issue of what kinds of memories a society decides to privilege, there is the question of how the past ought to be recalled. In some instances, societies have demanded that specific (often sacred) things from the past be remembered exactly and in great detail, even to the point of making membership in the collectivity contingent upon such memories. In other instances, it has been acceptable for people to remember in only a general or sketchy way, that is, in such a manner as to possess a rough knowledge of something in the past even if they cannot give an exact account of what they know. And in yet other cases, it has been permissible for entire populations to forget a wide range of vital, though often highly arcane information, so long as a small number of professional remembrancers were at work recalling it. In subtle and not so subtle ways, it is society as a whole that decides how and with what thoroughness certain facts or values are to be remembered, not each individual acting on his or her own, entirely separate from the group.

Third, society also helps decide the "charge" or affect a memory is to have, as well as the specific valuation to be placed on it. All of these decisions about what, how, and how intensely to remember some things and not others precede the appearance of any particular individual; they are embedded in the culture in which one is born and socialized. Even when an individual thinks he is freely choosing to recall certain aspects of his social past, he may, without realizing it, simply be recalling what his society has already singled out as noteworthy.

The reason societies have sought to ensure that whole populations remember and internalize certain things is that memory can be very effective as social cement. Wherever it is present as a binding force, there one can also expect to find cohesion, consensus, and solidarity. In fact, so important have these three qualities been as values over the centuries that it is not surprising to see how regularly societies have made it a point to foster what they take to be the right kinds of memories, and therefore the right kinds of collective sentiments, among their members.

One of the oldest and most primitive means employed to encourage the right kind of remembering has been the infliction of pain. As Nietzsche famously summarized it, it has been assumed from earliest times that "[i]f something was to stay in the memory, it had to be burned in: only that which never ceases to *hurt* stays in the memory."[2] Operating on this premise, many archaic societies made the body, especially the bodies of criminals or other violators of the social codes, a kind of *aide-mémoire* by means of cuttings, piercings, brandings, mutilations, or various dismemberments. The guiding supposition behind these acts of violence was that when ordinary people took note of such awful markings of transgression and recalled why they had been inflicted, they were more likely to make sure that their behavior complied with the social norms. A greatly toned-down variant of this approach to memory continued into the Middle Ages. In parts of France at that time, when important matters affecting a village community needed to be remembered, a public gathering was convened so that all could hear firsthand the information it was imperative to recall. In such instances, as Georges Duby has written, "great care was taken to have very young children present and to slap them, sometimes violently, at the height of the ceremony, hoping that the memory of the spectacle attached to the memory of pain would cause them to forget less quickly what had transpired before their eyes."[3] Here, too, pain, though in a less extreme manner, was used as an inducement to memory.

Another way, developed at a later point in time, that societies of the past instilled the memories they required was by means of what might be called positive rather than negative reinforcement. Here the approach just mentioned was reversed, as generally pleasurable feelings were intentionally linked, in however rudimentary a fashion, to "memorable" ideas or events on the theory that when the pleasurable feelings were later recalled, so too would be the ideas or events associated with them. In early modern Europe, for example, the pomp and circumstance surrounding royal pageants, coronations, and triumphal entries into cities were designed to leave a literally unforgettable impression on the observing crowds. There are numerous descriptions of just how overwhelming these spectacles were, especially for commoners who in their daily lives were unaccustomed to witnessing such stunning displays of grandeur.[4] But precisely what favorable emotions were these displays designed to evoke? Basically, of course, those that worked to the advantage of the social and political elites who planned and staged the ceremonies: for instance, a sense of awe at how majestic the rulers seemed on such occasions, and thus how right and proper it was that they be, as it were, on top.

By the nineteenth century, other, seemingly more proficient, methods were devised to foster the requisite collective memories. With the introduction of compulsory schooling in most of western Europe and North America around mid-century, educational institutions began to be effective transmitters of social and political memories. In primary and secondary schools, children were systematically taught both the historical facts deemed worthy of recall and the normative values from the past to which they needed to pay allegiance.[5] Likewise, states began promoting memory through national commemorative days and other public fêtes, but in contrast to the spectacles of earlier times, these new days of remembrance were more participatory. Crowds no longer passively watched the goings-on from a distance, as was more typically the case in the seventeenth century and earlier, but actively joined in the celebrations themselves.[6]

By the beginning of the twentieth century, two other perhaps even more important things began to be understood. The first was that people, in order to remember at all, need to rely on mental frames or scaffoldings to help them search out and retrieve what they want to retain from the past. The second and related point was that, no matter how personally idiosyncratic these frames may appear to be when looked at on a case by case basis, they are in fact largely socially configured. Hence what an individual tends to think is memorable about the past is to a great extent what the social milieu designates it to be. As this kind of awareness began to take hold, some commentators became concerned about the danger of powerful groups gaining control of and then shaping to their own advantage the frames that people use to recover the past. Any group or interest that was successful in achieving such control would have gone a long way toward determining the tone and content of popular memory. Thus it became evident that the exercise of power did not have to mean brute force; it could also mean the subtlest manipulation of the frames that people utilize, mostly unconsciously, to think about and understand the past.

To be sure, in recalling not the historical or collective past but the personal past, individuals take a much greater role in devising their own frames. These frames, or schemata as they have been called, are to a considerable degree (though not entirely, as we will see later) based on the peculiarities of people's separate histories, and consequently no frame for private memory is exactly identical with any other. But in remembering the social or collective past, one's personally created schemata are obviously inadequate. For this broader, more extensive remembering one must turn to the frames that are ready at hand in one's social environment. But in adopting the schemata provided by society at large, one simultaneously adopts the biases and interpretations built into them, for no schema is neutral or disinterested. Each has its own categories and cuing mechanisms designed specifically to exclude some things from the past, selectively include others, and highlight still others.

By the late twentieth century the degree to which the social or cultural milieu itself furnishes people with the frames of reference and temporal markings they need to recall and "make sense of" the past began to be better understood. It became understood, too, that if whole communities internalize roughly the same frames, the remembered world that individuals within such communities share with each other will seem consistent and harmonious, since everyone will more or less agree on what the past was, and what it continues to mean. When these unifying frames break down, however—as happened in the West in the eighteenth and nineteenth centuries, when traditional communities began to dissolve under the impact of new economic and political realities—the world can suddenly appear chaotic and disjointed, since the schemata that map out a common interpretation of the past no longer seem to work. The result is that people tend to lose their grip on exactly that certain and dependable past which, in more stable times, individuals and collectivities are able to count on to help give them their bearings in the present.

Everything said above about the place of social schemata in human memory was hardly noticed by the earliest memory researchers. All of the nineteenth-century pioneers in the scientific study of remembering and forgetting—chief among them Wilhelm Wundt (1832–1920), Georg Elias Müller (1850–1934), and Hermann Ebbinghaus (1850–1909)—made great advances with respect to investigative procedures and modes of measuring and recording psychological phenomena, but they all neglected to take account of the social context in which most kinds of remembering and forgetting occur, and hence they overlooked the importance of social framing. By the beginning of the twentieth century, however, a number of psychologists (along with some sociologists) began to pay closer attention to the ways in which society at large is actively or passively present in most types of remembering. Indeed, some researchers eventually went in very nearly the opposite direction from their nineteenth-century predecessors by suggesting that when an individual remembers it is really society itself that remembers *through* him or her.

In France, for instance, the work of Pierre Janet, Charles Blondel, and others in the 1920s made considerable headway in placing individual memory within a group context,[7] but the most influential book within this new genre was Maurice Halbwachs's *Les cadres sociaux de la mémoire* (*The Social Frameworks of Memory*, 1925). In this work Halbwachs argued that the key not only to what is remembered but to how it is remembered lies neither in the psyche of individuals nor in some vague collective mind or collective unconscious, but in the "mental structures" that inhere in social groupings: structures which are then passed on from one generation to another through the normal processes of socialization. By virtue of being a part of specific families, classes, religions, political parties, professional organizations, and the like, one unwittingly acquires the frames and perspectives of these groups, and in time one begins to remember, naturally and without any particular effort, those things that are emphasized by each particular frame. (Actually, for Halbwachs, there are two kinds of social schemata: those shared by nearly everyone within a collectivity—for example, by Frenchmen in general—and those shared only by the members of smaller, more tightly knit groups within the social whole. It was mainly the latter type of schemata, each allegedly possessing its own "logic" and "*esprit*," that Halbwachs chose to explore in some detail.)[8]

According to Halbwachs, then, what we call individual memory is at bottom only a facet of social memory, or more specifically of group memory. When an individual recalls something, he always recalls it as a member of a group, and consequently he only recalls what the group (or groups, if he is a member of several at the same time) enables him to recall. If an individual completely forgets some aspect of the collective past, it is because the group has also forgotten it. Or if an individual leaves a group—say, the family in which he was raised—and is therefore no longer in daily contact with its mental frames, he will gradually forget what the family thinks memorable. Conversely, if the class to which an individual belongs changes its schemata for some reason and begins remembering new things, the individuals within that class will do likewise, and they will remember these new things in ways that are consonant with the class's newly devised mental configurations. Of course, Halbwachs does acknowledge that memory is still a "cerebral process," or as he also put it, a subjective "mental operation."[9] But since individuals are always members of groups, and since the group is the actual preserver and conveyor of memory, what an individual recalls when he remembers always comes from the group, and cannot be other than what the group makes possible.

Thus in Halbwachs's seminal work of the 1920s, the collectivity, whether construed on a small or large scale, is in a sense the true agent of every act of recollection, for the collectivity preserves and sustains the material that individuals recall. The individual seems at times to be little more than a conduit through which the group's memories are made manifest. Even when an individual thinks that he is remembering on his own, it is usually the case, according to Halbwachs, that he is really recalling the memory of some social group, since mentally every individual unavoidably carries the group with him at all times, even at those times when he is entirely alone.[10]

In England, the work of Frederic Bartlett in the early 1930s very much paralleled that of Halbwachs. In his *Remembering: A Study in Experimental and Social Psychology* (1932) Bartlett argued, in contrast to the assumptions underlying most nineteenth-century memory research, that "the manner and the matter of recall are often predominantly determined by social influences."[11] More specifically, when we remember, we grasp patterns in or impose patterns upon the material remembered; what we ultimately recall is what the patterns bring out, while what we forget is what the patterns prevent us from grasping or even discerning. These determinative patterns do not usually emerge spontaneously from the psyches of individuals, but rather are acquired from society and thus depend on the prevailing customs, conventions, and institutions of one's time and place. For Bartlett as for Halbwachs, we chiefly recall what the group induces or conditions us to recall, whether we are actually in the presence of other people or not. In the last analysis, it seemed to both that the psychological constructs we acquire from society shape what we remember—though we still have some leeway, based on individual temperament and character, to decide how we use and interpret the social frames we employ.

In the United States in the 1940s, a view similar to Bartlett's was put forth by Ernest Schachtel, a recent émigré from Germany. Like Bartlett, Schachtel believed that individual memory was decisively shaped by the prevailing social schemata. But whereas Bartlett thought of these schemata as constantly shifting in relation to changing historical circumstances and group interests, Schachtel, writing for a post-World War II American audience, tended to see social frames as generally locking individuals into rigid, stereotyped memories, thereby giving them not a flexible and constructive but rather a fixed and frozen perspective on the past. In Schachtel's opinion, not only does society indicate what we ought to recall about our collective past; it also encourages us to remember even our own personal past according to the frames and markers provided by society. For Schachtel, virtually every kind of memory we can have is "socialized"; the social or cultural world in which we live gives us the signposts without which we would hardly be able to remember anything at all. These signposts tell us which events of both the past and present are significant, and how they ought to be recalled. Schachtel put it this way:

> [T]he memories of the majority of people come to resemble the stereotyped answers to a questionnaire, in which life consists of time and place of birth, religious denomination, residence, educational degrees, job, marriage, number and birth dates of children, income, sickness, and death. . . . In the course of later childhood, adolescence, and adult life, perception and experience themselves [as well as memory] develop increasingly into rubber stamps of conventional clichés. The

capacity to see and feel what is there gives way to the tendency to see and feel what one expects to see and feel, which, in turn, is what one is expected to see and feel because everybody else does. Experience increasingly assumes the form of the cliché under which it will be recalled because this cliché is what conventionally is remembered by others. . . . There are people [for example] who experience a party, a visit to the movies, a play, a concert, a trip in the very words in which they are going to tell their friends about it; in fact, quite often, they anticipate such experience in these words. The experience is predigested, as it were, even before they have tasted it. . . . [As a result,] the processes of memory substitute the conventional cliché for the actual experience.[12]

Viewed in retrospect, it may be that Halbwachs, Bartlett, and Schachtel greatly overstated their respective cases. For instance, it is surely inaccurate to say flatly, as Halbwachs does, that "the memory of the group realizes and manifests itself in individual memories," as if the memories of any particular individual were nothing more than an extension of social memory.[13] Likewise, Schachtel undoubtedly exaggerates when he contends that the social memory frames most of us make use of radically narrow our relation to the remembered past, often reducing our memories to hackneyed clichés. Nevertheless, even allowing for overstatement, it is thanks to such theorists of social memory that we now have a much better understanding than the nineteenth century did of the following points: first, that although there may be no such thing as a "collective mind" in a Jungian or Durkheimian sense, there are nonetheless social schemata that lead us to recall the historical past, and at least some of our personal past, in prescribed ways; second, that these schemata are both general (belonging to a large collectivity, such as a nation), and group-specific (belonging to families, classes, or ethnic communities subsisting within the larger collectivity); third, that different groups or collectivities tend to foster the mental structures most suitable to their purposes, and that when these structures are used in thinking about the past they produce different kinds of memories; fourth, that when social schemata become internalized as an integral part of an individual's psyche, a natural "flow" develops between social and individual memory which often makes it difficult to distinguish which memories are strictly personal or private, and which are social or collective; and fifth, that just as individuals remember particular things with the aid of social frames, so too they are led to forget or occlude other, seemingly irrelevant, things, owing to the specific nature of the memory frames they employ.

In light of these relatively new understandings of how memory works, it should now be evident that if we are to talk about memories other than autobiographical ones, we cannot exclude the social dimension. Social or collective memory is simply too crucial, and it comprises too large a part of what we recall, to be left out of the discussion. With this in mind, I want to suggest that two developments which have become manifest over the past two or three centuries in the West with regard to social memory have had a great bearing on what and how individuals are likely to remember today. Here it would be useful to summarize each development by means of a separate argument (stated in very brief form) and then provide, in the following two chapters, the evidence that I think supports each argument.

First, there has been in recent times a general lessening of the need to remember both on the social and individual plane, and along with this lessening a widespread devaluation of memory itself. Though we are on occasion enjoined to recall collectively certain events from the historical past invested with symbolic meaning, these moments of remembrance have now become increasingly infrequent. What's more, given what seems to be a growing anti-memory mood in late modern society as a whole, such moments of collective remembering no longer carry either the societal importance or psychical intensity they did in earlier eras.

Second, social memory, even though much diminished when viewed from the perspective of the *longue durée,* has by no means disappeared, nor has it been entirely discredited. Rather, the frames and schemata of memory continue to exist, thus indicating that we have not yet become the culture of forgetting some have proclaimed us to be. Still, the kinds of memory most actively promoted now are memories of very different things than prevailed in the past. Within an overarching framework that has brought us a decrease in the value of memory as such, some social memory continues on today, but it has been so greatly reconfigured that it is possible our ancestors would not recognize what we now call "social memory" as a legitimate form of memory at all.

Both of these arguments, even if they seem contradictory at first glance, are relevant to the questions I have been raising throughout this book regarding the role that remembering and forgetting should play in one's life. I want to continue addressing these questions as we proceed, but now within a broader social and historical setting. In the final chapter of this book I intend to return to the issue of individual remembering and forgetting, but before that point it is imperative that the social and cultural dimensions of memory be discussed in greater detail, mainly in order to gather the information needed to speak more meaningfully about remembering and forgetting as values at the present moment. My goals for the two remaining chapters in this section are, first, to provide a better understanding of just how individuals living in the contemporary age have been affected by the unique memorial—or as it seems, anti-memorial—context of late modernity; and second, to determine what cultural significance remembering and forgetting now have in comparison to the significance they possessed in former times. That completed, it will be possible, in the conclusion to this book, to end the journey where we started: with the situation of the individual as he or she exists today, but now seen from a larger and more inclusive historical vantage point.

Memory in Historical Perspective

As we have already seen in part, for the great swath of time between the Neolithic Age and the beginning of the modern period, remembering was thought to be the single most important source and underpinning of all value. Indeed, without the aid of memory, it seemed inconceivable that values of any kind could even exist, for values were understood to be by definition things that were passed down from forebears and preserved more or less intact, not things that could be created *de novo* in the present.

In archaic times, for instance, nearly every aspect of life was oriented in some fashion toward habits of recollection. On the mundane level, the things recalled might be specific skills or modes of practical knowledge transmitted orally from one generation to the next; or they might be the norms, traditions, or symbolic meanings which were considered indispensable to communal solidarity; or, more abstractly, they might be the real or mythical origins or the heroic deeds of a tribal founder, each of which had to be kept in mind in order to give the group a sense of common lineage. (Even as late as the first century A.D., Tacitus described the manner in which certain Germanic tribes such as the Semnones met at fixed times throughout the year to recall their distant origins and thereby reinforce their bonds of kinship and sense of collective *Herkunft*.)[1] On a higher and more spiritual level, the recollections might be of essential cosmological truths deemed necessary for an understanding of existence itself, having to do with how the world originated, how it is sustained, and what place human beings have in the order of things. In remembering these truths, prehistoric and early historic peoples developed a profound sense of indebtedness to divinities who had set everything in motion and were thought to be palpably present everywhere. Partly as a result of such beliefs, remembering led to the taking on of numerous duties and obligations designed to propitiate the gods. In time these obligations came to provide some of the key rites and rituals that not only held archaic societies together but also gave them a sense of their own identity and purpose.

To forget any or all of these matters, whether practical, mythical, or metaphysical, was to lose touch with most of what was important in life. It is for this reason that Eliade was right to observe that in the earliest human communities memory was "the preeminent form of knowledge."[2] Without memory, archaic peoples would have had no guidelines for behavior, no framework for thinking, no substantial information with which to work. In this respect, the present for them did not merely follow upon the past temporally or sequentially, but depended on it for almost everything vital or necessary to existence. Thus every effort was made, individually and collectively, to bring the past actively into the present by means of commemorations and festivals of memory. By such methods, the apparently empty "now" of immediacy could be suffused with a worthier "then" of the past, and in this way achieve a certain borrowed validity which the present, it seems, did not possess on its own.

Seen in this light, forgetting in any form appears to have been one of the greatest transgressions imaginable. If the forgetting was related to everyday matters, such as how to make fire, forge weapons, or adapt to a hostile environment, it endangered group cohesion or perhaps even group survival. If the forgetting concerned tribal origins or the vaunted "ways of the fathers," it threatened to separate the living collectivity from those who had gone before. In the archaic *Weltanschauung,* what the dead knew must not be allowed to fade into oblivion; at all costs it had to remain alive and available (in communal customs or traditions, for example) so that it could "flow back to the living in the form of a memory."[3] To lose touch with this deep knowledge was to be cut off from everything that was considered culturally and socially life-sustaining. If, finally, the forgetting was of sacred matters, or of the indispensable ritual practices bound up with them, then what was put at risk was the community's relationship to the cosmos itself, or to the spiritual forces believed to operate therein. This kind of forgetting was arguably the most devastating, since it led not just to social or political disintegration but to moral chaos. Without ties to the realm of the holy or divine, no one would know what "right order" was, or what the gods intended, or what they asked of individuals or communities. Life itself, stripped of a spiritual or transcendent dimension, would become merely profane, and in such a condition no one would be able to determine which values to honor, or what the purpose of life on earth is or ought to be.

If this is how prehistoric peoples thought about such matters, then remembering was the only acceptable way to situate oneself in the world, and forgetting the main thing to be avoided. This point of view was strongly reinforced by the community as a whole and by the leading institutions in it, most of which tended to establish their own legitimacy on the basis of their connection to or continuity with the past. Not only was memory widely emphasized as a value, but the collectivity was careful to define what it was that individuals within the group needed to remember, and how and under what conditions they were to express or embody their memories in terms of actual social behavior. Since the unity of the whole was so important, little room was allowed for divergences from the communal norm. Under the circumstances, it seems likely that the vast majority of early peoples took their cues regarding the importance of remembering from the general orientation of the societies in which they lived. When remembering as a practice was held up as an ideal, we can assume that few were likely to have dissented, for what the collectivity wanted or needed was for the most part what the individuals within the collectivity thought they wanted and needed as well. Hence to the extent that, in this comparatively primitive context, memory was considered a value, forgetting was regarded as an anti-value. The individual who continually forgot what the group insisted be remembered appears to have been viewed as at best a lax and undesirable figure, and at worst a threat to the social and moral order.

Memory was no less important for the Jews of the first and second millennium before Christ. Virtually every aspect of early Jewish life was permeated by the imperative to remember—an imperative so powerful and unchallenged that it is difficult to find evidence that the opposite, anti-memory, perspective was ever seriously entertained.

What was it that the Jewish people as a collectivity felt obliged to remember? Three things stand out as especially noteworthy. First, there was the need to recall the numerous prescriptions and injunctions of Jewish law such as "Remember the Sabbath and keep it holy," which are found throughout the Torah. Second, there was the need to remember the acts that God had performed in history. For the Jews there was only one God (Jahweh), and he manifested himself not through the medium of nature, as was the case with the divinities of many other early religions, but almost exclusively through the medium of time. The events of history, from the rise and fall of empires to the punishment of some types of collective behavior and the rewarding of others, were believed to reveal the nature of God's will and intentions better than anything else. Thus by first discerning and then conscientiously remembering the meaning of God's many temporal interventions, one could grasp the broader patterns of his designs for mankind in general and the Jewish people in particular. Third, there was the need to be mindful of and collectively remain faithful to the greatest of God's interventions in history, namely the unique Covenant he established with the Jews, his chosen people. Once the Covenant was made and sealed at the time of Abraham, it was binding on every succeeding generation. All Jews for all time were enjoined to recall both what Jahweh expected of them (to worship him exclusively, to keep his Commandments) and what, historically speaking, he had done for them (delivered them from bondage in Egypt, helped them smite their enemies, permitted them to prosper when they had honored and obeyed him). To forget the Covenant and all it entailed was an act not only of ingratitude but of rebellion. When, at various times, the Jews did in fact break the Covenant and lived outside its terms, the worst disasters befell them. It was at moments such as these that the prophets spoke up, reminding Israel that it had alienated itself from God, that collectively it was living in sin, and that sin was by its very nature an aspect of willful forgetting. Especially within the prophetic tradition, the solution to Jewish woes was almost always to repent "in sackcloth and ashes." But the first and most essential step toward repentance was very simply to remember again what had been forgotten.[4]

These needs to remember applied to the Jewish people as an entire community. For that community, memory was crucially important religiously, socially, and politically. But when the cognitive structures of any people are so heavily dependent on memory as a value that the desirability of being anchored in the past achieves the status of a self-evident truth, one may naturally expect that memory will be just as highly esteemed on the individual or personal level as it is on the social. This proved to be the case in ancient Israel. For the Jews of biblical times, the good person was the one who continually remembered God in his prayers and acts, who recalled the blessings that had been bestowed upon him, and who kept in mind his past misdeeds and showed contrition for them. The reprobate individual, by contrast, repeatedly forgot what God had done for him, failed to examine his conscience, and showed little or no remorse for the wrongful behavior of his past. If one wanted to transform oneself from a sinful forgetter into a righteous rememberer one could not do better than imitate the example of Jahweh, who was himself portrayed as a model of remembering. In fact, in most instances in the Old Testament where the verb "to remember" *(zakhor)* was used, it applied to Jahweh as the subject or initiator of a memory. In some instances he remembered individuals in order to show them mercy or deliver them from harm. In others he recalled events such as the afflictions of Israel or the offerings and burnt sacrifices made to him.[5] But most of all, and most significantly, it was the Covenant that Jahweh remembered, and when he did he also recalled both those occasions when the Jews violated its terms (and hence deserved punishment or retribution) and those times when they lived up to their promises (and hence deserved his favor). By and large, Jahweh tended to reward people when they remembered him and became, like him, rememberers themselves; and he tended to strike out against them when they forgot and thus became unlike him. One might say that just as God became most fully himself when he remembered, so too the Jews became most fully themselves—and most pleasing in the sight of God—when they remembered his will and followed it explicitly.

As different as ancient Hellenic culture was from the Hebraic, it nonetheless placed a similar high value on social memory. From earliest times, for example, Greek aristocratic families stressed the importance of genealogical memory, since for them an individual's identity and status were intimately bound up with his or her ancestry. The further back through the ages a prominent *genos* extended, the more respect accrued to the living descendants of that line. To forget one's genealogy, or to have none that could be called illustrious, was to stand outside the chain of social life that linked the past to the present. Indeed, to have no significant lineage that one could remember and recount was literally to be nothing, to hardly exist at all.[6] Later on, to be sure, the concept of *genos* was transferred from family and kin to the emerging polis. In many places in Greece by the fifth and sixth centuries B.C., one's identity came to be tied more directly to the city-state to which one belonged than to the family connections one inherited. When this happened, the various poleis began developing a better historical as opposed to mythological sense of their place within a larger temporal frame. With the aid of numerous markers, monuments, and memorials, city-states such as Athens, Sparta, and Corinth increasingly called attention to the founding events and key personages of the past that helped make each polis historically unique. Of course, for centuries the Greeks remained aware of their common identity as "Hellenes," but they did so without forfeiting the more specific memories of those things that marked them off from one another politically and historically.

Besides genealogical, local, and regional memory, there were other types of memories the Greeks thought important. There was, for instance, the memory of model forms of behavior exemplified by real or legendary heroes from the past, and kept alive by *rhapsodes* whose task it was to transmit this vital information from one generation to the next by means of epic stories. There was the memory of divine admonitions that had to be kept in mind by leaders and commoners alike if the worst kinds of misfortune were to be averted. There was the memory of fundamental religious and symbolic meanings as well as of more mundane but still indispensable traditions and customs that the Greeks believed they could not do without, since their absence would produce an anomic mode of existence that would scarcely be endurable. And finally, there was the memory of important legal and juridical precedents, which were to be recalled not by everyone but by *mnemons,* or professional rememberers (and after the advent of writing, by *anagrapheis,* or "inscribers"), whose responsibility it was to preserve publicly and for the sake of consistency court decisions from the remote past.[7]

Given the influence of so much social or collective remembering, it is no wonder that memory was vitally important to the Greeks on a personal level as well. The historian Jean Pierre Vernant has described in detail the role memory played in what might be called the private realm. For the poet, or the creative individual in general, memory was a source of inspiration. It was the means by which, with the help of the goddess Mnemosyne, one became at least partially aware of all that had ever happened and all that was yet to come (information which the inspired poet could then turn into "divine song"). Likewise, for the spiritually questing individual, memory was thought capable of bringing back to consciousness knowledge of the previous lives one had led before birth. By recalling who one had been in the prenatal past, including all the faults and defilements of one's earlier existences, many Greeks believed it possible to rid themselves of the weight of former transgressions through rites of expiation and purification, and in this manner prepare the soul for a higher destiny after death. Here *in nuce* one can note the intimate connection between memory and spirituality discussed in chapter 2. Though this connection has been variously described over the centuries, one thing has remained constant throughout most of the Western tradition, namely that remembering has been positively associated with discipline and *askesis,* leading to redemption, while forgetting has been negatively associated with moral softness, or *hédonè,* leading to spiritual vacuity.[8]

Similarly, for thinkers such as Plato and his followers, memory was presumed to link one not to the former lives one lived but to the eternal truths of which one was cognizant before birth. Memory as *anamnesis* was valued because of the way it tied the individual to an unchangeable reality. By so doing, it allowed one to escape from the superficiality and transitoriness of everyday life in order to ground oneself in the realm of pure Being, which for Plato was the only reality worthy of the name.

During the classical age of Greece and after, some individuals began questioning the strong emphasis placed on memory in its many forms and manifestations. To at least a few outspoken critics of ancient Greek life, the present seemed to offer something more interesting and stimulating than the legacy of the past. But for most people throughout the long span of Greek history, the value of both social and individual memory was rarely doubted. On the whole, the ancient Greeks were, in the words of the Dutch classicist B. A. van Groningen, locked "in the grip of the past," and yet this grip was a friendly and nourishing one. To be connected to the past through the bonds of memory was for most Greeks not a dilemma or a curse but something desirable and enriching, since it was memory more than anything else that anchored one in the foundational things that mattered.

The Romans were perhaps even more respectful of the past than the Greeks, and thus even more susceptible to the pull of memory. This respectfulness was particularly evident in the way the Romans revered tradition. For them *traditio* (from the word *tradere,* "to transmit") meant a handing down of something valuable from one generation to the next in such a fashion as to keep it secure and intact. Tradition implied a sense of continuity, an unbroken connectedness to the past. When it was operative for any length of time, it was invested with almost unquestioned authority because it came from ances-tors, who were thought of as *maiores,* or "the 'greater ones' by definition."[9] The Romans took it for granted that the ideas or values one's forebears had forged and passed down to posterity must not only be best but must also be used as the frame for interpreting nearly everything that happens in the pres-ent. To forget tradition, which meant in effect to "break faith with the dead," not only jeopardized an entire world of inherited meanings; it was also an act of ingratitude, an unforgivable violation of trust. For this reason the Romans, when they migrated from ancestral homelands to take up residence in new colonial towns, were careful to bring with them clods of earth from the land inhabited by their forefathers. These clods, which were treated as sacred soil, were then ceremonially thrown into trenches dug where the new towns were to be. Symbolically, the earth of the mother country, which was believed to contain the *manes* of progenitors, was mixed with the earth of the colony. This procedure turned out to be an ingenious way of remaining in touch with the past, for instead of abandoning the land of their ancestors, the Roman colonists brought it with them when they emigrated in order to remain spir-itually tied to what it represented. Piety, fidelity, a strong sense of duty, and deference to the *authoritas* of the past were all cardinal virtues for the Ro-mans, and each was rooted in the primacy of remembering as a social as well as personal value.

Besides recalling and venerating what the ancestors stood for, the Romans were also strongly focused on two other kinds of remembering. The first was of the earliest beginnings of things, especially the most important beginning of all as far as the Romans were concerned: the founding of Rome itself.[10] This founding, which had both a mythological and historical dimension (the Romans never forgot that the Republic came into being in 509 B.C.; they marked this as the first significant date on their historical calendar), was mo-mentous because it meant the establishment of a *novus ordo seclorum* superior to anything that had existed before. Now there was finally law, order, and civilization, not just the obduracy of nature or ancient forms of political tyranny.

But over the course of centuries the Romans could not help noticing how frequently they slipped away from the greatness of their origins. Too often the promise of the beginnings was not only not realized but actually contravened in practice. From the Republic through the Empire there were numerous political disasters, decades of decline and disintegration, and periods in which the Roman people seemed to lose their sense of purpose. The solution to this breakdown of order was that Rome needed to renew itself by returning to the mystique of its beginnings. And it needed to see these beginnings in the same way that archaic peoples saw theirs: as rich with possibilities, a font of creative vitality and moral energy. For the Romans, the aim was almost invariably to return to or retrieve that which was implicit in the origins, since what was present there *ab ovo* represented something good and valid for all time. Quite literally, to the Roman way of thinking the origin was the goal, for ontologically the origin never had been and never could be surpassed.

To one degree or another, most Romans shared this view of beginnings and the imperative to remember them. Even Machiavelli, a thousand years after the fall of Rome, expressed sentiments which his predecessors would have had no trouble embracing. "Those [republics]," he wrote, "are best organized and have the longest life that through their institutions can often renew themselves. . . . The way to renew[al] is to *carry them back to their beginnings,* because all the beginnings of religions and of republics and of kingdoms must possess some goodness by means of which they gain their first reputation and their first growth. Since in the process of time that goodness is corrupted, if something does not happen that takes it back to the right position, such corruption necessarily kills the body."[11]

The second kind of memory centered on what the Romans called *exempla,* that is, historical examples of exceptional moral courage or patriotic self-sacrifice shown by political leaders, military figures, or even ordinary citizens of the Roman past. If contemporary individuals recalled and took to heart the meanings of such *exempla,* the Romans reasoned, they would be inspired to repeat them in the present. In this way, memory would produce virtuous conduct, or at least the type of conduct that the Roman state considered virtuous, for it was the state above all that benefited when the populace remembered or reenacted heroic ideals. At the same time, Roman educational institutions and the very important Roman rhetorical tradition also played a role in reinforcing a public awareness of *exempla.* In the streets great orators swayed crowds and in the senate great speakers won arguments by recalling and using to rhetorical advantage the exemplary deeds of the past.[12] The point of this sort of public remembering was not just to encourage ethical behavior, though this was always an important consideration. It was also to promote Roman civic culture, strengthen social cohesion, and tie the individual more firmly to an enduring political community. To remember and be moved by the same examples was to participate in a common identity. By contrast, to forget the *heroum laudes et facta parentis* (the glories of the heroes and the deeds of the fathers) was to be alienated from precisely those shared values that were regarded as essential for a meaningful collective life.

Generally it was not necessary throughout the Middle Ages to encourage people to remember socially or culturally, since an orientation toward the past was presumed to be part of everyone's natural attitude. What Marc Bloch has called the "folk memory" ran deep,[13] though it sometimes had to be reinforced by more formal modes of recollection. One example of such reinforcement was the local communal assembly which in some parts of Europe was convened on fixed dates throughout the year with the aim of inducing all adult males to recite publicly the customs of the seigniory and to rehearse the many contractual obligations that bound them to one another. By means of arrangements such as these, medieval people were helped to recall their social duties. Occasionally such rituals of memory were open to women and children as well in order to involve the entire community in preserving and passing on its "heritage of remembrances."[14]

But aside from the underlying constancy of communal memory, there were some notable changes in the types of memory deemed important in the Middle Ages. The most obvious, of course, was that memory was "Christianized."[15] In the realm of thought and belief what now became essential to recall were, first and foremost, the key events of Christ's life on earth, such as the Incarnation, the Last Supper, the Passion and Crucifixion, and the Resurrection. Second, it was crucial to remember Christ's *exempla* as recorded in the Synoptic Gospels, particularly his acts of love, generosity, and humility (all placed on a quite different register of value compared to the more political and heroic *exempla* espoused by the Romans). Third, it was imperative to recall the lives of the Christian saints and martyrs through the ages who were now also regarded as models of behavior, and along with these the lives of dead family members and benefactors who deserved to be remembered in *libri memorialis,* necrologies, and liturgical commemorations. And finally, it was necessary to remember the doctrines of the Catholic Church as they developed over the centuries, since it was one of the principles of faith that these had to be embraced if one was to have a chance of gaining eternal salvation.

Besides the new kinds of religious memories, older types of memories reappeared in new guises. In aristocratic circles during the twelfth and thirteenth centuries, for instance, there was a revived interest in genealogy. As in ancient times, the further into the past a nobleman could trace his family lineage, the greater stature he acquired in the present. In its medieval French and German context, this drive for status led to the putative recollection of illustrious blood lines going back to the Carolingian Age, or even to the great Frankish families established around the time of Clovis. Where evidence of eminent lineage was hard to come by, it was often fabricated by enterprising clercs adept at creating just the family trees their aristocratic employers desired.[16] Simultaneously, in the emerging towns, guilds strove to keep alive the memories of particular craft skills, techniques, and cultural traditions, while elsewhere in Europe trained remembrancers, such as those who were part of the Gaelic learned orders of Ireland and Scotland, sought to recall common law precedents and prescriptive social norms considered indispensable for the grounding of everyday life.[17]

For most people in the Middle Ages the old was esteemed and the new was approached with caution or suspicion, as one would expect in a society where the regular and recurrent, the venerable and well-tested, were especially respected. To turn away willfully from what the past bequeathed to the present was tantamount to clearing the way for cultural and moral degradation. Those who embraced the "new" or the "modern" (both terms, *novus* and *modernus,* carried generally negative connotations in the Middle Ages) were censured rather than applauded. One of the accusations leveled against medieval heretics, the so-called *novi doctores,* was that they were too innovative, too quick to embrace novel or untested ideas and doctrines, which, from a traditional perspective, meant forgetting the very truths that it was imperative to keep in mind and honor in practice if one wanted to remain free from error.[18]

These long-standing certainties concerning the inherent value of memory began to be questioned in significant ways only at the dawn of the modern age, during the Renaissance and the Reformation. Indeed, it might be said that modernity itself came into being in large part because of this very re-thinking of the value of memory.

At first glance, neither the Renaissance nor the Reformation seems to be a movement that challenged the importance of memory. Both were, after all, backward-looking in the sense that they were intent on recovering something lost, or almost lost, in order to make it relevant once again. For projects that defined themselves in this way, remembering would appear to be essential to their *modus operandi.* Still, what made memory in both cases different from, say, medieval memory was the special emphasis placed on the memory not of existing continuities but of alleged discontinuities—that is to say, of ideas and values believed to have been meaningful at an earlier point in time, but which had since been obscured or discarded.

For the Renaissance, what needed to be remembered and recuperated were not only the great literary and philosophical texts of the classical world, but also the attitudes, values, and modes of life of the ancients which had, or so it was claimed, been lost sight of for nearly a millennium. For the Reformation, what had to be recovered were the truths of Scripture and the "pure" Christianity of the early Church, both of which had supposedly been forgotten through centuries of false accretions and doctrinal misunderstandings. (According to Luther, and in this he was typical of many other Reformers, nearly the whole of what an individual needed to remember was written in the Bible; almost everything else, as he expressed it in his *Treatise on the Mass* of 1521, could be put out of mind, since it was likely to be "an addition of the devil.")[19] In the Renaissance, old material was reorganized under new categories in such a manner that, when brought forward into the present, it yielded new meanings. In the Reformation, old ideas or beliefs never successfully preserved in ongoing traditions were rediscovered and reappropriated in such a way that they were experienced as novel or even transformative. In both cases the past was ostensibly retained as a value, but it was a different past than most people would have been familiar with throughout the Middle Ages.

The Renaissance and Reformation were more firmly grounded in the present than their leading spokesmen might have liked to admit. Each movement had a strong sense, based on contemporary needs and expectations, of what the "authentic" past was supposed to look like. Consequently each selected and highlighted from the past those elements that best conformed to their preconceived views, and at the same time dismissed or radically reconfigured other conceptions of what the classical world or the age of the apostles was really like. As a result, the meaning of the past, which was once presumed to be fixed and unchanging, was significantly altered. Instead of being seen as given, the past became a reality that to a great extent one created for oneself in response to the needs and demands of the present. This, again, is not to deny that either the Renaissance or Reformation were movements of memory, for both definitely were. Nevertheless, under the auspices of cherishing and retrieving old ideas or outlooks, new ones were in fact smuggled in, and these had the effect of weakening and undermining other ideas and memories that had for a long time sustained a traditional world view. Thus, rather than being solely movements of recovery and return as they at first appeared to be, the Renaissance and Reformation actually helped prepare the way for a reconceptualization of many of the legacies that in the Middle Ages were simply taken for granted as part of "the way things are."

Signs of a serious questioning of the value of memory itself began to appear in the later sixteenth and early seventeenth centuries. As a result of the new skeptical mood emerging in Europe at that time, at least among the intellectuals, it was not surprising that an individual like Montaigne could wonder if remembering the past in *any* shape or form was really as useful as had been claimed. Perhaps, he speculated in an essay of 1580, those who have the best memories also possess both the weakest intellects and the least capacity for sound judgment—a notion that exactly reversed the assumption of previous centuries.[20] Along similar lines, Cervantes, in his novel *Don Quixote* (1605), tried to show how absurd the results could be when one remembered past ideals too well. As a model rememberer who tried to embody in practice the knightly values he recalled in great detail, Quixote turned out to be not a heroic but a comic figure. The very same acts that in earlier times produced glory and renown were now shown to exhibit, under the new conditions of modernity, all the characteristics of social pathology. Cervantes' contemporary, Francis Bacon, likewise expressed grave doubts about both the personal and social usefulness of memory. In works such as *The Advancement of Learning* (1605) and *The Great Instauration* (1620), Bacon acknowledged that remembering can help give one bearings in the world and provide a reservoir of information that may prove advantageous in some situations. But he was even more concerned to point out the degree to which memory could harm or limit an individual. To rely on it too much was, Bacon thought, one of the worst mistakes a person could make. For memory, by ensconcing one in a questionable fund of received ideas, perpetuates errors and prejudices, discourages discovery, hinders the emergence of original ideas, and prevents one from developing those qualities of initiation and independence of mind that would benefit an individual—and mankind as a whole—the most.[21] Descartes, writing in France a couple of decades later, reached similar conclusions. In his *Discourse on Method* (1637) he suggested that the highest moral norms were not to be found in the prescriptions mindlessly passed down through cultural memory. In ethical matters as in much else, the past, because it provides "no adequate criterion for virtue,"[22] seemed to Descartes to mislead more than guide. If one wants to know how to behave, it was, in his opinion, necessary first of all to seek the aid of reason rather than *memoria*, for reason always uncovers the core principles of correct conduct, while memory simply perpetuates the misconceptions of the past.

To be sure, at the same time that these thinkers were raising concerns about the worth or utility of memory, most of official society continued to insist on its overriding importance. From the sixteenth through the eighteenth centuries, nearly all the leading political, ecclesiastical, and cultural institutions upheld the value of memory, particularly for the way it integrated and stabilized what might otherwise be a disorderly, normless world. Yet even this seemingly united front in support of memory was more a façade than a bulwark, for in fact numerous cracks and fissures had begun to appear in the once invulnerable pro-memory position.

Probably what undermined memory most in the early modern period was the ascendancy of capitalism. Though the origins of commercial capitalism go back earlier in time, it became a fully operative, self-sustaining economic system only in the sixteenth century. When that occurred, other institutions were increasingly drawn into its sphere of influence, and, if they wanted to survive as entities in their own right, had to redefine themselves in relation to the market or run the risk of being absorbed by it on its terms, not theirs. In comparison to previous types of economies, capitalism showed little respect for memory or for the past as such. Being fueled above all by the drive for profit, capitalism's natural tendency was either to take existing use-objects and turn them into commodities, or to create a plethora of entirely new things that were intended to be commodities from the beginning. In the first case, most items or human relationships that could not be commodified were deemed to be of little real worth, at least by market standards. Old objects, customs, values, traditions, memories, or loyalties that did not lend themselves to exchange relations were allowed to fall by the wayside or were pushed there no matter how ancient or venerable they might have been. In the second case, the market was and of course still is propelled mainly by a quest for the new or novel. It needs continuous innovation, or what Marx called "a constant revolutionizing of production," in order to keep growing and expanding. Even freshly created products need to be declared obsolete not too long after they enter the market to prepare the way for still newer, more "improved" products and commodities. Hence early capitalism had no interest in the memorable, the sentimental, or the nostalgic, though this would change to some extent by the twentieth century.[23] In its nascent stage, however, capitalism's chief concern was to keep producing and selling new things, and to do so in such a manner as to gain as high a profit as the market would allow.

Another force that eroded the importance of memory in the early modern period was rationalism. The capacity of the mind to reason, argued Descartes and others, stands apart from and does not need either sense experience or the accumulated remains of memory. In fact, mental residues of old sensations and opinions, marked as they necessarily are by ancient biases and prejudices,[24] were said to block the free exercise of reason and therefore move one away from the truths that needed to be known and acted upon. According to this way of thinking, it would be best if all that is not in conformity with reason were dispatched from contemporary life as quickly as possible. And as some also contended, it would be best too if modern institutions were made to operate strictly according to the guidelines of reason, based on rational procedures, a systematizing of functions, and a uniformity of rules and regulations rather than on the inertia of memory and precedent. The claim here was that this kind of rationalization, extending out beyond the mind itself and into the warp and woof of social reality, would result in something more efficient and dependable, and thus ultimately more satisfying to modern individuals, than the cultural, political, and economic irrationality that had for too long been ascendant in human history.

Still other developments were occurring in the early modern era that made social memory seem less important than it had once been—and consequently less worth defending. One was the growing awareness that it was not only possible but often highly desirable to "begin again." The idea that one had at all costs to remain true to some first beginning shrouded in myth or legend slowly lost its credibility. In its place came the notion that starting over, far from being an act of disloyalty to gods or predecessors, could actually open the door to new and better possibilities both for the individual and for the human race in general. (The existence of the New World as a place where one really could "start up again under fresh initiative, in a divinely granted second chance"[25] helped foster the idea that the past did not have to be determinative; it did not have to be treated as a virtual force of nature, but rather could be bracketed or nullified by any willed act on the part of an individual to begin anew.)

Another development of the seventeenth and eighteenth centuries that served to weaken the importance of social memory was the growing acceptance of the notion that the past must be thought of in terms of particular historical epochs, each one succeeding and replacing its predecessor over a long span of time. Every epoch that had ever come into being, or so it began to be held by many, had its own identity and character, and consequently none was directly comparable to what now came to be called the "modern age." Moreover, because each age was thought to possess its own kind of uniqueness, the past had to be seen as literally a different place, a foreign realm. From this premise it followed that the experiences of ancestors were incommensurable with those people living in the present. Hence there were no universally applicable "lessons of the past" nor any eternally valid models of behavior that were available to be learned or applied, and thus previous conceptions of what one should do or think could be more or less dispensed with. If the past was no longer needed to inform or structure contemporary life, the task of remembering what had gone before could best be left to historians or, even more appropriately, to antiquarians.

In one respect the concept of epochs was an old one with a long genealogy in Western thought. In Greece at the time of Homer, for example, the poet Hesiod had outlined what he called the four ages of man (the ages of gold, silver, bronze, and iron); in ancient Israel, the prophet Daniel had arranged all time within the framework of the four successive world monarchies; and later, at the beginning of the Christian era, Julius Africanus described the long duration between the creation of the world and A.D. 221 in terms of six epochs, taken from the six days of creation. Strictly speaking, then, the notion of epochs itself was not new in the early modern period. What was new, however, was the reinterpretation of this notion to mean, first, that each era generates the values it needs to address its own social and historical reality, and second, that when one epoch is replaced by another the set of values appropriate to the earlier era can no longer be considered suitable to the later one. In fact, to hold fast to the "old ways" in new circumstances would guarantee that, like Quixote again, one would become maladjusted to one's surroundings. In light of understandings such as these, it not only seemed impermissible to transport into the present the ideas or beliefs of another time and place; it also seemed that those concepts or world views that did happen to survive beyond the age that produced them would have to be treated merely as leftovers (or, as they later came to be called, "cultural lags") with little or no practical value in the present. What was novel about the modern concept of historical epochs was that it did away with long-standing certainties about the wisdom of the past and introduced the idea that the past represented something obsolete or out-lived. For the first time in the history of the West, large numbers of people began to think that they could not depend on the past to give them the directions they needed.[26] Being in the "modern age" *(Neuzeit),* and not for example in antiquity or the Middle Ages, they had to look solely to the present to give them the guidance they required.[27] This new awareness meant, among other things, that if masses of people were indeed cut adrift from the past as it seemed, they were also free to forget it—not entirely, perhaps, but to a great enough extent that it would no longer be a burden, hindering innovation and discovery in the only period that mattered, the period now labeled: modernity.

A last development worth mentioning, and one closely related to the notion of epochs, was the increasing importance given to the theory of progress. This theory maintained that each epoch had amounted to a notable advance over its predecessor.[28] Viewed from the perspective of the eighteenth century, the world seemed to be steadily improving materially, technologically, and for some even morally. If advancement really was the rule, there would be no compelling reason to remember the past, since it had been superseded; to hold on to what had once been would be merely regressive. Rather, the goal should be, as the Marquis de Chastellux put it in 1772, "to forget [or] . . . obliterate as much [of the past] as possible [in order to] raise that much more quickly the edifice of reason on the ruins of opinion."[29] For Chastellux, as well as for Condorcet and other Enlightenment figures, the present was mature enough to decide on its own terms the norms and values it wanted to embrace. But its maturity would never be complete until the present liberated itself from the shackles of the dead past, and for many thinkers of the eighteenth century that meant first and foremost that the present had to give up its seemingly childish reliance on memory.

Throughout the nineteenth century and into the early twentieth, new forces came into play that appeared to further reduce the importance of memory. These forces are familiar enough today that they need only be mentioned briefly here.

One of the most prominent of such forces was the emergence and spread of the Industrial Revolution, which dramatically sped up the pace of change in all areas of life and irreversibly fractured particular *milieux de mémoire* that had remained intact for generations. By transforming production and consumption, the Industrial Revolution either invaded and reshaped the traditional lifeworlds of the West or wiped them out altogether. As old, organic communities were increasingly undermined or gutted by outside forces, the stock of valued memories they once contained began to be depleted. One result of this development was that the recollection of inherited meanings or communal practices no longer seemed very urgent, at least not to those for whom the most pressing need was the acquisition of skills and attitudes better suited to an emerging industrial reality.

At the same time that village or rural *Lebenswelten* were being rapidly transformed, nineteenth-century cities were likewise undergoing important changes which also worked to the detriment of memory. Under the influence of a new breed of urban planners and architects, both European and American cities began to be revamped according to the idea of the "Rational Plan."[30] Among other things, this approach entailed a new and systematic "disciplining of space"[31] so as to eliminate disorder by regulating and rationalizing the urban environment as much as possible. Such planning often meant clearing away old buildings, neighborhoods, or entire districts, even if many of these sites had long served as markers of cultural and historical memory. Sometimes the removal of physical residues from the past was inadvertent, that is, merely a by-product of the larger and more encompassing drive to eradicate everything that appeared outdated. But sometimes it was more a matter of policy, since for many planners in the nineteenth century it was essential to remove all traces of nostalgia in the city so that people would not be distracted from the practical affairs of everyday life. As Leonard Courtney, a Liberal member of the British Parliament, expressed it in 1878 (in a speech opposing the protection of ancient buildings): "We cannot allow our lives to be overburdened and crushed down by the mere accumulation of the dead things of the past. . . . Let dead things go, let living things be kept."[32] Even Freud, though no expert on urban matters, noted the detrimental effects that historical sites in the city could have on individuals. As mentioned earlier, he worried that especially compelling "mnemonic symbols" in the city could lead people to become too emotionally involved in the past "instead of going about [their] business" as they would be better advised to do.[33] By the 1920s, some urban planners and architects spoke in still more disapproving terms about the desirability of *any* traces of memory being left in the modern city. Le Corbusier, for one, argued that the fully functional urban metropolis should include no references whatever to the past (except, if need be, in out-of-the-way parks), since the past represents a "danger to life" and must therefore be combated "without remorse."[34] The city as Le Corbusier envisioned it needed to be transformed into a "machine for living" which would address only the present or future needs of its inhabitants, not indulge their sentimental longings for an absent past.

Yet another factor promoting the erosion of social memory in the nineteenth century was the concerted attack on collective remembering put forward by the newly emerging technocratic intelligentsia. These intellectuals, among them engineers, economists, scientific managers, and "positivists," were the direct heirs of those who had espoused the theory of progress in the previous century. Almost in unison they stressed the inutility of memory in a modern age, chiefly because it encouraged backward attitudes and habits and consequently was a drain on production and economic growth. As they saw it, the proper aim for both individuals and societies was to accumulate for the future or be efficient and practical in the present without lingering over or lamenting what had been left behind. A life too focused on remembering what had disappeared would not only be enervating but inhibitory, since it would lead one to hold in check one's own best thoughts and actions. Even more importantly, those who, under the sway of memory, tried too hard to make their behavior compatible with what they retained from the past would almost certainly fail in modern life, whereas those who let go of old mental baggage would be much better positioned to move up the social or economic ladder of success.

For many such "progressive" thinkers of the nineteenth century, then, the best way to live a fruitful and productive life was by dispensing with the encumbrances of the past. The same judgment was likewise applied to whole societies, for it appeared that those cultures or civilizations that were unable to divest themselves of the weight of memory became stagnant and moribund, or at best suffered from what some called "arrested development." Ancient Egypt, the Late Roman Empire, China, and Byzantium were frequently cited as examples of "sick societies" freighted with an excess of memory. The single thing that might have made them creative or robust again would have been a heavy dose of forgetting. But since none of these civilizations was able to shake free from the dead hand of the past, none was able to gain a second wind or a new burst of energy. That being the case, there seemed to many interpreters to be no option for such societies but to slide further into a terminal state of entropy.

Finally, in the nineteenth and early twentieth centuries a strident assault on memory issued from a variety of modernist literary and artistic movements, each seeking to establish its own identity in relation to a past that appeared largely discredited. Many of these movements declared themselves in favor of the "absolutely new." Sometimes being new meant little more than remembering the old differently,[35] but at other times, and more characteristically, it meant negating the intellectual traditions of the past, since they prevented that which was novel or unique from coming into being. The assumption among many of the modernists was that just as no two moments can occupy the same point in time, so too for any contemporary artistic or literary movement to fulfill its potential, previous movements had to be displaced. The worst thing one could do was continue clinging to cultural forms that deserved to pass into oblivion. Thus one finds the French writer Jules Vallès declaiming in 1867: "The past, there's our enemy! Humanity would be no worse off if we burned down all the libraries and museums, . . . [for what they now represent is] merely ridiculous and an encumbrance."[36] Similar views were echoed in Italy by Filippo Marinetti in his Futurist Manifesto of 1909 ("We want nothing of [the past]. . . . Let the incendiaries come with their carbonized fingers!");[37] by the Russian constructivists of the 1920s (We are "leaving the past behind as carrion"); and dadaists from several European countries writing about the same time ("The abolition of memory *is* dada!").[38] For these as well as many other modernisms, the past was something to forget because, being "oppressive like darkness" (Mondrian), it prevented the highest possibilities of the present from being realized. Even for those who would not have agreed with such extreme statements in defense of forgetting, it was nevertheless clear that in a technological age that had no precedent in history, the past had little to offer in terms of artistic or literary models to emulate.[39] There was no good reason to remember a heritage which was neither useful for nor appropriate to the new conditions of contemporary life.

Still, this hostility to memory was not the whole story. There were countertendencies as well. For many, the fading away of the past from present consciousness was a calamity of the first order, since it produced not more freedom, autonomy, or innovation but rather more disruption, discontinuity, and anomie. In seeking solutions to the problem of an excess of forgetting virtually no one suggested that it would be possible to restore memory to the place of importance it had held in ancient or medieval times; that option, it seemed, was gone forever. But many did suggest that some of the most important aspects of social memory could be recuperated in order to establish a counterweight to what otherwise seemed to be the drift and emptiness of modern life. This kind of recovery meant neither a literal return to the past nor a restoration of memory to every nook and cranny of contemporary existence. It meant instead only a partial salvaging of as much collective memory as was feasible, and a better integration of this memory into what appeared to be an overly rationalized and vacuous present.

The Romantic movement at the beginning of the nineteenth century was one effort to reassess the value of memory in personal and collective life. But independent of Romanticism proper there was a proliferation of local historical or folklore societies in Europe in the early decades of the century, each seeking to preserve memories of a world that seemed to be disappearing. At the same time, both amateur and professional ethnographers began collecting not only old ballads and tales but also material artifacts which eventually came to be housed in museums such as the Musée des Arts et Traditions Populaires in Paris or its equivalents in other countries. Simultaneous with these developments, the nineteenth century in Europe and America witnessed the first efforts at historic preservation. The intent of the preservationist movement, if it can legitimately be called a movement at this point,[40] was to rehabilitate the physical structures of the past so as to reproduce the ambiance of former times. The main impetus behind historic preservation was the notion that every national community needs to be in touch with the remains of its own past. Without a palpable connection to its historically significant buildings, a nation would be like "a man without memory," as David Lowenthal has put it, because it would lack both a sense of its own identity and an awareness of its place in the temporal scheme of things.[41]

Around the middle and later part of the nineteenth century there were still other indications of a reprising of memory in the West, one notable example being a new mood of social nostalgia that gripped some elements of the population. Without denying that "advancement" was by and large a good thing, or that there was progress in history, some people began to develop a wistful interest in the distant past. This interest in historical memory manifested itself in, for instance, the mid-century vogue of neo-Gothic, neo-Renaissance, and (in America) neocolonial architectural styles; a reawakened fascination with the Middle Ages and the idealized forms of life that were believed to be found there (knighthood, chivalry, and so forth); a burgeoning concern with family genealogies; a popular embrace of a number of arts and crafts movements that strove to recover seemingly lost skills from preindustrial times; and a fashionable turn toward antique collecting, including, for the few who could afford it, the collection of premodern *objets d'art*.[42]

For those swept up by these various enthusiasms, memory gained new importance as a link to the past. Of course, the historical past was still perceived as "other," but this very otherness was what made it alluring. Even in its difference, the past appeared to be a home to which one could on occasion retreat in order to escape, as the French commentator Raoul de La Grassiere expressed it, the "frenzy" of forward movement, or the drive toward "incessant progress."[43] In this respect at least, the spell of *nostos* made what seemed over and done with attractive once again.

Finally, historians, too, responded to the apparent excesses of forgetting in the nineteenth century. Like others of their time and place, European and American historians witnessed firsthand the reduction of memory that accompanied modernity. For those historians especially distressed by this "crisis of memory," there was an urge to repair the situation in some manner, if possible through the medium of history itself.

There were two main ways historians thought they could recover vanishing social memories. The first was by retrieving, through exhaustive historical research, as much of the factural detail of the past as possible. (This was the approach of the positivist historians who felt driven to establish the "truth" of the past exactly and scientifically.) The second was by fashioning grand narratives that stressed the underlying continuities of history. The overriding concern of those who approached history in this latter way was to mend the perceived rupture with the past by capturing in totalizing historical accounts what Leopold von Ranke called "the connectedness of history in the large."[44] By focusing on the coherences and unifying threads of the *longue durée,* the descriptive historians of the nineteenth century believed that they could make what they called "historical consciousness" a substitute for the once vital traditions and customs that were withering away. If this effort were successful, they reasoned, written history "in the large" might eventually provide the integrative glue that traditional forms of memory had once provided.

By the early twentieth century both of these modes of historical remembering began to be called into question. It is true that some historians such as Carl Becker could still write in the 1930s that the historian's most important task was "to preserve and perpetuate the social tradition," or that history itself should be viewed as an "artificial" but nonetheless indispensable "extension of the social memory."[45] But other historians in Becker's day and later wondered whether there were really good and legitimate reasons to consider history an extension of social memory. By the 1990s, the list of history's inadequacies as a medium of collective memory had grown increasingly large, with each new notion of what history is *not* able to achieve seemingly more damaging than the one preceding it. For example, some now say that although history can recover the past to some extent, it can do so only in very circumscribed ways, owing to the extremely limited nature of the sources at its disposal. But even more problematic, the past that is "remembered" by the historian, it is now claimed, can never be the same one that people experienced in earlier times. For the past that the historian brings forth in written works is by its very nature so abstracted from its original context that it gives us not life as it was actually lived but only disembodied information *about* that life. Building on this criticism, others have gone further and argued that history, far from being an extension of memory as Becker assumed, is in fact memory's antipode. According to some historians today, memory (seen as natural, spontaneous, and embedded in the habitual practices of a lifeworld) and history (viewed as a critical-analytical product of the library and the study) cannot help but work at cross purposes. In the words of Yosef Yerushalmi, "Memory and modern historiography stand . . . in radically different relations to the past. The latter represents not an attempt at a restoration of memory, but a truly new [and deleterious] kind of recollection. . . . With unprecedented energy, [history] continually recreates an ever more detailed past whose shapes and textures memory does not recognize."[46] Similarly, the historian Pierre Nora has written that we are presently witnessing the "eradication of memory by history," since the true but unstated mission of an analytical historical method is not to bring us the subjectively remembered past more thoroughly or more completely, but to "suppress and destroy"—even "annihilate"—memory as the primary medium of information about the past in order to replace it with more accurate or verifiable forms of historical knowledge.[47]

If these two historians and others like them are right in saying that critical historical narratives abolish the very thing they purport to save, then history would indeed represent a failed attempt to rescue from obscurity the past as it was personally known or felt by those who preceded us. And one result of this failure would be that the fissure between the past as it was actually experienced and a present which can only know that past conceptually would unavoidably grow ever wider and deeper.

What is the situation of memory in the West as we enter the twenty-first century?

Despite the evidence of a pervasive hostility to memory since the early modern period, it seems indisputable that a considerable amount of social or collective memory is still alive and well today. It is clearly active, for instance, in many of our institutions: in schools, libraries, museums, seminaries, and conservatories, whose very *raisons d'être* are built upon an imperative to re-member. It is present as well in bureaucracies, in the rules and regulations, the procedures and protocols, that keep the past alive even in the process of routinizing it. Social memory is active too in law codes, legal statutes, and judicial precedents (the law itself being, in its totality, the juridical memory of the community). It is also active in the churches, at least to the extent that they preserve and carry forward the essential elements of belief through a continuity of dogmas, doctrines, and sacred texts. And it is active in political parties, labor unions, and other voluntary organizations devoted to, among other things, the promotion of class or ethnic interests.[48]

Social or collective memory is operative also in the enormous storehouse of information contained in the countless documents, records, files, and dos-siers collected by a host of agencies in both the public and private realms, and (on a still vaster scale) in computers and electronic data banks. Social mem-ory continues on, as many linguists have reminded us, in the very grammar and structure of our language, and in the way that assumptions and mental habits from the past are perpetuated in the concepts, figures of speech, and metaphors we use. It is likewise implicit in centuries-old symbols and images that have managed to survive into the contemporary period; hidden within these carryovers from the past, as the art historian Aby Warburg pointed out, is a residue of "mnemic energy" that yet speaks to us across the ages, whether we are fully aware of it or not.[49]

On a somewhat more pedestrian level, social memory is alive in some form or other in the current fascination with *le mode rétro,* in local and na-tional movements for historic preservation (now more broadly based than in the nineteenth century), and even in certain strands of postmodernist thought that have self-consciously reversed the modernist animosity toward the past. Instead of regarding the past as something that needs to be forgotten so that the new can achieve its own voice, many postmodernists have come to regard it as something that we need actively to return to, albeit in ways that may be entirely unfaithful to the past's original tone or spirit.

Social memory similarly persists in the highly successful "national heri-tage industry" in Britain, in the current vogue of *patrimoine* in France, in the efforts at "coming to terms with the past" in Germany, and in the recent American concern to recover the nation's "divergent histories," that is, the reputedly untold or unacknowledged stories of, among others, women, His-panics, African Americans, Asian Americans, and indigenous peoples. In the countries of eastern Europe over the past decade social memory has been active in the aptly named "revolutions of retrieval and recuperation" *(nach-holende Revolutionen),* which have brought to the surface traditions and val-ues that had been repressed and nearly forgotten during the Communist era.

And finally, outside the old Soviet system, social memory is active in the commemorations of certain key events of the recent past such as the Holocaust. For Jews and non-Jews alike, there appears to be a concern "never to forget" the horrendous occurrences that took place in Europe between 1941 and 1945. Especially for the Jews of the generation that suffered the Holocaust directly, that event has arguably become the single defining moment of their history. For some it has even become more constitutive of Jewish collective identity than the deliverance out of Egypt as recounted in Exodus or the destruction of the Second Temple by the Romans in A.D. 70.

Given all these indications of the persistence of social memory, it seems that a good case can yet be made that we are still very much a culture of memory and not a culture of forgetting. But before concluding too quickly that social memory is active today in much the same way that it was in the distant past, it would be wise to consider again the evidence that calls this point of view into question. For every example one could cite in which memory has continued more or less unabridged, there are many others that suggest much more has been forgotten than remembered. Even the so-called discourses of memory that are discernible today have emerged not from strong feelings that memory still securely grounds us but from deep-seated anxieties about the past having already slipped out of reach. As a rule, people begin making something the subject of a discourse only when it becomes problematic, but it becomes problematic not when it is thriving and healthy but when it is put in jeopardy.

Some observers see indications that the present is suffering acutely from what Jean-François Lyotard has termed "dememorization."[50] What seems to be happening in the late modern societies of the West is a more rapid turnover of ideas, values, and practices than at any other time in history. Breakthroughs in, among other things, the technologies of information processing, biogenetics, microelectronics, automation, and telecommunications are moving the present away from the past at an ever accelerating rate. Not only are many of the ideas, beliefs, and modes of life from the last century now being "relegated to the Stone Age,"[51] but so are those of even one or two decades ago. This speeding up of modern life has led to a kind of deritualization of experience that has itself been destructive of memory. For millennia, collective rituals were prime carriers of memory, but in the contemporary period there has been a noticeable drying up of public ritual, and with it an evaporation of public memory. To be sure, the media have stepped in with substitute rituals of their own; and many individuals and groups have, on their own initiative, cobbled together ritual forms that compensate privately for what is missing publicly. Yet neither alternative really makes up for the loss of certain kinds of collective memories that in the past were transmitted by means of widely practiced social rituals.[52]

Rather than simply marshaling additional evidence that the present age is more antagonistic to social memory than supportive of it, it might be better to look more carefully at the pro-memory position to see if it is shakier than it at first appears. Does the evidence pointing to the perdurance of social memory really hold up? Or are social or collective memories today actually shot through with a deeper kind of forgetting? In attempting to answer these questions, I have selected for brief treatment three examples of enduring memory in order to suggest that memory today may not be nearly as active as one might think.

The museum. A museum, particularly a historical or ethnographic one, is by definition a memory-intensive site, where the diachronic is stressed over the synchronic, the past over the present. In the West at the beginning of the twenty-first century it is obviously true that many museums remain in operation and an impressive number of new ones continue to built.[53] But the mere presence of museums, especially when they are relegated to the margins of contemporary life, does not in and of itself indicate an abiding concern with social or cultural memory. Even for those few who visit a museum once or twice a year, the impression received is not likely to be how valuable and important it is to remember the past. Instead, a visit may produce just the opposite effect: it may make clear how different the past is from the present, and how little one needs to be aware of it any more. In contrast to the first sponsors and promoters of museums, who sought to deepen visitors' historical consciousness, the museum now seems to widen rather than narrow the rift between what was and what is, thereby making the past appear both more distant and less usefully memorable than ever. Though one does seem to come into contact with the aura of the past by viewing the historical objects and artifacts on display, that aura, whatever one might think of it, tends to dissolve very quickly as soon as one reenters the quotidian world beyond the museum's walls.

In the nineteenth century, when many of the great public museums of the West were built, the museum's primary function was to serve as a "temple of memory." That is, its purpose was not simply to acquaint the broad masses with the achievements of the past but to communicate something of the sacredness of the past as well. By coming into contact with the vestiges of bygone ages in the traditional museum, an individual was expected not only to learn something about his or her historical roots, but to become cognizant of the ways in which the past still spiritually informed the present. But during the last two or three decades especially, a more up-to-date and less temple-like museum has come into being, and this type has become far more popular than its old-fashioned predecessor. In the most modern museums in Europe and North America, the very aim and purpose of museology has begun to change. Instead of trying to convey the atmosphere of former times by exhibiting their remnants and traces, the most innovative museums today aim to show how the past *has been represented or has represented itself* in different ways over time. Since, as is now increasingly assumed, what something is depends on how it is constructed, it follows that there is no autochthonous past possessing an inherent meaning of its own that a museum director can simply label and place on display for all to see. Rather, what the so-called *nouveau musée* has taken upon itself to show is that everything is a construction or a representation, and that there is nothing behind these constructions and representations but more of the same. As far as the past as an entity is concerned, there is really no such thing. The chief lesson that contemporary museology strives to teach is that there is not one but many pasts, each of them fashioned to serve particular needs at particular times, and consequently none of them truer or more authentic than any other.

In this regard, what one takes away from a modern as opposed to traditional museum is not so much a greater respect for the past as a strong sense of the superiority of the present over the past. For when all is said and done the message that is most emphatically communicated by the proliferating *nouveaux musées* is that it is the contemporary epoch and not any previous one that has grasped the constructed nature of all meaning, and therefore it is our epoch above all that deserves to be celebrated, even in museums that are ostensibly about the past.

The new museology has also sought to bring the most advanced technology into the heart of the museum. Though it is frequently argued that this technology (high-definition TV, computer consoles, holographs, and the like) helps make the past more accessible, many have reported that the sophisticated electronic and multimedia devices themselves often become the center of attention and fascination, especially for younger visitors whose interest is diverted away from the very past that such devices were designed to illuminate. As museums strive to compete with other sources of entertainment, they have turned themselves into what are now referred to as "total environments," housing, along with actual referents to the past, not only restaurants and gift shops but rooms devoted mainly to animatronics and computer simulation. In the rush to make the modern museum a place of fun and entertainment as opposed to the almost sacral place it once was, something of the traditional museum's solemn, reflective character has gotten lost. In the same vein, many of the recently established museums have come to focus less on the *res gestae* of the distant past than on the *histoire immediate* of popular culture. Apparently many more people visit museums devoted to sports, film history, rock-and-roll memorabilia, or even collections of kitchenware, street jewelry, and other bric-a-brac, than museums devoted, for example, to the history of the nation-state.[54] One result of these developments is that not just the specialized but also the "total museums" have become much more synchronous (and thus less memory-oriented) than the old-fashioned didactic museum, whose focus was entirely and exclusively on the past alone.[55]

Family memory. Family memory is probably far weaker today than most people imagine. (Here I am treating family memory as a form of collective memory, since the family is, after all, a kind of *Intimgruppe* that mediates between the individual and the larger social whole.) For family memories to remain strong, it is not enough that a photo album exist or that a few pieces of memorabilia be passed from one generation to the next. Rather, for family memories to endure and take on meaning, they must be repeatedly and actively reinforced with continuous interaction between an older generation that wishes to transmit memories and a younger one that is present and willing to receive them. This kind of family interaction in turn assumes some amount of rootedness in one place and reasonably frequent contact among family members so that the family has the opportunity to recall together important as well as trivial matters concerning its own existence in time. The importance of shared reminiscences in keeping family memories alive cannot be underestimated. A person reminiscing entirely on his or her own can, it is true, recall particular things from the family's past, but not nearly so well as can a family group *remembering together.* When a small group reminisces about its past, there is at least as much reminding as recollecting going on, for every intimate group tends to activate and sustain memories that would otherwise be forgotten by each individual member trying to recall, alone and apart from the collectivity, the things considered significant by the group. If the conditions that encourage this kind of collective reminiscence are absent, it becomes very difficult for memories to take hold at all, let alone be passed on from one generation to the next.[56]

Today the social conditions needed to perpetuate family memory are being severely eroded. The general pattern in the West is for families to disperse, separate, and lose contact with one another, except for the occasional phone call, letter, or e-mail message. What Halbwachs assumed to be a given in 1925 when he wrote *Les cadres sociaux de la mémoire*—namely, that the collective memory of the family has remained intact in the West, because families still share "the same daily life" based on "[c]onstant exchanges of impressions and opinions"[57]—is now no longer true. Broadly speaking, most modern families in Europe and America are not integral units anymore. With rare exception, they neither possess a clearly identifiable "mentality" (as Halbwachs also thought) nor have their own "logic and traditions" which remain constant over generations.[58] Instead, due to the pressures and demands of contemporary life, families have tended to become fragmented, with grandparents, parents, children, and siblings all moving in their own direction and in the process losing touch with other parts of the family unit. Such distancing, both physical and psychological, naturally leads people to think less frequently of their families, with the result that family memories deteriorate. For many people today, the very term "family" has become at best a concept, not a lived experience. Though some family narratives and some bits of family lore may continue to be transmitted from the old to the young, this information is usually not very significant to those who find themselves far removed temporally and spatially from the settings within which such information initially took on meaning. Simply put, when family memories are separated from their original contexts, they become abstractions, and like most abstractions they are easy to forget.

In rural areas of Europe and North America there appears to be a greater continuity of family memory owing both to the greater fixity of family structures and to what one might call the geographical fixity of the "homestead" or similar sites to which memories can readily be attached. There is much evidence, for example, that in some peasant milieus in Europe family memories extend back two hundred years or more. The reason is that many such memories are linked either to intrafamily conflicts (with the rival families remaining continuously in the vicinity, which helps keep memory alive) or to the nearly unchanging presence of physical markers such as farmhouses, hills, forests, or crossroads which, when encountered, evoke memories of events that happened there decades or even centuries before.[59] But these conditions obviously do not pertain for families that are constantly on the move, as are most urban or suburban American families, which, the sociologists tell us, change their place of residence on average seven times over the span of a lifetime. Where this kind of mobility is the norm, as it now increasingly is throughout most of the Western world, the resulting lack of proximity as well as infrequency of contact with other family members lessens the stock of memories available to all. It is no wonder that under such conditions many family memories fade and eventually disappear from consciousness.

Postmodernism. Postmodernism, which Frederic Jameson has termed our "cultural dominant" today, seems at first sight favorably disposed to memory.[60] Unlike so many strains of its predecessor movement, modernism, it has not viewed the past as stifling or tyrannical, and therefore carries no brief against it. Whereas many modernists waged war on tradition and the past in general, the postmodernists have felt no great animosity toward either. In fact, postmodernists are content simply to pick up and rearrange within a contemporary setting the pieces left behind by the modernist assault on the cultural forms of the past. What they have discovered is that these leftovers, instead of being treated as worthless, can be recycled or brought together in new combinations. If this kind of recuperative activity qualifies as memory at all, it is memory entirely dismissive of the actuality of the past, since precisely that actuality is what postmodernists ask one to forget. Rather than try to retrieve the original spirit or context of residual things, it is better, they say, just to take them as they are, reassemble them in novel ways, or treat them in an ironic, playful manner.

In all of this, the primacy of the present is taken for granted; little or no prestige accrues to the past as such, nor does the past carry anything of the aura it once did. When old styles or motifs are gathered up and reutilized, it is not their "pastness" that is valued but their quaintness, that is, the strange and sometimes *outré* qualities they seem to take on when viewed from some distance in time. In contrast, say, to neoclassicism (which, by preserving, reiterating, and updating the classical past showed that it had a high regard for the integrity of what it inherited), postmodernism has no sensitivity toward the past, no real esteem for it, and no desire to keep its spirit alive. In this respect the so-called *le mode rétro* mentioned earlier perhaps represents a characteristically postmodern outlook on the past. Though it seems to look backward for inspiration and thus appears to be much like earlier movements of revival, *le mode rétro* is in fact concerned neither to imitate nor repeat the past but to reinvent it—often with a commercial twist. As one commentator correctly put it, being rétro-chic means "play[ing] with the idea of a period look, while remaining determinedly in the here-and-now."[61]

Taken as a whole, postmodernism is atemporal and ahistorical. It has little interest in encouraging memory in the ordinary sense of the word because it does not take the past seriously. At best what matters for most postmodernists are the aesthetic reverberations of the past in the present. To borrow Lyotard's apt term, the past can be "dememorized" without much loss to anyone, so long as its defused and decontextualized remnants remain available for artistic or cultural refunctioning.

In light of what has been said above, it may seem legitimate to suggest, as Pierre Nora has, that we are now experiencing "a fundamental collapse of memory"; or that, as Sheldon Wolin similarly expressed it, we are rapidly becoming a "post-mnemonic society."[62] There is an element of truth in these suggestions, but they surely go too far, for as I tried to indicate earlier in this chapter, social or collective memory has by no means disappeared. Though there is clearly a privileging of the present over the past, and though the dominant institutions of our time no longer promote memory as they formerly did, memory is still with us, even if it is now framed in quite different ways than in previous eras. Because the framing is different, when people remember they are inclined to recollect a range of things not recalled, and not even thought worthy of being recalled, in earlier ages. This same point can also be made the other way around: as a result of the frames that prevail today, much that our ancestors once considered essential, and which they made every effort faithfully to commit to memory, now seems to be cheerfully and happily forgotten.

If it is correct to say with Halbwachs that we tend to remember the way our societies prompt us to remember,[63] then it would be important to look more closely at how social memory is ordered and arranged in the late modern period. Once the role played by social framing is taken more fully into account, we will be in a better position to determine, in the final chapter of this book, what the value of remembering and forgetting is or ought to be at the present time.

The Shapes of the Past

Social memory is always shaped, it has form, and it shifts and changes according to changing circumstances. Moreover, it is possible at all only with the aid of schemata, which help decide not only what is memorable (out of an almost limitless array of things that potentially could be remembered), but how such material should be thought about or interpreted. There is, as Jacques Le Goff has reminded us, no "unmediated, raw collective memory."[1] Though several competing schemata may exist simultaneously, one is usually dominant, and hence more effective in selecting and ordering what is considered noteworthy about the past.

The population at large generally accedes to the forms of memory encouraged by the prevailing schemata. For most people there is no good reason to question the frames that are in place so long as they seem to work satisfactorily. To be sure, there are always dissenters who reject the dominant schemata, claiming that what most needs to be recalled is what the schemata reject or suppress. Except for these few, however, the majority in every historical period have been content to remember roughly in the way the reigning frames dictate.

When large numbers of people appear to "vibrate in unison,"[2] it is easy to conclude, as Jung and Durkheim did, that there must be a collective mind, or a collective psyche, expressing itself. But there is no evidence to indicate that any such supra-individual entity exists, at least not in the same way that an individual mind capable of memory exists. What looks like the manifestation of a collective psyche is at bottom only a hypostatization of a multiplicity of many individual psyches recalling similar things through shared mental frames. There is nothing mysterious about this; when people utilize the same socially created cognitive structures in thinking about the past, they tend to remember that past in more or less the same way.

Seen from this perspective, frames of memory can be powerful instruments of control. The social group that can determine the regnant schemata can also exert a great deal of influence over how the rest of the population apprehends the past and, by extension, the present and future as well. Throughout history there have been both overt and covert struggles over who would decide what the predominant schemata ought to be. Different interests have come to the fore at different times to install the frames that would, in their estimation, engender the right kind of memories. As a rule, it takes a certain amount of time, probably several generations in most cases, for schemata to become entrenched enough that they begin to operate in ways that seem natural and normal. When this point is reached, there appears to be a match between what the frame selects as important or significant and what a given population seems to want to know about the past. No effort, in other words, has to be made to induce people to adhere to the schemata, for adherence happens as a matter of course. In times of crisis or rapid change, however, when it may appear that the prevailing schemata no longer give people the past they want or need, ruling groups tend to revert to force in order to compel a population to remember what they think must be recalled if stable social or political life is to continue.

To see evidence of this kind of *Schematenkampf* in history one need go back no further than the Middle Ages. At that time, the dominant frame was religious, owing to the hegemonic influence of the Catholic Church over most aspects of cultural and intellectual life. In practical terms, this dominance gave the Church a considerable amount of power not only to shape how the faithful would perceive the past but also to determine what in the past they would think worth remembering in the first place. Even later, at the time of the Reformation, the religious framing of memory remained securely intact, since for Protestants no less than Catholics the historical memories that mattered most were those bound up with the religious events of the past.

Of course, the prevailing religious schemata did not go unchallenged. Starting in the High Middle Ages, the rising states of Europe began to contest the validity of an exclusively religious ordering of memory. From the point of view of these new states, the political past was as important as the religious one and deserved to be honored equally. This at first modest and then increasingly aggressive contestation of the religious hold on memory went on during the post-Reformation era, with some of the allegedly more "advanced" sectors of the population shifting their allegiance over to a political frame while other sectors, especially in the countryside, remained resolutely loyal to the religious frames. Eventually, as the states were able to establish themselves as more powerful and influential institutions than the churches by the early modern period, they succeeded in replacing a religious framing of the past with a political one. Arguably, the supremacy of political schemata in the West lasted for approximately two hundred years, from the mid-eighteenth until the mid-twentieth century. During that span of time, the religious frame by no means disappeared, nor has it disappeared today, but it did become residual rather than dominant and thus lost most of its former capacity to shape popular perceptions of the past.

Not long after the state's political schematization of memory achieved ascendancy, however, it began to be challenged by a more subtle but highly effective new framing interest, that of the so-called mass media. The mass media, emerging as a collective force in the nineteenth century, are best seen as a social and cultural power existing apart from both the church and the state, since they reflect neither religious nor political but primarily market interests. Beginning with the expanding world of newspapers and magazines (the field of print journalism grew almost exponentially from one decade to the next throughout the nineteenth century), and later broadening to include the world of radio, film, and television, the mass media eventually became both an integral part and a direct expression of a growing capitalist economy. For the most part, what the media held up to be remembered were the forms and styles of popular culture, or at any rate those that had the greatest potential for turning a profit. From the outset there was something about media framing that was more democratic and down-to-earth than what was highlighted in the older religious or political schemata. Perhaps because the mass media seemed to be in tune with the egalitarian spirit of the modern age, they were able to acquire great influence over large collectivities in a relatively short period of time. Today it appears that media schemata have moved from their initial emergent status to a now dominant one, while the once hegemonic political framing of the past has fallen back into a residual status (though probably not quite as residual as the religious).[3] Put differently, both political and religious schemata have continued on in the contemporary era and both still have an effect on modern consciousness; but overall, such schemata, because they have been increasingly marginalized, now have far less influence over the reigning forms and contents of memory than they did in centuries past.

Though a strong case can be made that the value placed upon memory has declined significantly when compared to earlier eras, the church, the state, and the media still seem to be actively promoting it. Nevertheless, one must understand that the memories these institutions advocate are mainly those relevant to their own domain, while those outside each institution's area of concern are treated as unimportant. At the same time, then, that there has come to be less reliance on memory in general, memory itself continues to be advocated in late modernity, even if less vigorously than before. But since the media now have the greatest say in how the past is framed, they have come to exert the greatest influence on what people think worthy of being remembered and what they think it is permissible to forget.

With this said, I want to turn to the three modes of framing memory mentioned above, first to show how influential a schema can be in deciding what is recalled and how it is interpreted, and second to indicate both what the dominant media framing in the West looks like today and what effect this framing has on our perceptions of the past.

A diversity of overlapping familial, regional, and *ständisch* schemata existed at all social levels in the Middle Ages, but one frame stood above and informed all the others, and that was the religious. The aim of a religious framing of the past was to guide collective memory toward those events of former times that had a bearing on matters of faith or salvation. Thus singled out for remembrance were the major happenings in the life of Christ, doctrinally important occurrences within the history of Christianity, and secular events that in some manner or other had lasting religious significance.

It was clearly in the interest of the Church that people remember matters such as these when they recalled the past. To this end, the Church, once it had become a full-fledged *ecclesia* with an immense amount of power and influence over all areas of cultural life, employed a variety of means to evoke the memories it considered most appropriate. It was especially effective in the interpretative control it had over (1) the key sacred texts of the Western tradition, along with the methods of exegesis designed to explain their meaning; (2) the pivotal signs, symbols, and images that made it possible to render the past intelligible to the unlettered millions who relied on the Church for the construction of values; (3) the most important rites, rituals, and commemorations of daily life, including those centered on the liturgical calendar which helped shape in a religious fashion the contours of time itself; and (4) the curricula of an entire spectrum of educational institutions from the monastic and cathedral schools of the early Middle Ages to the great universities of the thirteenth and fourteenth centuries. With such extensive framing opportunities at its disposal, the Church at its apogee was able to configure the kind of past that most suited its institutional needs and, in its view, the needs of the faithful as well.

In the High Middle Ages this formidable religious schema began to be challenged by the newly emerging states of Europe. These states, each concerned with establishing the grounds for its own legitimacy, had a vested interest in recalling a political rather than a religious past. This being so, they began advocating an alternate set of memories, most of which were focused on what was called the *status regis et regni* (the state of the king and the kingdom).[4] These included such things as the memory of dynastic continuities, claims regarding the territorial extent of a realm or the traditional powers of the crown, matters involving jurisdictional and historical precedent, and the like. In the postmedieval period, states became still more emboldened. Among the absolutist monarchies of the early modern period, for example, one finds a more militant contestation of religious schemata in an effort to establish political authority outside and beyond the sanctions of religion. By the late seventeenth century, new political calendars came into being in Europe which annually recalled and commemorated not religious happenings but statist or national ones, such as, in England, the defeat of the Spanish Armada in 1588 and the foiling of the Gunpowder Plot in 1605.[5]

By roughly 1700 a political framing of the past had gained equal footing with, but had not yet displaced, a religious framing. A century later, though, the situation had changed more decisively in favor of the state, since by that point political schemata appear to have become generally ascendant in the West.[6] Whereas, paradoxically, collective memory was declining in other respects (in part because of the influence of the emerging market economy), it was nevertheless upheld by modern secular states for one important reason: it helped forge closer ties between the populations at large and the institutions of government that claimed to represent them. Since by the mid-nineteenth century many states had come to base their legitimacy on popular sovereignty rather than dynastic continuity, it began to be necessary that a citizenry identify with and not merely accede to the state's de facto authority. One way to make sure such bonds of identity took hold and worked as effectively as possible was to fortify them by means of shared political memories. If people recalled the same past in the same manner, and if such recollections were in tune with how the state also thought about its own existence in time, then a kind of fusion of interests would take place. The memories and sentiments advanced by the state and those actually present in people's minds would be similar enough to make governing the newly enfranchised masses a much easier task. Hence the politicization of memory was a highly desirable end, but for it to take root in a population and begin performing the tasks expected of it, the people had to become not just a populace but a nation; the state had to become not just any state but a nation-state; and memory had to be not just the memory of disparate events in the past, but the memory of the nation-state's "special and extraordinary place in history." All three of these things did in fact occur over the course of the nineteenth century.

The methods employed to evoke useful political memories have been dealt with by others and therefore need no more than passing mention here. They include the utilization of state-sponsored festivals and commemorations designed to, as Talleyrand put it, "awaken glorious memories [and] tighten the bonds of fraternity";[7] the erection of national historical monuments and memorials for the purpose of arousing patriotic sentiments; the establishment of national museums to help define the meaning of national greatness; the manufacturing of images, icons, and symbols intended to deepen the citizen's emotional allegiance to the nation-state; the invention of traditions devised to make the nation-state seem older and more venerable than it actually was; and the creation of an educational system, set up in part to validate national memory schemata while at the same time discrediting older local, regional, or religious ones.[8]

Admittedly, the United States did not follow this pattern to the same extent that European states did. In the decades before the Civil War, the federal government shied away from the role of custodian of memory, since there was too much grassroots opposition to the idea of a state imposing national memories from the top down. It is true that by the mid-twentieth century the American government did become more active in promoting an "official" interpretation of the past and in seeing to it that the entire nation shared a similar memory schema. But even here, because it had to respond constantly to a variety of domestic pressure groups and interests, the government seldom made use of the aforementioned methods of memory evocation as extensively or assiduously as it might have.[9]

In Europe, by contrast, many states went even further in the twentieth century than they had before in melding collective memory with national identity. In the 1920s and 1930s, for instance, it became evident particularly to those states that had gravitated to the far right that memory could produce not just political unity (this much had already become obvious in the nineteenth century) but *integral solidarity.* One can point to many examples of the management of the past toward the achievement of this kind of solidarity in fascist Italy, Spain, Romania, and elsewhere, but perhaps it was in National Socialist Germany that the political orchestration of memory reached its most extreme form. There, state-manipulated memories, forged and deepened by means of massive public rites and liturgies held throughout the year, from Reichspartei Day festivities to Heroes Remembrance Day, helped create a coordinated and regulated *Volksgemeinschaft* that supposedly embodied a solidified German consciousness.[10] Of course, in comparison to their eighteenth and nineteenth-century predecessors the Nazis had access to numerous advances in technology, including radio and film, which they used to good advantage. Probably for this reason, the way in which the Nazis were able to utilize their rituals of memory successfully for political ends made all earlier efforts, such as the *fêtes de la Fédération* of the French Revolution, seem highly amateurish by comparison.

The end of World War II brought with it a discrediting of statist memory, as the excesses of fascism and National Socialism made it clear to most people in the West that too much politicization of memory was not a laudable goal. To be sure, in the 1950s and thereafter a political deployment of memory continued, as the case of the Soviet Union shows,[11] for both domestic and Cold War reasons. But to a greater extent than ever before, modern states came to realize that their power and legitimacy rested more on their ability to satisfy the material needs of their respective populations (to "deliver the goods," as Herbert Marcuse put it) than on cultivating or mobilizing the memories of the past. At the same time, a mass-media temporal framing gradually made its presence felt as well. As already mentioned, the origins of this media framing can be traced back to the nineteenth century, but it was not until the period between the 1940s and 1960s that it became ascendant in North America and Western Europe and then hegemonic thereafter. For historical reasons, the instauration of a media framing of memory has lagged behind by thirty or forty years in Eastern Europe and the former Soviet Union.

By the terms "media" or "mass media" I mean the overlapping and inter-penetrating worlds of mainstream newspapers, magazines, tabloids, compact discs, videos, radio, film, and television that have by now become omnipres-ent in the postindustrial West. Today these media have become not only the chief purveyors of contemporary ideas and values but also the most influen-tial framers of what we now know or think about the past. The religious and political frames of memory have certainly survived, and at particular times and under the right conditions they are still able to shape the memories of large numbers of people. But they are forced to operate under the new rules of the game dictated by the mass media, since more often than not the media interpret what the religious and political schemata mean and decide how valid those meanings are.

What gives the media the power they currently enjoy is their ubiquity; no matter what the place or time of day, media sounds, images, and messages are continuously available to be heard or seen. They saturate virtually every as-pect of experience and work their way into the conscious or unconscious minds of most people who are exposed to them, thereby making modern Western society surely the most media-mediated society that has ever existed. This contention seems especially borne out with respect to the electronic me-dia, and above all television. Today, more than 95 percent of the households in the West contain one or more television sets. In the United States, we are told, an ordinary American spends approximately two thousand hours a year watching television (as compared to 2,900 hours sleeping), which amounts to almost 40 percent of one's waking life. In France, a man or woman born after 1970 is expected to devote 63,000 hours of his or her adult life to television, as opposed to 55,000 hours working. What these and similar statistics indicate is that in our era hardly anyone lives outside the televisual world. Watching television, as Stephen Heath recently put it, has become an obligatory require-ment for full membership in modern society.[12] As a result, the way that tele-vision frames and structures the past (and the present) has come to have an enormous influence on contemporary consciousness. Curiously, nearly all early theorists of collective memory either overlooked or failed to anticipate this new shaping power of the media. Halbwachs, for instance, writing as late as the 1930s and 1940s when the cultural importance of the press, radio, and film were plainly evident, had almost nothing to say about the effects of the mass media emerging in France and elsewhere during his own lifetime. In-stead, he confined most of his discussion to family, class, or small-group memories, each dealt with on its own terms apart from media influences. Halbwachs was unable to see that all these types of collective memory were about to be transformed by or subsumed into a much broader and more inclusive media framing of the past.

What the media in general and the electronic media in particular are most adept at conveying is information about popular culture, especially commer-cialized popular culture. To a considerable degree, information about sports, film, fashion, popular music, and the daily lives of celebrities has become the common coin of daily discourse. The stock of cultural knowledge stemming from these shared interests seems to do more to join us together in collectivi-ties than anything having to do with religion or politics. When religion was the main binding force of social life, the Church was there to organize and structure it. When national sentiments played the same role, the nation-state was there to direct them. But now that popular culture has become our new social cement, it is the media—backed, of course, by the corporate interests that fund and support them—that have come forward to be not only popular culture's chief boosters, but its chief shapers and framers as well.

However that may be, my concern here is not so much with the media's role in spreading the values and attitudes of popular culture as it is with their role in framing social-cultural memory. With regard to this issue, it would be well to keep the following three points in mind.

First, modem media, especially the electronic media, seem to prefer to focus on the present rather than the past; their primary concern, after all, is with what is happening now, not what happened long ago. The one exception to this rule is that the media do sometimes take an interest in the immediate past of popular culture, such as the relatively recent events in sports, fashion, or entertainment, but usually these kinds of memories go back only a few years or at most several decades. Beyond this short span of time the media treat even popular culture memories as too historically remote to be worth recalling, unless they can be recycled in such a manner as to become serviceable in a present-day context. In contrast, say, to religious memory (which often extends back centuries or millennia), the media offer us a greatly foreshortened temporal frame within which to think about or approach the past. Most of what falls outside this frame is consigned to oblivion.

Second, the media, and again the electronic media in particular, though themselves generally indifferent to long-term memory, are not averse to discrediting memories associated with or embedded in other, non-media schemata. What seems especially objectionable is what might be called untainted religious or political memories, that is, memories that have remained largely unaffected by media influences or resistant to media control. Whenever such autonomous forms of memory are dealt with by the mass media, they are almost always treated with disapproval if not disdain. From the perspective of most of the media, those memories that stand outside the shaping power of its own schemata are by definition irrelevant or insignificant. That the media can now label in a negative way the religious or political memories of which they disapprove, and then have the majority of the population accept such labels as accurate and credible whether there is sound reason for doing so or not, is itself a sign of the vast framing power the media have managed to acquire.

Instances of autonomous religious memory can be found, for example, in some of the fundamentalist sects and apocalyptic subcultures that still survive in the interstices of modern life. In small, half-hidden enclaves, old religious schemata continue to persist beyond the glare of media attention. (On those rare occasions when the media do take an interest in them, such schemata receive mainly critical and sometimes even scathing treatment, in part because the memories they encourage are neither appreciated by nor readily assimilable into mainstream culture.) Political memories unfiltered by the media have been equally disapproved. With few exceptions, purely political memories have been portrayed as either self-serving and therefore suspect, or fanatical and therefore dangerous. An example of the first kind of accusation is evident in the decades-long filmic, televisual, and journalistic assault waged on the French state by some elements in the French media for the way that the state, for its own political purposes, falsely remembered the Vichy period of the 1940s.[13] An example of the second kind of accusation is apparent in the recent news coverage of the conflict in the former Yugoslavia. A point that the Western media repeatedly made throughout the 1990s was that political memory untempered by other influences is always dangerous, because it arouses irrational sentiments which in turn lead to wars of revenge or recrimination. The Serbian memory of the Battle of Kosovo Polje in 1389, for instance, was often singled out as a typically misguided and perilous form of political memory. At Kosovo, a Serbian-led Christian force was vanquished by the invading Turks. Not only was the cream of the Serbian nobility lost, but, as present-day Serbian nationalists have viewed it, Christian civilization was set back more than half a millennium in the Balkans. According to the media, the memory of this defeat came to be woven over the centuries into Serbian myth and legend to such an extent that it eventually became an integral part of Serbian national identity. As a result of the recollection of this six-hundred-year-old political event, the Serbian government, even in the last decades of the twentieth century, vowed that it would never relinquish the Albanian-populated province of Kosovo where the battle occurred no matter what the costs might be in future suffering and bloodshed. To the media this attitude was an example of political memory run amok. Set against this sort of extremism, the more benign memories of popular culture, which the media are happy to cultivate, seem entirely wholesome by comparison.

The third point has to do only with that part of the media that deals primarily with images. Even on those relatively infrequent occasions when the visual media do undertake to recall the historical past by means of electronic images, they are unable to do so very successfully. Television in particular, despite its technological sophistication, is limited in its ability to produce memories that become deeply imprinted in the minds of those who watch it. The reason is that the information television conveys is transmitted so impressionistically, and within such an inadequate structure of relations for ordering and interpreting it, that it is difficult for the average viewer to retain. Furthermore, much of what is communicated via television is watched passively or with only fitful bursts of attention. Thus the multiplicity of images that enter one's field of vision rarely get registered or processed mentally, and hence are hard to recall at a later point in time. In this sense, television, both by overwhelming the viewer with disconnected bits of information and by asking so little in the way of involvement with what is presented on the screen, seems to produce forgetfulness at least as much as it produces memory.

Perhaps even more important, television has an inherently weak capacity for fostering social or collective memory because the electronic images on which it is based are simply not good conduits for transmitting lasting knowledge about the distant past. Televisual images can be effective when it comes to imparting synchronic information. They may in fact be unmatched in their ability to give individuals far removed from events a vivid sense of what is happening immediately and simultaneously in the world around them. But by the same token, images are not able to do the opposite very well, that is, render for viewers a sense of historical duration, sequence, or continuity. Nor for that matter are they able to preserve the vital content of collective memories, or tell people why such memories are worth retaining. It might seem that at least in television documentaries or docudramas the past is being transmitted by electronic means, but this too is a misperception. Mainly what one gets from even the best television programming is not anything like "organic memory" (*mémoire organique*), as the French poet Charles Péguy called it,[14] but either images of other images repeated in an "eternal cycle, an endless loop" of visual reference,[15] or images that appear to be from the past but are manufactured in the present and then projected backward onto some earlier historical period so as to create the illusion of coming authentically from the past. It is probably unfair to blame the medium of television for perpetuating this deception, for neither television's early nor its present-day advocates have ever claimed that the medium's goal is to give people real collective memories. At best, the claim has been that it could give people *representations* of such memories—some more or less true and others more or less false—and generally speaking television has made good on this claim.

If entire cultures may be classified by what they remember about the past,[16] many today would judge the late modern age harshly for the seemingly trivial nature of its memories. For as I have tried to indicate, the kinds of memories chiefly encouraged now are those selected by media schemata, and that means above all memories centered on the concerns and diversions of popular culture. This limited kind of remembering shuts out a much greater range of ideas, events, and values that never get much attention. It might be said that underneath the relatively small but prominent sphere of popular culture memory which appears to be thriving today there exists widespread social and historical amnesia.

Some critics of the contemporary era, seeing that what is considered memorable today is mostly determined by our dominant media frames, have urged that those frames be pushed aside or loosened up enough to make way for the recollection of other, presumably more important matters. What other matters, now nearly forgotten, would it then be possible to recall once again? Here a wide variety of answers have been given. Some defenders of discarded religious schemata have called for the revival of Christianized frames of memory with the intent of making them ascendant once more,[17] while apologists for a political framing of memory have wanted to see the state regain control of the interpretations of its own past. Some nationalist groups and associations in the United States as well as in Europe and the former Soviet Union have called upon the modern state to free itself from what they believe to be an excessive and unseemly dependence on the media and media images. As these proponents of a renewed political mode of remembering have argued, states themselves ought to again take charge of the memories they require and wield them for their own ends, as they did with notable success in the nineteenth century; they should not rely on commercially managed media interests to do it for them, and moreover to do it in such a fashion as to undermine the integrity of the state in the process.[18]

Aside from these two answers, some historians have proposed that efforts be made to retrieve not the memories of old religious or national traditions, which now often appear too narrow or confining, but rather *world* memories, or what one historian called "the legacy of everybody's past experience." For those who have embraced this point of view, it is the "memory of the whole of humanity," not parochial or merely Western memory, that has the capacity to free us from the errors and misdirections of the past, thereby preparing all humankind to live together more harmoniously in the twenty-first century.[19] On a more esoteric level, other thinkers, taking their cues from the writings of Theodor Adorno, have wanted to resuscitate memories of an intimate, fraternal relationship with nature which human beings supposedly once enjoyed, but which they have long since forgotten because they have lost touch with their "mimetic faculties." And yet others, especially contemporary followers of Heidegger, have wanted to see a restoration of the lost knowledge of "Being"—a kind of knowledge that is presumed to have slipped away twenty-five centuries ago with the advent of Western metaphysics, and then become even more obscured in modern times thanks to the triumph of technological rationality.

These various calls for a recovery of memories other than popular culture ones are by no means anomalous. A number of other interests outside the mainstream have likewise pleaded for a remembering of values and traditions that for one reason or another have been occluded or suppressed in the contemporary period. In light of this, it may be a legitimate undertaking to ask if these many things-to-be-recalled are truly important and pressing, or simply the product of notions spun out of the minds of intellectuals. But this is not the direction I wish to follow here. Instead, I want to raise the issue of whether *any* alternative to our predominant media remembering, tenable or not, has much chance even of gaining a hearing today, let alone being embraced by a significant element of the population.

Pessimists tend to think that memories not sanctioned by the media, particularly the electronic media, have virtually no opportunity of achieving wide adherence. The reason, they argue, is that people are so inundated by especially television images and interpretations that it is all but impossible to counteract their profound effect on modern life and consciousness with something that comes from outside of media control. The inevitable result is that other types of memory either go unnoticed or get rudely shunted aside. Among the young, who are growing up at a time when media schemata appear to hold undisputed sway, this suspiciousness of or lack of interest in other, non-media forms of memory is said to run especially deep. As a consequence, the younger generation may be developing far greater skepticism toward the older memories and values that inhere in rival frames than is the case with most of their elders. In contrast to those who came to maturity before, say, the 1930s or 1940s, many young people now have little or no first-hand knowledge of other kinds of schemata, but rather know about them only through media filters. To the pessimistic observer it seems that ever larger numbers of people, young and old alike, are losing interest in most of the memories that stand beyond the pale of popular culture. Or, if on occasion they do concern themselves with such memories, their concern appears to be laced with ironic detachment if not outright hostility.

Present-day optimists say that though the mass media now shape the content and scope of collective memory, they are neither as oppressive nor as overbearing as the pessimists maintain. Moreover, if one keeps in mind that the term "media" comprises not just a visual and aural but also a print dimension then it must be granted that a wide array of collective memories, some of them quite far removed from the realm of popular culture, do receive acknowledgment today, especially through the publication of books and specialized journals. Hence for many optimistic commentators, the public sphere, broadly understood, is not entirely moribund. There are places in modern life—in churches, meeting halls, university classrooms, book clubs, and even Internet chat rooms—where real "environments of memory" are still alleged to exist, though often in greatly reduced form. In many of these settings, the optimists claim, a past outside of and sometimes markedly different from that of popular culture is not dismissed as irrelevant but given a voice in the conversations of the present.

The differences separating these two camps can perhaps be summarized as follows: whereas the pessimists see media frames as both dominant and determinative, the optimists see them as dominant but not determinative. Today, evidence that these two perspectives continue to square off against one another is not hard to find. The so-called *Historikerstreit* of the 1980s in Germany could be cited as one example of this continuing dispute. This "quarrel among historians" was mostly carried on in the print media, particularly in select newspapers and some of the more learned magazines and journals, but in time it moved beyond the concern of intellectuals to ignite, at least momentarily, the interest of a relatively large reading audience. At the center of the controversy was the perceived need to deepen German historical memory. On one side, a neoconservative position emerged (articulated most thoroughly by Michael Stürmer, Hagen Schulze, and Ernst Nolte) which asserted that Germans today have an obligation to recall their past more conscientiously than they have in recent decades, because a healthy collective identity, which ought to be everyone's goal, can only exist where there is some depth of tradition and memory. But in order to establish as affirmative a German identity as possible, the neoconservatives maintained, memory must not only be long-term, as popular culture memory is not; it must also stress the positive aspects of the past more strongly than the negative. For those who espoused this side of the dispute, it seemed imperative that contemporary Germans begin recalling better and in greater detail the twenty or more centuries that constitute the whole of their history in order to highlight once again the great spiritual and intellectual contributions which they as a people have made to Western civilization. The kind of memory that must *not* get overemphasized, the neoconservatives averred, is the memory of the Nazi period. Stürmer and Nolte especially insisted that too much recollection of the years 1933–45 out of a span of nearly two millennia of German culture is counterproductive, unnecessarily burdening modern Germans with a crushing weight of "guilt obsessions" (Stürmer) and thereby hindering their ability both to cope with and take responsibility for the world they inhabit in the present. Thus it would be best to begin to "get out from under Hitler's shadow" by bracketing or otherwise historicizing the Nazi era in such a way as to play down what happened then in order to play up the rest of the now nearly forgotten German past.

In opposition to the neoconservative point of view, a liberal position (enunciated by Hans Mommsen, Eberhard Jäckel, and Jürgen Habermas, among others) quickly came to the fore. Those representing this view agreed that an abiding historical memory is something contemporary Germans need, but contended that such memory must not give up its focus on the Nazi period. For the liberals, the Nazi era was not simply an outbreak of irrationalism, as the neoconservatives preferred to think; it was rather an expression of certain deep-seated and disturbing tendencies in German life and culture which were present well before 1933 and which, by all appearances, had not entirely disappeared after 1945.[20] From this perspective it naturally became unacceptable to historicize or, as some of the neoconservatives put it, "normalize" the National Socialist past. In Habermas's words, the searing "image of that unloading ramp at Auschwitz" needs to remain a permanent part of German memory;[21] to put it out of mind, even to contextualize it too much, would be to forget something essential that Germans need continually to be aware of if they are to understand themselves as a people.

However different these two positions may appear to be, we can notice in retrospect that the disputants were perhaps closer to one another than they realized. Both sides, after all, argued that memory is a good thing; both wanted to see it promoted more extensively (though they differed with respect to the kinds of memories they thought should be encouraged); and both were hopeful that deeper forms of memory could be made to take hold among the

German people as a whole. But beyond these two parties at loggerheads with one other there was another camp that never directly entered the controversy, but which may be the true antipode to *both* of the contending groups. I am referring to the cultural pessimists who would maintain that the liberals no less than the neoconservatives have failed to call into question the same erroneous presuppositions. There is little or no chance that historical memory will develop either in Germany or elsewhere, the pessimists would claim, for what exists and will continue to exist throughout the West is the triumph of a popular culture mesmerized by electronic images. In a contemporary environment saturated internationally by what one critic called "Rock, rap, Rollerblades, Disney, and McDonalds," it would seem that no long-term memories other than those of popular culture can be expected, and even these often last only for very short periods of time before vanishing altogether.[22] The myopia of both camps in the *Historikerstreit*, the pessimists would insist, lies in their attempt to revive the "past-oriented individual." Resuscitation of this now nearly extinct type is a virtual impossibility, since almost everyone in this posthistorical or posttraditional era, the younger generation above all, appears to have lost the desire as well as the ability to recall any past not sanctioned by the prevailing media schemata.

This same split between the optimists and pessimists has also cropped up elsewhere. In many eastern European states, for instance, optimistic observers have noted the veritable explosion of forms of memory that were once expressly disapproved by the state and given little or no attention by the state-run media. Beginning in the late 1970s and continuing into the 1980s, Poland, to cite just one example, witnessed a surge of civic, Catholic, and national memories, most of which had been marginalized or suppressed since the late 1940s. Unexpectedly this flood of memory seemed to burst forth everywhere, indicating to some that the memories and traditions that many others thought had been undermined or defeated were in fact still alive, existing outside the control of the state bureaucracy and beyond the purview of the official media.[23] But pessimistic observers in Poland and elsewhere have offered a different interpretation. The public reappearance of memory, they have suggested, was due to the specific circumstances, not likely to be repeated, of Eastern Europe during the span of roughly a decade. The recovered memories and newly improvised public commemorations of past events during those few years were primarily a protest against the much-resented Soviet control of Polish culture and politics that had gone on since the end of World War II.[24] But once a post-Communist, market-oriented mode of life settles into fixed routines—and even more, once the electronic media begin exerting the same influence over the Polish population that they already exercise throughout the West—then it will be television more than anything else that will decide what is worth recalling and what can be forgotten. And, according to the pessimists, what will be thought worthy of recall will not be the temporarily revived religious or civic memories of the 1980s; it will be the memories and values promoted by a televisual culture that will itself play a central role in the larger, globalized culture of consumption.

A final instance of the split I have been discussing has become manifest in controversies concerning Jewish memory. Most commentators on modern Judaism agree that Jewish collective identity has always depended on the sustaining power of memory. Throughout their long history it was memory that held the Jewish people together spiritually and religiously, in part because they were so dispersed physically or geographically. The memory that performed this integrative function was of sacred texts, ritual traditions, common beliefs, religious and customary laws and practices. For three millennia, the recollection of these things was indispensable for Jewish self-awareness, but today, it seems, these conduits of memory have come to play a much diminished role in the lives of most Jews. No longer thinking of themselves as a "people of memory" but rather as up-to-date individuals living in late modern societies, increasing numbers of Jews have detached themselves from the old rituals, the rabbinical traditions, and most of the injunctions and interdictions of their faith. The result, according to some, has been an unraveling of Jewish collective consciousness, leading to a "decay of Jewish group memory."[25] For perhaps the majority of Jews in Europe and North America today, many observers fear, there may now be only a faint memory that there *once was* Jewish memory, and that it was deeply invested with religious and cultural importance. On the future of collective memory (or lack thereof) the optimists and pessimists within the Jewish community divide into opposing camps. The optimists naturally contend that despite the pressures of contemporary life many young Jews show signs of wanting to hold on to the memory of specifically Jewish values and legacies.[26] The pessimists are doubtful. In their view, the younger generation as a whole has already succumbed to a massive forgetting of their heritage stretching back to biblical times. But worse yet, to the extent that young Jews are indeed turning away from memory as a source of identity, they are said to be simultaneously turning toward the media and popular culture in search of new ways to discover what their interests are and what thoughts and ideas they will want to attach themselves to in the modern world. If this turn toward homogenization is successful, Jews will eventually be Jews in name only, but in attitude, outlook, and lifestyle they will have become indistinguishable from everyone else.

There is no need to elaborate any further the differences between the optimistic and pessimistic perspectives on memory. Only the future will tell which side has made the better assessment, but for the time being it seems to me that the optimists have come closer to describing the actual situation of social and collective memory today. For without underestimating in the slightest the hegemonic framing power of the mass media, I believe that many memories originating outside the realm of popular culture and generally devalued by the mainstream can and still do manage to win acceptance, even if only among relatively small numbers of people. Despite critics such as Guy Debord, who have argued that nothing gets remembered if the media wants it forgotten,[27] a good case can yet be made that some important memories barely acknowledged by popular culture or the mass media have nonetheless persisted, in however a precarious a fashion, in the nooks and crannies of modern life.

But to suggest that certain types of nonconformist memory still survive in what many consider a culture of forgetting is to raise again the larger question that I have been asking directly or indirectly since the first pages of this book. If memories not encouraged or shaped by the popular media are or can be made a living presence today, what ought we to think about the value of such memories? Is memory as such something that should ground us, as it did individuals and cultures long ago, or are we better off cutting our ties with the past in order to make room for a better apprehension and appreciation of the present? The discussion of remembering and forgetting in the late modern age that I have undertaken here cannot be considered complete until a satisfactory answer is given to this question. My own attempt at such an answer, bringing together some themes only partially developed thus far, is the purpose of the concluding chapter.

Memory in Late Modernity

We have taken a long detour in part II, but it has allowed us to see the importance of social and cultural frames and how they affect and shape individual memory. In the most important matters of life, an individual is not likely to recall the past in any way he or she wishes. Rather, unless one makes efforts to the contrary, one will probably recall those aspects of the past that the frames indicate are worth remembering and forget those things the frames screen out as irrelevant. Most memory, in other words, is socially mediated, which means that there tends to be a confluence between a collectivity's predominant schemata on the one hand and the mental structures of the individuals who live within that collectivity on the other. Just as the prevailing schemata shape private memory by helping to decide both what from the past deserves to be recalled and how it is to be remembered, so the manner in which millions of people individually remember the past helps entrench and normalize the structures of recall from which they take their memory cues in the first place.

As we come back now to the situation of the individual in this final chapter, we need to keep this social or collective dimension in mind. But at the same time we need to see that people are still free to remember outside the dominant frames if they choose to do so.

In some sense it is indolence, or the tendency to follow the line of least resistance, that leads people to remember in generally conformist ways. To say this is not necessarily to express a critical judgment, for it is simply a fact of human nature that individuals living in social environments find it easier to remember what others remember and to forget what they forget. But always available to anyone at any time is the freedom not only to remember in a manner unlike most other people but also to remember other and different things than are encouraged by conventional norms. This freedom is what Nietzsche meant by a "will to memory," and it implies going against the grain or diverging from the patterns of recall most others take for granted. Today, as we have seen, the dominant type of social or collective memory is the memory of the ephemera of popular culture, now fostered and sustained by the mass media. A divergent or oppositional memory would recall things about the past that are not commonly thought about and perhaps not even missed in the population at large. To remember differently, then, is no easy task. It takes effort, determination, and self-initiation to search out and hold onto countermemories at a time when most others are content with the memories that are already in circulation.

But there is at present a still more formidable impediment to dissonant forms of memory than the prevailing media framing of the past. The impediment I am referring to is the larger context in which we all live, which in its basic contours seems to discourage memory and promote forgetting. Because of the simultaneous electronic, technological, communications, and information revolutions that have taken hold in the West, we now appear to be moving away from the past at such an accelerated pace that remembering it no longer seems pertinent or useful. As we enter the twenty-first century, the world that is available to be experienced has changed fundamentally in many ways. At the very least, it is far more fluid, and thus far less stable or continuous, than it was for our ancestors. As a result, there is now the necessity on the part of many tens of millions of people to reassess their respective life situations, and then retrain or retool if that is called for—all of which require large amounts of forgetting. In the face of these pressing new necessities, the need and even the desire to remember atrophy. As Eric Hobsbawm has accurately put it in summarizing these developments, "the past . . . has lost its role [today]," for "the old maps and charts which guided human beings, singly and collectively, through life no longer represent the landscape through which we move, the sea on which we sail."[1] If this is so, then holding on to the remainders of the past would do nothing but weigh us down if it did not sink us. Under the circumstances, it would seem to make good sense to jettison the mass of facts, meanings, and values left over from a past that has been supplanted, since to retain and honor them could not help but be counterproductive in the short as well as in the long run.

When attitudes such as these come to predominate, as they have in late modern culture, the result is a pronounced tilt toward present-centeredness, with consequences that in our case are now plain to see. For one thing, our orientation today has increasingly become less diachronic and more synchronic (now even on a global scale), and hence we have lost much of our interest in the past, along with the reasons we once had for remembering it. For another, we in the West have dramatically shifted our attention from the old to the new, and in the process have shown a willingness to throw out the old with hardly a second thought when it is judged to have lost its utility. Further, there is a growing conviction that memory, by binding us to past determinations, makes us too rigid, too stuck in frozen habits. We seem persuaded now that in being too wedded to memory we only repeat but cannot initiate, whereas with forgetting we can become free, innovative, experimental, and multifaceted (if not necessarily "whole") human beings. Notions such as these appear to be widely held because so many people have come to accept an idea that earlier centuries would have found absurd, namely that *un*-learning is the way to growth. Personal development, according to this view, does not proceed by means of a gathering in or reappropriation of the past. Rather it comes about through a series of liberations from what one formerly was. Or put differently, it comes by shedding the qualities one had been forced to acquire through the socialization process in order to start over afresh, free of the stranglehold of memory, to become whatever, at any point in one's life history, one decides one wants to be.

With what I have just described apparently representing the new mood today, Heidegger's comment that we appear to be "put[ting] all our stock into forgetting as quickly as possible" seems apposite.[2] Memory, to a considerable extent, has simply ceased being the desideratum it was to our forebears.[3] (In those cases where information from the past *does* need to be retained, the widespread assumption now is that computers can do most of the remembering required, and they can do it better than humans.) As a rule, those who choose to adapt to contemporary conditions and, like the culture itself, come to play down the overall importance of memory for life will find themselves more "in the flow" of things. They will likely experience fewer tensions in relation to their surroundings and, as suggested earlier, will probably be happier and better adjusted than those who, for whatever reason, prefer to hold on to memories of the past. At the same time, however, they will almost certainly be narrower, emptier, and shallower. It would not be unfair to say that those who forget the past in order to adapt more comfortably to the world as it is resemble the animals in the grazing herd that Nietzsche alluded to in his 1874 essay *On the Advantage and Disadvantage of History for Life.* Being well fed and generally reconciled to life, these animals are not beset by problems. They "leap about, eat, rest, digest and leap again" all the while "know[ing little of] what yesterday and today are," and for this reason "feeling neither melancholy nor bored."[4] Living this sort of life, Nietzsche averred, may increase one's level of contentment, but because it is based on so much forgetting, it also makes one less deep, less rich with possibility.

If, by contrast, one were to decide not to adapt to the way things are, but instead to remember divergently, in a way that is not in conformity with current media schemata, then something different and more interesting could happen. Arguably, one could then become aware, as the forgetter cannot be, of what is *not* at hand, that is, of what is past and, being past, now appears strange and unfamiliar to late modern sensibilities. This awareness of the difference of the past could have the positive effect of distancing one from the constraints of present-day norms, thereby opening one up to a deeper or broader range of perceptions and possibilities than the present alone could hope to offer. But is this really what would happen? Would an intensification of memory, and the *Entfremdungseffekt* that it would presumably bring about, really be a gain, or would it in fact lead to something ultimately detrimental to the individual?

My aim here is to pursue just this issue—the value of memory even though it may estrange us versus the value of forgetting even though it may lull us into complacency—along two separate lines. The first is personal and concerns the worth or worthlessness of memory at the individual level; the second is social and has to do with the worth or worthlessness of collective memory. Even though there is considerable overlap between the personal and the social realms of memory, I have thought it best to deal with each type of memory separately in order to make my remarks as focused as possible.

In pursuing the first of these two lines of inquiry, I will not discuss those forms of personal memory that strictly adhere to conventional frames. This is not a particularly interesting type of memory, for here one recalls, even about one's own personal past, primarily what the dominant social schemata designate as important. As Ernest Schachtel summarized it, much adult memory does indeed frame the past according to the familiar milestones and signposts provided by the culture at large. In his essay "On Memory and Childhood Amnesia" cited earlier, Schachtel wrote "The milestones are the measurements of time, the months and years, the empty count of time gone by, so many years spent here, so many years spent there, moving from one place to another, so many birthdays, and so forth. The signposts represent the outstanding events to which they point—entering college, the first job, marriage, birth of children, buying a house, a family celebration, a trip. . . . [But] even these [milestones and] signposts themselves do not indicate the really significant moments in a person's life; rather they point to the events that are conventionally supposed to be significant, the clichés which society has come to consider the main stations of life."[5] This, it is true, is the way a great deal of personal remembering takes place, but for our purposes it is not compelling enough to merit much attention.

However, although all individual memory tends to be socially mediated to some degree, it does not have to be socially determined. There is room for play. All of us possess in unique combinations a mixture of dominant and residual frames that help us notice aspects of the life we have lived that the dominant schemata alone would not permit us to see. Thus we may break through the kind of frozen, conventional remembering that Schachtel described in order to obtain some leeway in how we recover our own past. In what follows, I will be concerned only with this relatively freer, less stereotyped kind of memory, not a kind that in formal and standardized ways dictates what we are supposed to recall.

With this said, the question of personal memory can be posed in the most straightforward terms: should we late moderns be advised to remember our past or forget it? The answer, unfortunately, is not clear and simple. Because personal memory can both enhance and burden us, be enabling and disabling and a source of pleasure and pain, it does not seem justifiable to recommend either remembering or forgetting in any blanket way. A recommendation in one direction or the other would have to take into account both what is remembered or forgotten and also how it is remembered or forgotten.

For example, one could recall an aspect of one's past—a particular event, a turning point that failed to turn, a relationship that ended badly—in such a fashion as to become overly invested in it. Should this happen, memory could well have damaging results, especially if, as a consequence of this overinvestment, one were to become morbidly fixated on the might-have-beens of one's past life, thereby making it impossible to ever fully *be* in the present. Here, obviously, memory would be something negative, even if it seemed to satisfy some inner pressing need.

Conversely, one could remember certain acts, experiences, projects, or commitments that might be usable as essential building blocks in one's personal development. In this instance, memory would have to be seen as beneficial, because it would give one the content out of which the identity of the self would be able to emerge. Here the Existentialists were no doubt correct when they claimed that one is nothing more, or less, than the sum total of one's past acts, thoughts, feelings, choices, and undertakings. If this is so, then the past we recall is constitutive not only of the meanings we attribute to our lives, but of what we in fact are as individuals. By grasping what we have been—our "being-in-time" so to speak—we come to see in what direction our life has been unfolding. We see our *durées*, our trajectories, and once these are noted, we become better able to affirm or change them as we think best. Without memory we would have no substantiality; we would know only what we are at a given moment but not apprehend the ways in which we are the outcome of our past.[6]

Finally, one could recall and dwell upon certain discreditable occurrences from one's past—not just mistakes or errors in judgment that might have had some embarrassing consequences, but also more injurious acts that may have had harmful physical or psychological effects on oneself or others. What would be important in determining whether it is best to remember or forget such occurrences would be some sense of how one should personally respond to these memories. Would it be with guilt, self-loathing, or a sorrow that goes beyond all bounds of reasonableness? If so, then memory should perhaps not be advised unless the seriousness of the acts or events remembered fully warrant this kind of reaction. Or would it be with remorse, followed by an urge to mend, repair, or correct the harm that was done? Perhaps in this case memory should be encouraged, for by keeping present and alive the wrongs of the past that need to be remedied, memory could help lay the foundation for a sense of what ethical responsibility toward others (or oneself) might mean.[7]

On the other side of the ledger, forgetting presents similar problems. One could, for example, forget things from one's personal past which, if remembered, would give courage or inspire one to excellence. By recalling what one once did (and hence could do again) one might gain the confidence to move forward in life. Forgetting, by contrast, erases the awareness of one's own capabilities, thereby making one excessively cautious or doubtful about nearly every undertaking. On the other hand, an individual might choose to forget old fears or anxieties which, when honored, would lock him or her into deadening habits or routines. Here forgetting would appear to be salutary, for it would free up the individual (as Lifton, Gergen, Hilman, and others have argued) to become more flexible, plastic, and protean. Or put differently, it would permit a person to remake or reinvent himself or herself in ways that, by late modern standards, would seem to represent something unqualifiedly good. Finally, an individual could, as Freud showed, "actively forget" major or minor traumas experienced in the past, but do so in such a fashion that their harmful affects linger on in the unconscious. In this case, forgetting—or the apparent forgetting produced by repression—would obviously not be something to encourage, since it would likely undermine the self one had become by poisoning it from within or turning it in a pathological direction.

Taking all of the above into consideration, we seem to be left in some confusion regarding the general desirability of remembering or forgetting at the present time. If one could still believe in the kind of deep memory that Plato discussed—that is, a memory that leads one to discover through *anamnesis* the highest truths of existence—these difficulties would be resolved, for that sort of memory would of course be something entirely positive. But today when we speak of memory, this is not the kind we mean. Rather, memory now means the recollection of things that are, comparatively speaking, more mundane and ordinary: past events, past feelings, earlier sense experiences, and the like. With these as the contents of our recollections, it is not easy to say, in a way that would apply to all individuals, whether there is on the whole a gain or a loss in remembering them.

One way out of this dilemma would be to dispense with the notion that the matter is reducible to an either/or choice, and say instead that sometimes remembering makes sense and at other times forgetting does. Kierkegaard took this approach when he recommended the "art of remembering *and* forgetting" in equal measure, believing that each individual, in order to be complete, must live as much in the hope that stems from forgetting as in the continuity that is produced by recollection.[8] Nietzsche likewise spoke up for the importance of "remember[ing] at the right time" and "forget[ting] at the right time," but he did so somewhat more assertively than Kierkegaard. According to Nietzsche, there are some things from our past that should always be remembered because they "quicken" life, and other things that should always be forgotten because they stifle or deaden life.[9] Beyond comments such as these, however, there is in both thinkers a noticeable lack of specificity. For all their interest in guiding modern individuals toward either religious (Kierkegaard) or vitalistic (Nietzsche) ends, neither nineteenth-century thinker directly addressed the issue of whether it would be better *as a rule* to remember one's personal past or to forget it.

Despite the difficulties and uncertainties surrounding this issue, perhaps it would be best now to offer an answer to the question of what, in the last analysis, the value of memory is today. That answer too is double-edged. If one believes, as I do not, that we, as supposedly autonomous and independent selves, are created out of the present moment in spontaneous interaction with our immediate surroundings, then it would seem best to be a forgetter, for there would be no need, no substantive or convincing reason, to cling to the excess baggage of the past. But if on the other hand one believes, as I do, that the past one has lived is not, after all, superfluous but provides the very ground and core of whatever self-knowledge one is able to achieve, then it would clearly be better to be a rememberer.

Memory of both the positive and negative aspects of our past gives us the material with which to work in composing the self we want to be. Memory helps give form to the meanings we see in the temporal structure of our lives, and thus it shapes how we think about ourselves. If we did not have memory as a base, we would live only on the surface of our selves, without much in the way of a personal history or stable identity. Moreover, remembering, unlike forgetting, makes possible a certain amount of reflectiveness in an individual, which in turn allows one not only to take notice of the good of one's life and build upon it, but also and just as importantly to become aware of the shortcomings or missteps of one's life and work through them in such a manner as to make sure they do not persist with damaging effect. Real, meaningful personal growth may well come about only by way of what the medieval theologians called a *via negativa:* that is, by straightforwardly confronting and dealing with what one would rather not face, instead of simply forgetting or dismissing it.

And not least of all, remembering enables one to see, again in a way the forgetter cannot, roads not taken in one's life, possibilities cut short, potentialities left undeveloped. Memory permits an individual not simply to visit again these futures that did not happen, but actively to take them up once more if one so chooses. St. Augustine would not have become the person we know in the *Confessions* had he not been able to go back, through the faculty of memory, and retrieve those spiritual threads from boyhood which he had let go of in adolescence and early adulthood. Similarly, without the power of memory the character Michel in Proust's *Remembrance of Things Past* would not have been able to recover and bring to artistic fruition particular lines of thought and experience which he had failed to attend to in the middle years of his life. The same is true for anyone. What might be termed the retroactive reappropriation of one's personal past could be an extremely important event in the unfolding of one's life history, for such a recollection and reappropriation could prompt one to bring forth, and then carry through with, projects or commitments that ought to have been fulfilled earlier but which for one reason or another were either abandoned or derailed. In its own way, this kind of undertaking could lead to what Kant referred to as an individual's "full, human maturity" *(Mündigkeit);* but if so it would be a maturity that comes about not so much, as Kant famously argued, by "daring to know" *(sapere aude)* as by "daring to remember" *(memor aude).*[10]

Turning to the collective realm, one discovers the same difficulties in staking out a firm position on the value of remembering and forgetting.

Certainly there is much to be said in favor of forgetting the collective past. As already noted, such forgetting can free one from traditions of acrimony and prejudice which once burdened or impaired previous generations that remembered all too well. Given that many wars and conflicts have begun as a result of some group's need to right remembered wrongs, often to the detriment of all involved, it would seem that such forgetting must be counted a good thing. Forgetting also allows one to see one's present condition with fresh eyes, unencumbered by old legacies or interpretations, and this in turn appears to make one better able to appreciate and effectively engage the world as it actually is, "warm with life and immediately around us."[11] Equally important, forgetting can help an individual perceive future possibilities in a present situation, for by letting go of the past, one necessarily becomes more cognizant of existing or emerging opportunities that lie directly at hand. As advocates of forgetting have long contended, it is these opportunities and possibilities that should be the primary focus of one's attention, since that which is coming into being will in the long run be more important for the individual than what has already passed away.

Each of these alleged benefits of forgetting seems convincing on its own terms, which may be one reason why the pro-forgetting outlook appears to be the prevalent one in the Western world today. But precisely because a stance favorable to forgetting has perhaps been too facilely and unquestioningly embraced by so many, it may be all the more imperative that we take a second look at what might be called the gains of collective remembering over those of collective forgetting. Two such gains stand out, and in what follows I will confine my comments only to these two. First, social or collective memory gives us a greater depth and breadth of awareness which can personally enrich us and stimulate creative thought and action. Second, such memory permits us to acquire a standpoint outside the present from which we can better see— and criticize—the shortcomings and aporias of the contemporary age. These two gains come, however, not by enmeshing oneself in the memory of popular culture, but by remembering what is *excluded* from the ruling memory schemata of our time.

Theodor Adorno spoke of the kind of memory I have in mind as "a remembrance of the forgotten."[12] But a better, or at any rate less vague, term than "the forgotten" to refer to the *disjecta membrae* of present-day consciousness might be the "noncontemporaneous." This admittedly cumbersome word denotes that which is "from another time" and thus discordant with the present.[13] The assumption built into most uses of this term is that what is discordant or does not "fit in" with the tenor of the present must be eminently forgettable. Though, to be sure, "noncontemporaneity" as a concept is not always exactly synonymous with "the forgotten" or "the excluded," it is close enough in meaning to serve our purposes here. Hence, what I want to suggest is that the type of memory that carries unacknowledged creative and critical potential today is a memory of the noncontemporaneous.

In the next few pages I elaborate on this term in more detail. Following that, I return to the two gains of collective memory just mentioned and deal with each in turn, beginning with the notion that collective memory is, or can be, a spur to creativity.

Before the coming of modernity, people were certainly able to distinguish between the past and the present, but they had a generally weak sense of what really *belonged* to the past as opposed to the present. With the triumph of modernity, the lines between these two temporal domains became much sharper, with the result that people in the West began to understand that some things are "modern" and therefore in tune with the times, while other things are "unmodern" and hence out of step with the age, or noncontemporaneous. What engenders noncontemporaneity is the advance of modernity itself, and the more rapidly the modern replaces the premodern, or the late modern replaces the early modern, the more sizable amounts of noncontemporaneity get produced. Still, not all noncontemporaneity is of uniform weight or importance. To simplify a complicated matter, one could say that today it is possible to delineate three different kinds of noncontemporaneity.

First, there is what might be called *absolute noncontemporaneity.* By this I mean that part of the past that has been completely obliterated except for a few shards or fragments preserved in museums. What we now know of this "lost" past can be ascertained only abstractly, by means of historical or archaeological reconstruction. Though we can still speak of the "world of the Scythians" or the "world of the Celts," these archaic forms of noncontemporaneity lie entirely beyond the realm of present-day experience. To cite Adorno's colleague, Max Horkheimer, this type of noncontemporaneity might be referred to as *das ganz Andere,* "the totally Other."[14] Any past that can be thus described would be not only unconditionally over and done with but, for just this reason, radically unlike anything one could be intimately or personally familiar with today.

Second, there is what might be termed *relative noncontemporaneity.* By this I mean a part of the past that, while also over and done with, has nevertheless left behind more immediately and continuously experienceable physical or cultural traces than those housed in museum displays. When premodern or early modern *Lebensformen* fell into eclipse or were defeated by the forces of modernity, they came to an end as ways of life, but sometimes the palpable evidence that they had once existed never vanished. Bits and pieces of these earlier life forms often persisted, and still persist even within our own time, though when one encounters them they may seem odd or out of place. Among such lingering residues of relative noncontemporaneity are not only certain physical artifacts still in use despite their obsolescence, but also vestiges of preindustrial habits of mind, residues of old-fashioned codes of honor, antiquated spiritual outlooks, scraps of ancient cosmologies, or shreds of ritual practices from traditions now defunct. Traces of all these superannuated forms of thinking and acting continue on today, but being mere aftereffects they are now discontinuous with the past from which they originated. The best way to regard them at the present time is as broken or fractured remains of wholes that have themselves disappeared. None of these fragments should be construed as living, vital traditions because, by being separated from the surroundings of which they were once an integral part, they are not in any true sense natural extensions of the past. Nevertheless, as a result of being alienated from the life- and value-worlds in which they had once made sense, such survivals can become something other than what they were initially; that is, they can become *referents* to a past that is no more. Today this newly acquired referential power might be considered the real value of these surviving remnants of relative noncontemporaneity. For by beginning with traces that are immediately at hand, individuals in the present may work their way back imaginatively to the lost wholes and former registers of meaning that such traces indirectly recall, and in this manner bring back to consciousness the otherwise absent reality of the past.

Third and last, there is *enduring noncontemporaneity,* which denotes those modes of thinking and behaving that have somehow managed to survive not piecemeal but intact into the present age. Where one encounters enduring noncontemporaneity (which will usually be in out-of-the-way places) one comes into contact with the continuous and living presence of the past, however strange or antiquated it may seem by present-day standards. This continuity will by definition be disjunctive with the contemporaneous, since it preserves that which is *unzeitgemässig,* or "out of sync," with the times. To survive at all, elements of enduring noncontemporaneity must often retreat from the mainstream, either to the periphery of social life—to rural enclaves, ethnic subcultures, or religious sects, for example—or, if there is serious risk of suppression or persecution, underground. Yet, as difficult as it may be to access many of these hiding places, they do nevertheless serve one important purpose: they sequester and thereby protect still-living modes of noncontemporaneity, enabling them to continue on, in no matter how reduced a condition, within the context of a present that in most respects is antagonistic to them.

What do these three modes of noncontemporaneity have to do with my contention that collective memory is, or can be, a stimulus to creativity? The answer is that by taking note of the referents to the past that have survived into the contemporary era, however few and fragile they may be, one discovers a reality that is temporally much richer and more multilayered than can be known by the forgetter. And, I would maintain, the awareness of this richer, more complex reality provides the groundwork for both the depth of experience and breadth of vision that seem always to be present as central ingredients in creative achievement.

If one's memory happens to be spurred by encountering pockets of enduring noncontemporaneity, one becomes aware that contemporary life is filled with more traces of temporal difference than is evident from what is highlighted in the media, especially the electronic media. (Whether one agrees or disagrees with what is found in these sites of otherness is not the central thing; just to know about or to engage them has the effect of widening and diversifying one's sensibilities.) More importantly, though, if memory is spurred not by enduring but by relative noncontemporaneity, then what one becomes cognizant of are not so much the marginalized worlds of the present as the seemingly lost symbolic ones of the past. When read correctly, the mnemonic residues of these lost worlds still strewn across our present-day landscape can become ciphers to the vanished ways of living and being that still resonate in them. As Walter Benjamin put it, it is yet possible to "look through [these surviving traces] into their distances,"[15] by which he meant that one can view the remnants of the past on at least two levels simultaneously: first on the level of what they are in their immediacy, and second, on the level of what they can tell us about the dissolved totalities of which they were once an essential part. To the degree that one is able to develop this kind of double vision with the aid of historical memory, one learns to take in more of the meaning and associative richness that is actually present, though not easily discernible, in one's surroundings. Arguably, in the process of doing so, one also—and without directly intending it—puts oneself in what may broadly be called a creative condition.

A heightened sensitivity toward the noncontemporaneous gives one something else that is unavailable to the forgetter. It gives one a feel not only for what has already passed away, but for what is now in the process of disappearing. The rememberer, one might say, has a better sense of evanescence than does the forgetter, which in my opinion ought to be considered a gain, for it may be that only by grasping the fleetingness of existence, both material and human, does one learn to appreciate the true value of what is perishing.

In a manner not easy to describe, value is often intimately linked to imminent loss. I mean by this that the falling away of something frequently tends to augment its worth, objectively and subjectively. Thus the individual who simply takes things as they come, unobservant of the transience of the people or objects around him and incurious about what that transience might ultimately mean, will probably have a weak or dubious hold on value, while the individual who is highly attuned to what is slipping away will more likely perceive the worth of passing things. If creativity has anything to do with a sensitivity toward fading value, as I believe it does, then the rememberer is surely situated more creatively in the world than is the forgetter.

The poet Charles Baudelaire, writing in the middle of the nineteenth century with modernity in full swing, was one of the first to take note of the connections among evanescence, memory, and creativity. For Baudelaire, modernity was by definition inimical to the past; it assumed that for the new to achieve a secure footing, everything old and outworn had to be swept away. In the nineteenth century such an attitude often implied outright destruction of the past. Especially in "progressive" circles in Europe, demolition was the preferred mode of dealing with outdated survivals, as was evident in Baron

Haussmann's approach to the renovation of Paris in the 1850s and 1860s which Baudelaire witnessed firsthand. As the premier urban planner of his day (or *artiste-démolisseur* as he preferred to call himself), Haussmann razed a large portion of *vieux* Paris in order to create a modern, streamlined capital city. In the course of doing so he not only tore down ancient buildings and ripped up old streets, squares, and passageways that had been a part of the Parisian *habitus* for generations; he also abolished the long-standing personal and communal relationships existing in and around these sites. For those who experienced the shock of such transformations of the environment, the world began to look and feel quite different. As old stabilities and certainties were destroyed, life began to seem not anchored and dependable, but, as Baudelaire put it, increasingly "ephemeral, fugitive, and contingent."[16] By dismantling the world they had inherited, Haussmann and other modernizers ushered in a completely new contemporaneity, one that made the formerly "natural" physical and social world it supplanted suddenly seem noncontemporaneous by comparison. And once something is categorized as noncontemporaneous, it becomes easier to treat it as irrelevant and therefore no longer worth preserving. This was exactly the attitude Haussmann took toward many of the old buildings and neighborhoods in Paris, making it easier for him to reduce both them, and the modes of social and cultural life associated with them, to rubble.

But not all forms of noncontemporaneity were smashed to pieces. To the extent that some survived, it became possible for individuals to live in two different "nows" at the same time: the now of modernity, and the now alluded to by the premodern remnants that had refused to disappear. Not only old physical structures but, more importantly, old values, meanings, and practices that were incompatible with modern notions of contemporaneity have lived on, mainly at the fringes of social life or underground and out of sight. What is especially interesting about this perdurance, however—and Baudelaire noticed it already in the middle of the nineteenth century—is that nearly all the examples of enduring noncontemporaneity to which one could point had (and still have) lost their ability to define themselves. Instead, as modernizers took control of most registers of valuation, they were able to label that which appeared new and up-to-date "good", and that which seemed stuck in the past "bad". Thus it was unsurprising to Baudelaire that most of the forms of enduring noncontemporaneity that he was yet able to experience in the interstices of Parisian life were disparaged or denigrated, particularly in comparison to what now began to be termed "modern."

For Baudelaire there was one social class more than any other that had not only come to control the valuative and devaluative judgments built into all cultural discourse but had also learned how to use such judgments to undermine those older meanings referenced by the extant remnants from the past, and that class was his *bête noire,* the nineteenth-century bourgeoisie. According to Baudelaire, it was above all the bourgeoisie who "went along" with modernity. Consequently, it was this class too that was more than willing to deprecate any type of noncontemporaneity, whether surviving cultural lags or traces of lost wholes. As Baudelaire saw it, the bourgeoisie's position was quite simple: it was to embrace the new because the new was associated with value as such, and to shun the old because it was by nature without value. But for Baudelaire this point of view led to an unacceptable narrowness, a flat one-dimensionality. His alternative was not only to become, on a personal level, as aware as possible of the still-surviving residues of noncontemporaneity but indeed to *go over to and poeticize out of them.*

Baudelaire believed that by siding with what has been shunned, defeated, or rejected, one acquires a better sense, from the inside as it were, of what evanescence means. For him, the transience of life is best perceived by attaching oneself to what is falling away, not by latching onto what is new or novel; and when one grasps transience from within, one gains access to a wealth of insights and awarenesses unavailable to those whose overriding goal is to forget what is departing in order to "keep up with the times."

By committing himself to what was about to perish, Baudelaire was able to see at the very least two things that were essential for a creative relationship to the world. The first was the "moral worth" *(valeur morale)* of what was passing from the scene, and the second was the special beauty of what was vanishing precisely because it was vanishing. According to Baudelaire, it was not just the value but also the beauty of things, ideas, and people that became manifest or even heightened as they were about to disappear. If one paid no attention to what was coming to an end or had already ceased to be, one missed a whole sphere of beauty that called out to be recognized. This indifference, in Baudelaire's estimation, explained why the life of the typical bourgeois had no aesthetic quality to it. The modern bourgeois had chosen to harness himself almost exclusively to what was new or au courant, and by doing so had blinded himself to the deepest sources of the beautiful.

The German poet Rainer Maria Rilke, writing in the early twentieth century, adopted a perspective on memory and creativity similar to Baudelaire's. He too saw the modern world laced with often barely noticed material traces from the past that contained noncontemporaneous meanings and messages. As Rilke expressed it in his *Duino Elegies,* we have around us pillars, pylons, towers, houses, fountains, gates, jugs, and much else that has survived from earlier times, but now, within modernity, these things have taken on the appearance of strange, decontextualized objects, since the past in which they were fashioned and where they once had a place is gone.[17] When we encounter them today, they often seem to be ungrounded or stranded objects because, being detached from their previous surroundings, they have been deprived of their original referents.[18] But their detachment does not prevent them from continuing to signal backward to human worlds of meaning which would otherwise be lost from view.

Nevertheless, Rilke detected a problem here—in fact two problems in one. First, by the beginning of the twentieth century fewer and fewer people appeared to be aware that fragments of past lifeworlds are actually carriers of memory, and hence only this dwindling number were able to hear or feel the reverberations of the past in surviving objects. Second, and even more serious, residual objects were themselves increasingly disappearing as modernity made them obsolete. To Rilke, the fact that ever greater quantities of old things were being taken out of circulation as soon as they showed the slightest signs of age or wear meant that people would eventually be deprived of the opportunity to make contact with the memories that echoed in them. And by losing contact with such memories, whole populations would be cut off from the worlds of value and meaning with which those memories were intimately associated.

In Rilke's view, this loss of contact with the past was part of the crisis of the modern age, but the crisis did not have to be suffered passively. For at least the most poetic types in the contemporary era, there were, Rilke thought, a couple of things that could be done. One was simply to take notice of and cherish all that was becoming outworn before it disappeared completely. The other and more important task was to remember what was being *dis*membered, and to do so in the most profound manner possible, which was by bringing the meaning of disappearing objects inward, into the core of the self. Only in this way, by means of what Rilke called a "flight into inwardness" *(Flucht nach Innerlichkeit),* could the problem of transience, including the sense of loss and anguish that transience frequently brings, be solved in a creative fashion. As Rilke saw it, there was no other way for either the remainders of the past or the irreplaceable values they contained to be rescued from oblivion except by absorbing them into one's very being and making them an integral part of oneself. Rilke referred to this undertaking as *Herz-Werk,* meaning the process by which one internalizes the things that are vanishing so as to make them rise again invisibly in one's innermost consciousness. As a result of this kind of heart-work, Rilke believed that the past could not only be saved from general erasure but brought to completion. For by reappearing in us subjectively, the past might, Rilke hoped, achieve something of the fullness that was denied to it objectively when, owing to the inherent limitations of earlier times, it was never able to realize its highest possibilities.[19]

In sum, both Baudelaire and Rilke contended that the memory of a past that is slipping away could lead to something creative, or potentially creative, for the individual. One is stimulated to be creative, they implied, when one has a creative relationship to the world. But for a creative relationship to the world to exist the right conditions must be present. Foremost among such conditions is some feeling for the inexhaustible richness and variety of the life around one, since it is this feeling more than anything else that draws individuals out of themselves and toward a creative engagement with their surroundings. But in order to be attuned to the richness of life, one must have some awareness of temporal depth and be able to see other realities besides that of sensual immediacy. The conclusion to this line of reasoning was that since memory gives one access to these other realities, it also deepens and broadens what one experiences, thereby setting the conditions that make it possible for an individual to have even the chance of being creative.

Still, to express the matter so apodictically is to leave everything at the level of generalities. One can, I think, extrapolate from Baudelaire and Rilke to say that memory is indeed a stimulus to creativity, because, by making one aware of how much even contemporary life is shot through with resonances from the past, it allows one to see that the world is far more textured and polysemous than it may at first appear. Moreover, memory not only increases one's awareness of the impermanence of all things (which can in turn enhance an individual's appreciation of the value of what is passing), but it also permits one to glimpse the uncompleted possibilities of the past in the present, and such insight, if responded to in an inspired way, carries its own kind of creative power. If memory were able to produce even some of the results just mentioned, it would have to be seen as highly conducive to a creative outlook. Forgetting, by comparison, would have to be regarded as generally unconducive to creativity, for by shrinking both one's range and depth of perception, it leaves the potentially creative individual with much more impoverished and circumscribed forms of experience within which to operate.

Earlier I suggested that collective memory, in addition to laying the conditions for creative thought and action in the present, provides us with something else at least equally important: it allows us to develop a much-needed standpoint outside of modernity from which we can better see and critically analyze the deficiencies of modernity itself.

In saying this I do not mean to imply that all kinds of collective memory are critical by their very nature, since it is clearly not true that the recollection of virtually anything from the past carries critical weight. Rather, in referring to the critical power of memory, I have in mind a particular type of memory that does not normally receive much attention because it seems to lack utility, namely the memory of what is estranged from and discontinuous with the present.

As the proverbial locomotive of history has moved forward ever more rapidly, it has left behind modes of thinking, valuing, and experiencing that were once cherished by our ancestors but are now considered obsolete. Obviously, some of the past that has been supplanted dates back to distant times, while other aspects of it, no less "transcended," come from relatively more recent periods. Within the former category one might include the lingering reminders of the classical or medieval periods. Within the latter one could include the world of the preindustrial peasantry in Europe which was still largely intact in 1850 but is now approaching extinction; or the world of Jewish *shtetl* culture in eastern and central Europe which was thriving as late as the 1930s, but was then wiped out as a result of war and Nazi exterminationist policies; or even, for that matter, the America of three or four generations ago, now almost completely effaced by postindustrial transformations. In Hegelian terms, this cast off "stuff" of history represents merely the refuse of the dialectic, the wreckage left over after the "Worldspirit" *(Weltgeist)* has departed from the scene.[20] Being superseded, such historical debris tends to be seen as irrelevant or irrational, since it no longer corresponds to contemporary realities. Very much like Hegel two hundred years ago, we today also appear to be more interested in the forward-looking side of the dialectic. For the most part, we warm to those aspects of the past that anticipate the present or point in the direction of a future yet to come, and we lose interest in those that have become passé. As for the residues or leftovers of earlier social formations, many now fully agree with the view expressed by Jean Baudrillard when he wrote that it would be best to make the past truly past as quickly as possible so that we can finally do what we should have done long ago—forget it.[21]

In contrast to this perspective, I want to suggest that the transcended past, seemingly comprising unreconciled or unassimilated remains, continues to be important for us at the present time not only because of the qualities of otherness or difference to be found there but because of what I would call the past's generally unacknowledged "truth value." As even a cursory glance at the many earlier struggles over beliefs, convictions, and ways of life will attest, neither "truth" nor "value" ever depends simply upon which ideas or systems of thought happen to win out historically. Success alone determines very little, for by almost any standard of measurement significant numbers of both true and valuable things have been consigned to the dustbin of history, while much that is worthless has triumphed. But these discarded things perhaps ought not to be neglected and forgotten just because they lost out to purportedly more advanced historical forces. In returning by means of memory to that which is different from the present, one not only pays respect to what has failed or been silenced but also acquires a standpoint from which to criticize the contemporary age—an age that does not seem much inclined to encourage criticism of any kind, above all criticism of itself.

How does one go about critiquing the age in which one lives? Or more precisely, how does one obtain the necessary leverage to make such a critique effective? The brief answer is that one needs a credible vantage point from which to frame what one wants to criticize. Broadly speaking, there are three such vantage points available to any potential critic. The first is one that operates from a position outside of time itself, from the perspective of, for instance, reason in the abstract or even God himself (as with the prophets of the Old Testament who criticized Israel from what they understood to be Jahweh's point of view). The second vantage point is from a projected ideal or utopian future to be arrived at from inside the historical process by the unfolding of certain immanent possibilities thought to be locked within the present. If a critic selects this as his framing perspective, he may censure his era for all the ways in which it blocks its own potential and prevents its most promising tendencies from being actualized. The third vantage point is based not on what might or could be, but on what was. A critic using this approach might juxtapose the strengths of some bygone period to the shortcomings of his own in order to accentuate those deficiencies of the present that would otherwise go unnoticed. Each of these modes of critique has its own degree of effectiveness, but in what follows I will be concerned only with the last of them, which is the one that most relies on memory.

Every substantive critique of the present undertaken from the standpoint of the past must begin with some grasp of what I have called the truth value of the past. Many today have certainly acknowledged the importance of "keeping watch" over superseded values and meanings in order to make sure they do not completely disappear from human consciousness.[22] But simply keeping watch is not enough to engender a critique, since this stance could lead to something merely custodial. In order to move beyond the mere urge to preserve and on to something like a real critique, the eclipsed truths of the past would have to be counterposed to the untruths of the present in such a way as to give what has been discarded real contestatory power. Should this happen, the remembrance of what once had been (extinguished traditions, lost causes, abandoned ways of living or thinking, and the like) might be able to produce, by means of contrasts or comparisons, enough leverage to call many of the givens of the present into question. If one should develop a special attachment or commitment to the absent past because of what one finds there, then a new, still more intense level of critique might result. For to the extent that what Péguy called a "fidelity to fallen things" takes hold inwardly, one becomes increasingly past-oriented—not just intellectually but viscerally—and thus also increasingly out of step or out of joint with the age in which one lives.

Of course, disadvantages may follow from too great an orientation toward the past. For one thing, such a stance obviously hinders a person's ability to fit in, and for another, it has, or seems to have, a dampening effect on one's capacity to be "happy," at least as this term is defined in present-day consumer culture.[23] But the benefits that come with being critically distanced from one's age are arguably more important than the drawbacks. First, thanks to memory a person becomes better positioned to see through reifications, whose workings forgetters especially fail to notice. If it is true, as Adorno succinctly expressed it, that "all reification is a forgetting,"[24] then one would expect remembering to be a first and indispensable step toward de-reification. Second, because of the critical effects of memory one becomes less susceptible to manipulation by either the economic or political powers-that-be. Manipulation of any kind occurs more readily, and is generally more successful, when people know only sheer presentness. When one possesses some depth of memory, it becomes easier to break free from the tyranny of the concrete, for a good memory allows one to recall the way things were before the present took shape and consequently to become aware of how one's thoughts and actions can be shrewdly managed unless one takes measures to prevent it. And third, one is better able, should the occasion arise, to go further and actually resist that which is illegitimate in the present, once one has determined that it is in fact illegitimate. When memory is dispensed with, everything tends to be accepted more or less at face value. With the aid of memory, however, one is able to see, in Nietzsche's words, just "how unjust [may be] the existence of some thing—a privilege, a caste, a dynasty for example"—and how much it might deserve to be opposed or abolished altogether.[25]

To be sure, "hold[ing] on to the debris"[26] in the manner just described does tend to make one untimely, since it places one in contradiction the age instead of permitting one to flow with it. But even though this untimeliness may justly be called beneficial (at least to the extent that it fosters a critical as opposed to a conformist outlook on the present), it is nevertheless true that two potential dangers exist which could nullify the gains that come with memory. One is the danger of so idealizing the past that one becomes excessively mournful about its disappearance. Here the result could be an exaggerated nostalgia for what is no longer present, which, were it to get out of hand, could lead to an unproductive obsession with the past. The other danger is that one might want to raise up the dead and bring back to life what has been left behind, even though the conditions of the present make any such *restitutio in integrum* all but impossible. Both extremes, in my view, need to be avoided.

One can remember and abide with what is absent without either pining for the past or believing that it can be reinstated.[27] That particular values or truths now seem to belong to a past that is no more should not prevent one from adopting them as one's own, or even using them with critical intent against the established reality of late modernity. By doing the latter one may be better able to apprehend the present not as some would like it to be, or as others work hard to make it appear, but as it actually is.

Today the champions of memory are on the defensive. According to one recent study, only 1 percent of the U.S. population currently define themselves as "past-oriented," while 33 percent describe themselves as future-oriented, 9 percent as present-oriented, and 57 percent as maintaining a "balanced orientation half way between the present and the future."[28] Yet despite such evidence that the value placed on remembering the past has lost importance, we have not become a full-fledged culture of forgetting. As I have tried to show, memory still plays a role in popular culture, and some key institutions of the present, among them universities, law courts, government bureaucracies, and corporate data-collecting agencies, continue to stress the worthiness of at least certain forms of social or collective memory.

Even so, the dominant tone of life today is hostile to memory. On a personal level, the reigning advice now is to let go of and not dwell upon what is absent; "closure" is the new catchword, meaning a willingness to block off or forget what cannot be comfortably assimilated. Likewise on the social level, one sees a growing suspicion of or incredulity toward a large number of once venerated legacies, heritages, and continuities. To remember what has by all appearances been superseded is increasingly regarded as a hindrance to development, however that term may be defined, since most of the meanings and messages stemming from the past are coming to be thought of as too temporally remote to matter. Notions such as these have by now become commonplace in the throwaway cultures of the West, where the mechanism of consensus, rather than the mechanisms of tradition or memory, is more and more relied upon to unify existing collectivities.

In light of the foregoing, it seems imperative that the value of memory be reaffirmed. For memory provides a counterweight to the blind power of the actual. It gives us the wherewithal to refuse the given where that is called for. And it allows us to recover and unfold again aspects of the past that, claims to the contrary notwithstanding, are perhaps not yet over and done with. Finally, memory makes it possible for us to do what Kierkegaard described metaphorically in *Either/Or*, which is to "play at battledore and shuttlecock with the whole of existence." In order to play this intriguing game, one must first, as Kierkegaard makes clear, perfect "the twin arts of remembering and forgetting." This being so, it would seem that battledore and shuttlecock is not a game that can be played very well today, since only half of what it requires, the perfection of forgetting, is now generally encouraged. But if memory were to regain some of its former importance, this game—which for Kierkegaard is really about deciding on and putting at stake one's very being—may be able to be taken up once more and played with the seriousness it deserves.

Notes

Introduction: The Past in the Present

1. The term "late modern" (or "late modernity") as I use it throughout this work refers roughly to the period since 1950. It denotes the most recent stage in the history of modernity in the West, in which most of the ideals, values, and aspirations of the last three centuries have been exhausted without being transcended. The result is that many of the earlier goals and enthusiasms of modernity are now approached more or less ironically or playfully. In my view, we in the West have not as yet moved into a so-called postmodern condition as some have claimed. Though at a later point I will refer to various postmodern "movements" or "tendencies" in our own time, each of these, it seems to me, still subsists within, not beyond, the framework of modernity.

2. "More or less intact" would be the correct way to express it, since ancient and medieval theories of memory did not deny that there could be impaired or faulty memories, that is, memories that were cloudy or inexact either because they were not adequately registered from the very beginning or because they were improperly stored over the course of a lifetime. See, for example, Plato's *Theatetus,* 191^d and 194^c–195, in *The Collected Dialogues of Plato,* ed. Edith Hamilton and Huntington Cairns (Princeton: Princeton University Press, 1973), 897, 901; also Aristotle's *De Memoria et Reminiscentia,* esp. 453^{a}31, in Richard Sorabji, *Aristotle on Memory* (Providence, R.I.: Brown University Press, 1972), 60, 114.

3. A typical statement in this respect is Israel Rosenfield's: "Memories are not fixed but are constantly evolving generalizations—or recreations—of the past." See Israel Rosenfield, *The Invention of Memory: A New View of the Brain* (New York: Basic Books, 1988), 76. A similar point of view is expressed in Gerald M. Edelman, *The Remembered Present: A Biological Theory of Consciousness* (New York: Basic Books, 1989), 110–12, and in his more technical *Neural Darwinism: The Theory of Neuronal Group Selection* (New York: Basic Books, 1987), 242–44, 265–70.

4. See Friedrich Nietzsche, *On the Advantage and Disadvantage of History for Life,* trans. Peter Preuss (Indianapolis, Ind.: Hackett, 1980).

Chapter One: Varieties of Memory

1. Maurice Merleau-Ponty, *The Structure of Behavior,* trans. Alden L. Fisher (Boston: Beacon Press, 1963), 125.

2. Homer, *The Odyssey*, trans. Richard Lattimore (New York: HarperCollins, 1991), 92.

3. Ibid., 139–40.

4. To be sure, on one occasion Odysseus himself "forgets home" while with Circe on the island of Aeaea. But this forgetting is only temporary; eventually he recovers his memory and once again sets sail for Ithaca. Ibid., 164–65.

5. Sophocles, *Antigone,* in *The Three Theban Plays,* trans. Robert Fagles (New York: Penguin, 1984), 82.

6. On Aeneas's memory of ideals, see John Crossett, "Love in the Western Hierarchy," in *The Concept of Order,* ed. Paul G. Kurtz (Seattle: University of Washington Press, 1968), 222.

7. St. Augustine, *Confessions,* trans. Henry Chadwick (Oxford: Oxford University Press, 1991), 15, 56, 86, 170–71.

8. Ibid., 152.

9. See Dante's account of these meetings in his *Vita Nuova,* trans. Mark Musa (New Brunswick, N.J.: Rutgers University Press, 1957), 5–16, 23–24.

10. See, for example, Dante's *Purgatory,* cantos 30–31. Here Beatrice becomes something like Dante's personal conscience, reminding him of what he needs to do to be virtuous. Dante Alighieri, *Purgatory,* pt. 2 of *The Divine Comedy,* trans. Mark Musa (New York: Penguin, 1985), 321–25, 330–34.

11. Dante, *Vita Nuova,* 80.

12. See the *mémorial* included in Blaise Pascal's *Pensées,* ed. Philippe Selliers (Paris: Mercure de France, 1976), 432–33.

13. Johannes Hofer, "Medical Dissertation on Nostalgia" (orig. pub. 1688), trans. Carolyn K. Anspach and reprinted in the *Bulletin of the History of Medicine* 2 (1934), 384.

14. Ibid., 390.

15. Marcel Proust, *Remembrance of Things Past,* trans. C. K. Scott Moncrieff and Frederick A. Blossom (New York: Random House, 1934), 1:1003.

16. Ibid., 2:994.

17. Ibid., 2:992.

18. Marcel Proust, from his *Pastiches et mélanges* (Paris: Éditions de la Nouvelle Revue Français, 1919), 197; see also Georges Poulet, *Studies in Human Time,* trans. Elliott Coleman (New York: Harper and Row, 1959), 298.

19. See Thomas J. Cottle, *Perceiving Time* (New York: Wiley, 1976), 22–23.

20. See Ludwig Binswanger, "The Case of Ellen West," trans. Werner M. Mendel and Joseph Lyons, in *Existence: A New Dimension in Psychiatry and Psychology,* ed. Rollo May, Ernest Angel, and Henri F. Ellenberger (New York: Simon and Schuster, 1958), 295–298.

Chapter Two: Memory and Modernity

1. See Otto Gerhard Oexle, "Memoria und Memorialüberlieferung im frühen Mittelalter," *Frühmittelalterliche Studien* 10 (1976): 70–75, and Patrick J. Geary, *Living with the Dead in the Middle Ages* (Ithaca, N.Y.: Cornell University Press, 1994), 2, 78–

87. The connection between medieval piety and memory is well expressed by Geary: "The gifts the living had received from the dead were so great as to threaten the receivers unless balanced by equally worthy countergifts. The gifts of the dead included nothing less than life itself, property, and personal identity. Without suitable countergifts [i.e., the gift of remembrance], the imbalance would become intolerable" (78).

2. In both the Middle Ages and the Roman world, "prudence" *(prudentia)* did not mean "frugality" or "provident and cautious management" as it does today. Rather, it meant the ability to distinguish right from wrong. Cicero, for example, defined prudence as "the knowledge of what is good, what is bad, and what is neither good nor bad." Cicero, *De inventione,* Loeb Classical Library, ed. and trans. H. M. Hubbell (Cambridge: Harvard University Press, 1949), 2:53, 160. Likewise, Aquinas, Albertus Magnus, and other medieval thinkers treated prudence as one of the moral virtues. To these individuals it meant the ability to make wise judgments about ends and then determine the proper actions required to reach those ends. See St. Thomas Aquinas, *Summa Theologica,* I–II, Q. 57, art. 5, *resp.,* and Mary Carruthers, *The Book of Memory: A Study of Memory in Medieval Culture* (New York: Cambridge University Press, 1990), 65–70.

3. Aquinas, *Summa Theologica,* I–II, Q. 57, art. 5, *resp.* See Carruthers, *Book of Memory,* 66.

4. Carruthers, *Book of Memory,* 69.

5. See, for example, Aristotle's *Nicomachean Ethics,* trans. David Ross and revised by J. L. Ackrill and J. O. Urmson (New York: Oxford University Press, 1980), 28, 271–72, and Aquinas, *Summa Theologica,* I–II, Q. 54, art. 4.

6. See Jean Pierre Vernant, *Myth and Thought among the Greeks* (London: Routledge and Kegan Paul, 1983), 108.

7. Ibid., 92. See also Michelle Simondon, *La mémoire et l'oubli dans la pensée grecque jusqu'à la fin du Ve siècle avant J.-C.* (Paris: Société d' Éditions "Les Belles Lettres," 1982), 154–60.

8. Bernardo Gui, "The Life of St. Thomas Aquinas," in *Biographical Documents for the Life of St. Thomas Aquinas,* ed. Kenelm Foster (Oxford: Blackfriars, 1949), 50–51.

9. See Geoffrey Galt Harpham, *The Ascetic Imperative in Culture and Criticism* (Chicago: University of Chicago Press, 1987), 13, 42, 73, 95–96. Harpham persuasively argues that, especially for Late Roman and early medieval ascetics, holiness was essentially a matter of recalling and replicating the models of saintliness portrayed in the *Lives of the Saints,* Athanasius's *Life of Saint Anthony,* and similar works.

10. See Carruthers, *Book of Memory,* 4, 192–93.

11. See J. A. Natopoulos, "Mnemosyne in Oral Tradition," *Transactions and Proceedings of the American Philological Association* 69 (1938): 465–93, and Eric A. Havelock, *Preface to Plato* (Cambridge: Harvard University Press, 1963), 98–103.

12. As one psychologist typically argued in the 1880s, "the same sensations can be combined in a thousand ways to take account of objects that surround us." What we remember as "fact" is in part an invention of our own minds. See Dr. Favuelle, "Volonté, conscience, idées, mémoire," *Extrait du Bulletin de la Société d' Anthropologie* (Paris, 1885): 40, cited in Matt K. Matsuda, *The Memory of the Modern* (New York: Oxford University Press, 1996), 84.

13. The first scientific studies of what is now called "false memory syndrome"

date to the last three decades of the nineteenth century. On what was then termed "misremembering," see A. Pick, "Zur Casuistik der Erinnerungsfälschungen," *Archiv für Psychiatrie* 6 (1876): 568–74; Emil Kraepelin, "Über Erinnerungsfälschungen," *Archiv für Psychiatrie* 17 (1887): 830–43, and 18 (1888): 199–239, 395–436; and Ludovic Dugas, "Sur la fausse mémoire," *Revue philosophique de la France et l'étranger* 37 (1894): 34–45.

14. Friedrich Nietzsche, *Advantage and Disadvantage of History,* 24.

15. See Albert Guillon, *Les maladies de la mémoire: Essai sur les hypermnésies* (Paris: Librairie J.-B. Bailliére & Fils, 1897), 83, 85–86; see also Michael S. Roth, "Remembering Forgetting: *Maladies de la Mémoire* in Nineteenth-Century France," *Representations* 26 (Spring 1989): 58.

16. Guillon discusses both types of hypermnesia, the type in which quantities of memories overburden and confuse, and the type in which an intensity of memory disorients or disturbs. *Les maladies,* 175–217. Ribot is more focused on the latter type, which he calls "exaltations of memory." See Théodule Ribot, *Les maladies de la mémoire* (Paris, 1881), trans. William Huntington Smith as *Diseases of Memory* (New York: Appleton, 1890), 174–91.

17. Eugène Minkowski, *Lived Time,* trans. of *Le Temps Vécu* (orig. pub. 1933) by Nancy Metzel (Evanston, Ill.: Northwestern University Press, 1970), 150.

18. Aristotle, *Nicomachean Ethics,* 28 (my italics).

19. Typical in this respect are John Todd's *Hints Addressed to the Young Men of the United States* (1845); Samuel Smiles, *Self-Help* (1859), *Character* (1871), and *Duty* (1880); and Paul Radestock's *Die Gewöhnung und ihre Gewichtigkeit für die Erziehung* (1882).

20. In his *Principles of Psychology,* James set forth one of the last firm defenses of habit in Western thought (though he somewhat modified his views on this subject in later works). Habit, he wrote, is a "precious conservation agent. . . . It alone is what keeps us all within the bounds of ordinance. . . . It alone prevents the hardest and most repulsive walks of life from being deserted by those brought up to tread within." For individuals personally, James continued, habits are important to develop because they simplify movement and diminish fatigue. Even more significantly, they are important because they "hand over" the details of everyday life "to the effortless custody of automatism," thereby setting free our "higher powers of mind . . . for their own proper work." In light of all this, James advised his readers to "*make [your] nervous system [your] ally instead of [your] enemy . . . [by] mak[ing] automatic and habitual as early as possible as many useful actions as [you] can*" (James's italics). William James, *The Principles of Psychology* (New York: Henry Holt, 1890), 1:112, 121–22.

In the twentieth century, only John Watson and his behaviorist followers continued to emphasize the importance of habit so strongly. For them, personality itself "is the product of our habit system." Without the cultivation and reinforcement of right habits by means of social conditioning, we can neither live in harmony with our surroundings nor be guaranteed that the patterns of conduct we associate with civilized behavior will be passed on to future generations. See John B. Watson, *Behavior: An Introduction to Comparative Psychology* (New York: Henry Holt, 1914), and B. F. Skinner, *Beyond Freedom and Dignity* (New York: Knopf, 1971).

21. Henri Bergson, *Two Sources of Morality and Religion,* trans. R. Ashley Audra and Cloudesley Brereton (New York: Doubleday, 1935), 20 (my italics).

22. Proust, *Remembrance,* 2:754, 839.

23. Ibid., 2:112.

24. Particularly influential were Ribot's *Diseases of Memory* and Guillon's *Maladies de la mémoire.* Other works in the same vein were Henri Piéron, *L'évolution de la mémoire* (Paris: Flammarion, 1910); Ludovic Dugas, *La mémoire et l'oubli* (Paris: Flammarion, 1919); Ludwig Wille, *Über die psycho-physiologischen und pathologischen Beziehung des Gedächtnisses* (Basel: F. Reinhardt Verlag, 1901); and Paul Ranschburg, *Das kranke Gedächtnis* (Leipzig: J. A. Barth Verlag, 1911).

25. The Italian art historian Giorgio Vasari adopted this line of reasoning in his *Lives of the Artists* (1550). Similarly, the German Reformer Melanchton called Dürer a melancholic in order to underscore his genius, and contemporaries of Raphael assumed that the artist was "inclined to melancholy" because he was so exceptionally talented. See Rudolf Wittkower and Margot Wittkower, *Born under Saturn* (New York: Random House, 1963), 104.

26. For the religious perspective on melancholy, see John Owen King III, *The Iron of Melancholy* (Middletown, Conn.: Wesleyan University Press, 1983), esp. 13–82.

27. Menard Boss, *Psychoanalysis and Daseinanalysis,* trans. Ludwig B. Lefebvre (New York: Basic Books, 1963), 210.

28. Minkowski, *Lived Time,* 160–61.

29. See Max Scheler's discussion of the relationship between resentment and powerlessness *(Ohnmacht)* in his *Das Ressentiment im Aufbau der Moralen* (1915), trans. Lewis B. Coser and William W. Holdheim as *Ressentiment* (Milwaukee, Wisc.: Marquette University Press, 1994), and Scheler's essay "The Meaning of Suffering," in *Max Scheler, 1874–1929: Centennial Essays,* ed. Manfred S. Frings (The Hague: Nijhoff, 1974), 121–63.

30. Friedrich Nietzsche, *On the Genealogy of Morals,* trans. Walter Kaufmann (New York: Vintage, 1969), 124.

31. Ibid., 39.

32. Nietzsche's views on remembering and forgetting are much more complicated than I have indicated here. Though he did defend what he called "active forgetting," he also at times strongly argued for the importance of memory, above all for the memory of promises. More will be said about Nietzsche's perspective on remembering and forgetting in a later chapter.

33. Typical of this genre were Lucien Arréat's *Mémoire et imagination* (Paris: Félix Alcan, 1904); Frédéric Paulhan's *La fonction de la mémoire et la souvenir affectif* (Paris: Félix Alcan, 1904); and Eugène d'Eichthal's *Du rôle de la mémoire dans nos conceptions métaphysiques, esthétiques, passionnelles, actives* (Paris: Félix Alcan, 1920).

34. Sigmund Freud, "Mourning and Melancholia," *Standard Edition,* vol. 14 (London: Hogarth Press, 1957), 243–58.

35. See Sigmund Freud and Josef Breuer, *Studies in Hysteria* (1895), in *Standard Edition,* vol. 2 (London: Hogarth Press, 1955), 48–105.

36. Sigmund Freud, *Five Lectures on Psycho-Analysis* (1910), in *Standard Edition,* vol. 11 (London: Hogarth Press, 1957), 16–17.

37. Freud and Breuer, *Studies in Hysteria,* in *Standard Edition,* 2:7 (Freud and Breuer's italics). Later, in *Five Lectures,* Freud repeated this sentence in slightly different form, also italicized: "our hysterical patients suffer from reminiscences." *Standard Edition,* 11:16.

38. Henri Bergson, *Matter and Memory,* trans. of *Matière et mémoire* (orig. pub. 1896) by Nancy Margaret Paul and W. Scott Palmer (London: Allen & Unwin, 1911), 90, 195.

39. Bergson, *Two Sources,* 10–11, 63–64.

40. Bergson, *Matter and Memory,* 98.

41. Ibid., 198, 323.

42. Ibid., 198.

43. Ibid., 227–28.

44. Ibid., 118, 197, 201, 216–17.

45. See Walter Benjamin, "On Some Motifs in Baudelaire," in *Illuminations,* trans. Harry Zohn (New York: Schocken, 1969), 157–63. For a fuller treatment of Benjamin's notion of experience, particularly his discussion of *Erlebnis* and *Erfahrung,* see Irving Wohlfarth, "On the Messianic Structure of Walter Benjamin's Last Reflections," *Glyph* 3 (1978): 148–212, and John McCole, *Walter Benjamin and the Antinomies of Tradition* (Ithaca, N.Y.: Cornell University Press, 1993), 272–78.

46. See Walter Benjamin, "Aus einer kleinen Rede über Proust," *Gesammelte Schriften,* II, 3, ed. Rolf Tiedemann and Hermann Schweppenhäuser (Frankfurt: Suhrkamp, 1977), 1064, 1066.

47. Benjamin, "Motifs in Baudelaire," 159.

48. See George Stambolian, *Marcel Proust and the Creative Encounter* (Chicago: University of Chicago Press, 1972), 56, 60, and Milton Hindus, *The Proustian Vision* (Carbondale: Southern Illinois University Press, 1967), 68–72. Though the indictment of habit in *Remembrance of Things Past* is clear, Proust was nonetheless ambivalent about the place it should occupy in his own life. Personally he seemed to need the regularity of habit in order to work, even though he implied in *Remembrance* that habitude kills creativity.

49. Proust, *Remembrance,* 2:996.

50. Ibid., 2:994.

51. Ibid., 2:114.

52. Ibid., 2:990–1007.

53. Poulet, *Studies in Human Time,* 298.

54. Martin Heidegger presented what amounts to an apologia for memory in his call to overcome the *Seinsvergessenheit,* or "forgetfulness of Being," that he thought had taken hold in the contemporary era, but the type of memory he had in mind was more ontological than personal; certainly it had nothing to do with the kinds of autobiographical memories I have been discussing in this chapter. There was also a vigorous defense of memory put forth by some members of the Frankfurt School during the 1930s and elaborated in greater detail in the 1950s and 1960s. Building on some notions in Freud while at the same time pushing them in new directions, Theodor W. Adorno and Herbert Marcuse in particular developed a radical theory of memory which was in many respects unique. This is not the place to expand upon the Frankfurt School's view of memory, however, especially since its focus was less on

a strictly private concept of memory than on a more broadly historical or collective one.

Chapter Three: The Vagaries of Forgetting

1. One gets a good idea of the attitude toward forgetting in earlier centuries by noting the complex memory schemes people devised in order to prevent forgetting. See Francis A. Yates, *The Art of Memory* (Chicago: University of Chicago Press, 1966), 1–81.

2. Carruthers, *Book of Memory,* 13.

3. Plato, *Meno,* 81a-e, in *Collected Dialogues,* 363–64.

4. Plotinus, *Enneads,* trans. Stephen Mackenna (London: Faber and Faber, 1962), 4:3, 22.

5. Janet Coleman, *Ancient and Medieval Memories: Studies in the Reconstruction of the Past* (Cambridge: Cambridge University Press, 1992), 121–36.

6. Richard Terdiman has insightfully discussed the nineteenth century's strong antipathy toward outside determinations of any sort in his *Present Past: Modernity and the Memory Crisis* (Ithaca, N.Y.: Cornell University Press, 1993), 48–49, 159–60, 177–81, 243–45.

7. Nietzsche, *Genealogy of Morals,* 57–58.

8. Anthony Giddens, *Modernity and Self-Identity: Self and Society in the Late Modern Age* (Stanford: Stanford University Press, 1992), 78.

9. Louis Lavelle, *The Dilemma of Narcissus,* trans W. T. Gairdner (London: Allen & Unwin, 1973), 101.

10. Mircea Eliade, *Myth and Reality,* trans. Willard R. Trask (New York: Harper and Row, 1963), 30.

11. Ibid., 32.

12. Vernant, *Myth and Thought,* 127; see also Michelle Simondon, *La mémoire,* 77–80, 99–127.

13. Vernant, *Myth and Thought,* 76–80.

14. Carruthers, *Book of Memory,* 38–39, 192.

15. Edward Gibbon, *The Decline and Fall of the Roman Empire* (New York: Modern Library, 1932), 2:1304; William Wordsworth, Preface to *Lyrical Ballads,* 2d ed. in *Movements, Currents, Trends: Aspects of European Thought in the Nineteenth and Twentieth Centuries,* ed. Eugen Weber (Lexington, Mass.: D.C. Heath, 1992), 28.

16. Abraham Maslow's statement that "the ability to become 'lost in the present' seems to . . . be a *sine qua non* for creativeness of any kind" typifies this viewpoint. Abraham Maslow, "The Creative Attitude," in *Explorations in Creativity,* ed. R. L. Mooney and Taher A. Razik (New York: Harper and Row, 1967), 46. See also Kurt Wolff, *Surrender and Catch* (Boston: Reidel, 1976).

17. The term "original," from the Latin *originalis,* once meant "harkening back to origins," or "faithfulness to beginnings." In our own time, however, the term has come to mean the reverse, that is, begetting something that does *not* resemble any origin but is instead utterly different from everything that existed before. See Roger Shattuck, "The Demon of Originality," in *The Innocent Eye: On Modern Literature and the Arts* (New York: Farrar, Straus and Giroux, 1984), 72.

18. Remy de Gourmont, cited in Władysław Tatarkiewicz, "Creativity: History of the Concept," *Dialectics and Humanism* 4, no. 3 (Summer 1977): 59.

19. Cited in Shattuck, "Demon of Originality," 74.

20. Piéron, *L'évolution*, 332–33.

21. See, for example, the various essays in the *Handbook of Creativity*, ed. John A. Glover, Royce R. Ronning, and Cecil R. Reynolds (New York: Plenum Press, 1989), and *Creativity and Its Cultivation*, ed. Harold H. Anderson (New York: Harper and Row, 1959).

22. See Thomas S. Kuhn, *The Structure of Scientific Revolutions* (Chicago: University of Chicago Press, 1962), and Gary Gutting, ed., *Paradigms and Revolutions: Appraisals and Applications of Thomas Kuhn's Philosophy of Science* (Notre Dame, Ind.: University of Notre Dame Press, 1980).

23. In a recent collection of essays on the "nature of creativity," memory as a factor in the creative process was mentioned in passing by only one of seventeen contributors, and even he redefined memory (beyond recognition) as simply "problem solving." See Robert J. Sternberg, ed., *The Nature of Creativity: Contemporary Psychological Perspectives* (Cambridge: Cambridge University Press, 1988). R. Ochse's *Before the Gates of Excellence: The Determinants of Creative Genius* (Cambridge: Cambridge University Press, 1990) does not mention memory even once as a factor in "creative genius."

24. Melanie Klein has been one of the more influential writers advancing such claims, particularly with regard to the periods of infancy and early childhood. See *The Writings of Melanie Klein*, 4 vols., ed. R. E. Money-Kyrle (New York: Free Press, 1964–75).

25. See Sigmund Freud, "Remembering, Repeating, and Working-Through," in *Standard Edition*, vol. 12 (London: Hogarth Press, 1958), 147–56.

26. Sigmund Freud, *Psychopathology of Everyday Life*, in *The Basic Writings of Sigmund Freud*, ed. A. A. Brill (New York: Modern Library, 1938), 103.

27. Ibid., 61, 102. By "forgetting" Freud sometimes meant something closer to selective inattention. Like many others of his day, he believed that nothing once committed to memory is ever truly forgotten. Traces of every experience remain lodged somewhere in the mind; once registered, they may later be "rearranged" or "retranscribed," as Freud wrote to his friend Wilhelm Fliess in 1896, but they never wholly disappear. See Freud's letter of December 6, 1896, in Sigmund Freud, *The Complete Letters of Sigmund Freud to Wilhelm Fliess, 1877–1904*, trans. and ed. Jeffrey Moussaieff Masson (Cambridge: Harvard University Press, 1985), 207.

28. Freud's younger contemporary, Pierre Janet, took a similar position in his early work. The proper response to painful memories, he initially argued, was to excise or liquidate them. Memories that have the power to damage one's psychological health needed to be brought forth not in order to "narrate" them, but in order to expunge them by means of an emotional catharsis. Later, however, Janet, like Freud, came around to the view that although some amount of conscious forgetting can be beneficial, it is generally better to remember and assimilate into one's whole life history even the hurtful events and experiences of one's own past. See Ruth Leys, "Traumatic Cures: Shell Shock, Janet, and the Question of Memory," in *Tense Past: Cultural Essays in Trauma and Memory*, ed. Paul Antze and Michael Lambek (New York: Routledge, 1996), 103–45.

29. Lawrence L. Langer, *Holocaust Testimonies: The Ruins of Memory* (New Haven: Yale University Press, 1991).

30. One of the strongest recent defenders of this position is Norman O. Brown. According to him, the motive force behind the longings and acts of every individual is the drive to feel pleasure, or put more prosaically, to "be happy." But for one to experience happiness, every trace of guilt must be eradicated, for wherever guilt exists there also is anxiety, morbid reflectiveness, depression, self-torment, and aggressiveness toward oneself (masochism) or others (sadism). See Norman O. Brown, *Life against Death: The Psychoanalytic Meaning of History* (Middletown, Conn.: Wesleyan University Press, 1959), 19, 32–39, 262–72, 307–22.

31. Friedrich Nietzsche, *Twilight of the Idols,* in *The Portable Nietzsche,* trans. and ed. Walter Kaufmann (New York: Viking, 1962), 554.

32. One exception to the rule that linked memory with character can be found in medieval monasticism. In the monastic setting an individual was said to increase both in character and in stature before God when he completely obliterated the memory of the self he had been before entering the monastery. Nearly everything having to do with autobiographical memory was viewed as irrelevant, which was why too much recollection of one's involvement in worldly experiences not only did nothing to advance one toward salvation but actually put one at risk of losing one's soul. See Janet Coleman, *Ancient and Medieval Memories,* 117–36.

33. Erik Erikson, *Identity: Youth and Crisis* (New York: W. W. Norton, 1968), 92; see also his *Childhood and Society* (New York: W. W. Norton, 1963), 247–74.

34. Robert J. Lifton, *The Protean Self: Human Resilience in an Age of Fragmentation* (New York: Basic Books, 1993), 51.

35. Carl R. Rogers, *A Way of Being* (Boston: Houghton Mifflin, 1980), 339–56, and *On Becoming a Person: A Therapist's View of Psychotherapy* (Boston: Houghton Mifflin, 1961), 122, 187–90.

36. See Lifton, *Protean Self,* esp. 50–92. Lifton's perspective on remembering, forgetting, and the decentered self has by now been replicated by dozens of other psychologists who write for mass-circulation journals and magazines. Typical of the genre is Kenneth J. Gergen's "Multiple Identity: The Healthy, Happy Human Being Wears Many Masks," *Psychology Today* 5, no. 12 (May 1972): 31–35, 64–66. Gergen later expanded his defense of decenteredness into a book, *The Saturated Self: Dilemmas of Identity in Contemporary Life* (New York: Basic Books, 1991).

37. Even Rimbaud's own short life added up to a series of distinct identities, each seemingly unrelated to every other and each representing a repudiation if not an absolute negation of the one preceding it. See Leo Bersani, *A Future for Astyanax: Character and Desire in Literature* (Boston: Little, Brown), 230–31, 239.

38. Proust, *Remembrance,* 1:1095.

39. Ibid., 1:510. But for the artist, at least, traces of these lost or "forgotten" selves are not completely obliterated. Rather, they slip into an "unknown region" (the realm of the unconscious) where they are preserved in their "pure state." *Remembrance,* 2:114, 996. At some later point they can become accessible to an individual through the medium of involuntary memory.

40. M. Scott Peck, for example, in his popular *The Road Less Traveled* (New York: Simon and Schuster, 1978), advises his readers that if they want "new selves" to come

into being, they must set aside their old ones and eventually be prepared to let them "die." According to Peck, it is only by giving up an "old self" that an individual can achieve the kind of real "mental and spiritual growth" needed to become a "mentally healthy" human being (69–70, 75).

41. James Hillman, *Archetypal Psychology* (Dallas: Spring Publications, 1988), 51–53.

42. See James Hillman, *Re-Visioning Psychology* (New York: Harper and Row, 1977), and James Ogilvy, *Many-Dimensional Man* (New York: Oxford University Press, 1977), esp. 99–115, 149–58.

43. On this point, see Hillman's work and David LeRoy Miller, *The New Polytheism: Rebirth of the Gods and Goddesses* (Dallas: Spring Publications, 1981), 76–77.

44. Two excellent discussions of this view regarding creativity are Harold Bloom's *The Anxiety of Influence: A Theory of Poetry* (New York: Oxford University Press, 1973) and George Kubler's *The Shape of Time: Remarks on the History of Things* (New Haven: Yale University Press, 1962).

45. Søren Kierkegaard, *Either/Or,* trans. Howard H. Hong and Edna H. Hong (Princeton: Princeton University Press, 1987), 1:103, 290.

46. Joseph A. Amato II, *Guilt and Gratitude: A Study of the Origins of Contemporary Conscience* (Westport, Conn.: Greenwood Press, 1982), xix.

47. Dostoevsky developed this point brilliantly in *The Brothers Karamazov.* Throughout this novel and in other works, as Diane Oenning Thompson has shown with great skill and insight, Dostoevsky stressed the "salvational power of remembered good deeds." As a writer he sought time and again to demonstrate the salutary effect that memory—especially childhood memory—can have on later behavior. According to Dostoevsky, memories are like seeds planted in the soul: after lying dormant for a period of time they can and often do "suddenly [spring] to life" in "a moment of spiritual crisis," and in this way take on a "redemptive function." Those characters in *The Brothers Karamazov* who have no early memories of exemplary individuals or of loving and generous acts to hold on to and revere (Ivan, Smerdyakov) are shown to lack spiritual depth and to have a generally poor grasp of ethics, while those who do possess such memories (Alyosha, Mitya) are shown to have a highly developed ethical sense and to be spiritual or ethical individuals. See Diane Oenning Thompson, *The Brothers Karamazov and the Poetics of Memory* (Cambridge: Cambridge University Press, 1991), 75–76, 103, 116, 119–25, 154–56.

48. Georg Simmel, "Faithfulness and Gratitude," in *The Sociology of Georg Simmel,* trans. and ed. Kurt H. Wolff (New York: Free Press, 1950), 388.

49. J. W. von Goethe in his toast to memory, in *Goethes Gespräche,* ed. Flodoard Freiherr von Biedermann (Leipzig: Biedermann, 1910), 3:37, cited in Ernest G. Schachtel, *Metamorphosis: On the Development of Affect, Perception, Attention, and Memory* (New York: Basic Books, 1959), 281–82.

50. For some today, the personal computer has become an unexpected facilitator of this quest for the heterogeneous over the integrative. According to Sherry Turkle, for example, ever larger numbers of people are now "presenting" themselves to others on-line, in multiple-user dialogues. In doing so they have begun playing with being alternate on-line selves, especially the kinds of selves they may find it difficult to be in their normal, everyday lives. Through the medium of the computer, one can experi-

ment with as many personae as one would like, but in the course of assuming these "virtual identities" each individual has momentarily to put aside—or "forget"—the others so as not to confuse one self with another. See Sherry Turkle, *Life on the Screen: Identity in the Age of the Internet* (New York: Simon and Schuster, 1995).

51. In an 1885 fragment, Nietzsche wrote: "The assumption of one single subject is perhaps unnecessary; perhaps it is just as permissible to assume a multiplicity of subjects, whose interaction and struggle is the basis of our thoughts and our consciousness in general? . . . [Hence] *my hypothesis:* the subject as multiplicity." See Nietzsche, *The Will to Power,* trans. Walter Kaufmann and R. J. Hollingdale, ed. Walter Kaufmann (New York: Vintage, 1968), 270. Postmodernist interpreters have made much of this and similar passages. They have argued that such statements indicate that Nietzsche was an early proponent of the notion that every individual contains a plurality of selves, and that for any of them to come into their own, the others have to be at least provisionally set aside or forgotten. Some interpreters also claim that for Nietzsche there is no such thing as a self at all, only a force-field of drives, impulses, and tensions without any focus or unity; and they add that what has traditionally been referred to as a "self" is, for Nietzsche, merely a grammatical fiction, a "seduction of language."

To be sure, ideas such as these do appear sporadically throughout Nietzsche's writings, especially his later ones. Nevertheless, at the core of his work is the presumed existence of a self, or an "I," that can think, reason, reflect, set goals, keep promises, will, affirm life, "organize the chaos," and of course remember its own past and interpret it, as needed, for the present and future.

52. Nietzsche, *Advantage and Disadvantage of History,* 10. In this passage Nietzsche is speaking not just about one's personal past but the historical past as well.

Chapter Four: The Social Frames of Memory

1. According to Émile Durkheim, there is such a thing as an objectively real collective consciousness *(conscience collective)*. This consciousness is not merely the aggregate of individual psyches but something separate from any and all individual minds. As Durkheim put it, the *conscience collective* is a "subject" in its own right, with its own "distinctive properties" and its own "mode of development." It is "[t]he totality of beliefs and sentiments [that form] a determinative system which has a life of its own. . . . [The *conscience collective*] has specific characteristics which make it a distinct reality . . . independent of particular conditions in which individuals are placed; they pass on and it remains, . . . thus [making it] an entirely different thing than particular consciences, although it can be realized only through them." See Émile Durkheim, *The Division of Labor in Society,* trans. George Simpson (New York: Free Press, 1964), 79–80 (translation slightly altered).

Carl Gustav Jung proposed something similar to Durkheim's *conscience collective,* but he termed it the "collective unconscious." Unlike Durkheim, however, Jung usually did not treat the collective unconscious as an objective psyche; rather, it was first and foremost an internal reality, a deeply embedded mental structure in individual psyches that was passed on from one generation to another phylogenetically. The forms of this internal collective mind, the so-called archetypes, were said to go back in some cases not only centuries or millennia but perhaps tens of thousands of years. To the extent that these archetypes supposedly carried forward the accumulated deposits of former experiences, they appeared, at least superficially, to resemble memory traces similar to those already discussed on the individual level. The main difference between ordinary and Jungian memory, however, is that the archetypal traces were said to come not from personal experience but from the archaic experiences of the larger collectivity. This notion that certain mental forms and patterns stemming from the distant past could be inherited and remain in the minds of modern individuals had a bearing on Jung's view of collective memory. For just as the primitive individual as Jung described him does not "think," but rather "something thinks in him" (namely the group unconscious), so too a contemporary individual fully attuned to his archetypes does not remember by his own efforts, but rather *something greater remembers in him;* and according to Jung, that something has remained intact since the remotest ages, "outlasting all generations." Thus, even though Jung did not posit a collective mind that exists literally outside and independent of individual psyches, he did suggest that there are forms and deposits fixed in the mind that precede individual experience, coming as they do from the experiences of forebears going all the way back to the primordial past. See Carl Gustav Jung, *Psychological Reflections,* ed. Jolande Jacobi (New York: Harper and Row, 1961), 36–45.

2. Nietzsche, *Genealogy of Morals,* 61.

3. Georges Duby, "Memories with No Historians," *Yale French Studies* 59 (1980): 8.

4. See especially H. H. Scullard, *Festivals and Ceremonies of the Roman Republic* (Ithaca, N.Y.: Cornell University Press, 1981); Roy Strong, *Art and Power: Renaissance Festivals, 1450–1650* (Berkeley: University of California Press, 1984); Bernard Guenée and Françoise Lehoux, *Les entrées royales françaises de 1328 à 1515* (Paris: Éditions du Centre National de la Recherche Scientifique, 1968); Ralph E. Giesey, *Cérémonial et puissance souvraine: France XVᵉ-XVIIᵉ siècle* (Paris: Armand Colin, 1987); and Jean-Marie Apostolidès, *Le roi-machine: Spectacles et politique au temps de Louis XIV* (Paris: Éditions de Minuit, 1981).

5. See my discussion of education and memory in "Temporality and the Modern State," *Theory and Society* 14 (1985): 68–70.

6. The assumption here was that when people are experientially involved in memorable events they will remember them better and longer. This notion seems to have gained wide acceptance in the nineteenth century, though the advantages of participatory memory did not go unnoticed earlier. For example, medieval royal entries were at times symbolic "dialogues" between the people and their rulers, not just overt displays of power. Similarly, premodern pageants, processions, and the like sometimes made room for commoners to enter at the end, though usually they were not an integral part of the event. Also, many of the civic festivals in Italy during the Middle Ages and Renaissance were open to representatives of virtually all sectors of the population, from the lowest guild member to the highest official of the city. Likewise at least minimal involvement was permitted in the rituals of public punishment in the early modern period, with bystanders being allowed to shout at, jeer, and throw stones or dung at those being punished. But usually in premodern times the major and most magnificent spectacles were to be watched; the lessons they were supposed to teach about majesty or the unbridgeableness of social difference were to be taken in visually,

not performatively. After the French Revolution, however, and into the twentieth century—culminating in the Nazi period—spectacles became much more participatory, but at the same time arguably more managed as well. For a discussion of this shift in emphasis, toward both greater participation and greater management, see Mona Ozouf, *Festivals and the French Revolution*, trans. Alan Sheridan (Cambridge: Harvard University Press, 1988); Jean Duvignaud, "La fête civique," in *Histoire des spectacles,* ed. Guy Dumur (Paris: Gallimard, 1965), esp. 240–56; and George L. Mosse, *The Nationalization of the Masses: Political Symbolism and Mass Movements in Germany from the Napoleonic Wars to the Third Reich* (New York: Howard Fertig, 1975).

7. See Pierre Janet, *L'évolution de la mémoire et la notion du temps* (Paris: A Chahine, 1928), and Charles Blondel, *Introduction à la psychologie collective* (Paris: Armand Colin, 1928). Also typical of the new turn in memory research were J. Nogué's "Le problème de la mémoire historique et l'influence de la société sur la reminiscence," *Revue Philosophique de la France et l'Étranger* 99 (1925): 389–424, and D. Elkine's "De l'influence du groupe sur les fonctions de la mémoire," *Journal de Psychologie* 26 (1927): 827–30.

8. See Maurice Halbwachs, *On Collective Memory* (a partial translation of *Les cadres sociaux de la mémoire*), ed. and trans. Lewis A. Coser (Chicago: University of Chicago Press, 1992), 52–59, and *The Collective Memory,* trans. Francis J. Ditter, Jr. and Vida Yazdi Ditter (New York: Harper and Row, 1980), 44–49.

9. Halbwachs, *On Collective Memory,* 38–39.

10. See Halbwachs, *The Collective Memory,* 33–35, and *On Collective Memory,* 38–40, 52–54. Halbwachs does admit what seems undeniable, namely that we all have idiosyncratic memories which stem from our unique location within the social whole and which for that reason cannot be exactly replicated by any other mind. Yet even here Halbwachs offers a social explanation for individual differences in memory, to wit, that since we all belong to a great variety of social, economic, or political groupings, and consequently always stand "at the intersection of several currents of collective thought," we cannot help but be affected by the competing and overlapping stores of information housed within us. *The Collective Memory,* 45. Because of the unique and unduplicatable combinations of frames we each possess, we all remember differently. Even when we recall the same things as others, we always recollect them from a somewhat different "personal" angle of vision. Ibid., 48.

11. Frederic Bartlett, *Remembering: A Study in Experimental and Social Psychology* (Cambridge: Cambridge University Press, 1964; orig. pub. 1932), 244.

12. Schachtel, "On Memory and Childhood Amnesia," 287–91 passim.

13. Halbwachs, *On Collective Memory,* 40.

Chapter Five: Memory in Historical Perspective

1. See Tacitus, *Germania,* sec. 39, in *The Agricola and the Germania,* trans. H. Mattingly and rev. S. A. Handford (New York: Penguin, 1970), 133–34; see also the commentary by L. L. Hammerich in his "Horrenda Primordia: Zur Germania c. 39," *Germanisch-Romanische Monatsschrift* 33 (1952): 228–33.

2. Eliade, *Myth and Reality,* 90.

3. See Bruce Lincoln, *Death, War, and Sacrifice: Studies in Ideology and Practice*

(Chicago: University of Chicago Press, 1991), xiii. A common assumption among proto–Indo-European peoples was that immediately after an individual died, his or her soul passed through a river on the way to the "other world." The waters of the river washed away all memories, but they did so in such a way as to prevent them from being lost entirely. Instead, the deceased's accumulated memories were carried by hidden streams and springs back to earth where they became "a source of the deepest wisdom and the most profound inspiration" (57). The message here was two-fold: first, that the dead are not really dead, since the memories they had once had remain accessible to the living; and second, that these memories, if taken in and acted upon, can be "the source of true wisdom, the wisdom that is based on the full sweep of human experience rather than just the idiosyncratic events of one human life" (58).

4. On these three aspects of collective memory in ancient Israel, see especially Brevand S. Childs, *Memory and Tradition in Ancient Israel* (London: SCM Press, 1962); Yosef Hayim Yerushalmi, *Zakhor: Jewish History and Jewish Memory* (New York: Schocken, 1989), esp. 5–26; and P. A. H. de Boer, *Gedenken und Gedächtnis in der Welt des Alten Testaments* (Stuttgart: W. Kohlhammer Verlag, 1962), 9–11, 64–70. It is no accident that many of the *mitzvot*, or injunctions of rabbinical Judaism, have to do with recalling acts of God in history ("Remember what happened at Horeb," "Remember the wrath of the Lord in the desert," "Remember what the Lord did to Miriam," and so forth).

5. A. G. Hebert, "Memory," in *A Theological Handbook of the Bible*, ed. Alan Richardson (London: Macmillan, 1950), 142–43.

6. See B. A. van Groningen, *In the Grip of the Past: Essay on an Aspect of Greek Thought* (Leiden: E. J. Brill, 1953), pp. 47–56.

7. See William V. Harris, *Ancient Literacy* (Cambridge: Harvard University Press, 1989), 74, 77.

8. See Vernant, *Myth and Thought*, 75–105.

9. Hannah Arendt, *Willing*, pt. 2 of *The Life of the Mind* (New York: Harcourt Brace Jovanovich, 1978), 215. For the Romans, the absolute priority of the *mos maiorum*, the "customs of the ancestors," cannot be underestimated. As Karl Galinsky has rightly put it, the guidelines laid down by predecessors had to be followed in almost every area of life from "the realm of values and morals . . . [to the realm of] legislation and politics." Karl Galinsky, *Classical and Modern Interactions* (Austin: University of Texas Press, 1992), 78.

10. The Romans, it is true, never became indifferent to cosmological beginnings; they continued to recall such beginnings periodically in ritual observances and sacred *fasti*. But unlike archaic peoples before them, and unlike the Jews of biblical times as well, the Romans directed much of their attention to a political notion of beginnings. As a result, they brought the concept of origin into the framework of human time instead of locating it in some primordial "time before time" inhabited only by supernatural beings (or, in the case of Judaism, by the creator God described in Exodus).

11. Cited in Bruce Jennings, "Tradition and the Politics of Remembering," *Georgia Review* 36, no. 1 (1982): 170 (my italics).

12. On the importance of *exempla* among Roman rhetoricians, see Coleman, *Ancient and Medieval Memories*, 39–59.

13. Marc Bloch, *Feudal Society,* vol. 1, trans. L. A. Manyon (London: Routledge and Kegan Paul, 1965); see esp. chap. 6, "The Folk Memory" (88–102).

14. Duby, "Memories with No Historians," 8–9.

15. See Jacques Le Goff, *History and Memory,* trans. Steven Rendall and Elizabeth Claman (New York: Columbia University Press, 1992), 68.

16. See Karl Leyser, "The German Aristocracy from the Ninth to the Early Twelfth Century: A Historical and Cultural Sketch," *Past and Present* 41 (1968): 25–53; Georges Duby, "French Genealogical Literature: The Eleventh and Twelfth Centuries," in *The Chivalrous Society,* trans. Cynthia Postan (Berkeley: University of California Press, 1977), 149–57; Leopold Genicot, "La noblesse au Moyen Age dans l'ancienne 'France,'" *Annales: Economies, Sociétés, Civilisations* 17, no. 1 (1962): 1–22; Jane Martindale, "The French Aristocracy in the Early Middle Ages: A Reappraisal," *Past and Present* 75 (1977): 5–45; Jean Dunbabin, "Discovering a Past for the French Aristocracy," in *The Perception of the Past in Twelfth-Century Europe,* ed. Paul Magdalino (London: Hambledon, 1992), 1–14; and Wilhelm Schwer, *Stand und Ständeordnung im Weltbild des Mittelalter* (Paderhorn: Schöningh Verlag, 1934). Some scholars have recently suggested that the search for genealogical roots was not widespread in the tenth and eleventh centuries (a time when horizontal or synchronic family connections may have been more significant than diachronic ones) but did become important later during the High Middle Ages. See, for example, Patrick J. Geary's chapter, "Remembering and Forgetting in the Eleventh Century," in *Phantoms of Remembrance: Memory and Oblivion at the End of the First Millennium* (Princeton: Princeton University Press, 1994), 23–47, 50–51.

17. Otto Gerhard Oexle, "Liturgische Memoria und historische Erinnerung. Zur Frage nach dem Gruppenbewusstsein und dem Wissen der eigenen Geschichte in dem mittelalterlichen Gilden," in *Tradition als historische Kraft: Interdisziplinäre Forschungen zur Geschichte des früheren Mittelalters,* ed. Norbert Kamp and Joachim Wollasch (Berlin: Walter de Gruyter, 1982), 323–40, and M. T. Clanchy, "Remembering the Past and the Good Old Law," *History* 55, no. 184 (1970): 165–76.

18. See A. J. Gurevitch, *Categories of Medieval Culture,* trans. G. L. Campbell (London: Routledge and Kegan Paul, 1985), 98, 124. For a more complete view of the meaning of the term "modern" in the Middle Ages, see W. Hartmann, "'Modernus' und 'Antiquus': Zur Verbreitung und Bedeutung dieser Bezeichnungen in der wissenschaftlichen Literatur vom 9. bis zum 12. Jahrhundert," in *Antiqui et Moderni: Traditionsbewusstsein und Fortschriftsbewusstsein im Späten Mittelalter,* ed. A. Zimmermann (Berlin: Walter de Gruyter, 1974).

19. Cited in Yves Congar, *The Meaning of Tradition,* trans. A. N. Woodrow (New York: Hawthorn, 1964), 45.

20. Michel de Montaigne, "On Liars," in *Essays,* trans. J. M. Cohen (Baltimore: Penguin, 1961), 28.

21. On Bacon's views, see Charles Whitney, *Francis Bacon and Modernity* (New Haven: Yale University Press, 1986), 5–12, 56–60, 98–99.

22. René Descartes, *Discourse on Method* (1637), in *Discourse on Method and Meditations,* trans. Laurence J. Lafleur (Indianapolis: Bobbs-Merrill, 1960), 7.

23. Today consumer capitalism has learned to do what sixteenth-century capital-

ism did not know how to do, namely package and sell sentiment and nostalgia as well as real or fake memories. See my *Past in Ruins: Tradition and the Critique of Modernity* (Amherst: University of Massachusetts Press, 1992), 75–76.

24. See René Descartes, *Meditations concerning First Philosophy* (1641), in *Discourse on Method and Meditations*, 69, 75.

25. See R. W. B. Lewis, *The American Adam: Innocence, Tragedy, and Tradition in the Nineteenth Century* (Chicago: University of Chicago Press, 1955), 5.

26. By the eighteenth century many, perhaps even most, of the leading secular intellectuals in Europe and America had developed attitudes of the kind I describe; during the nineteenth and twentieth centuries, however, the anti-historical ideas and opinions initially entertained by a relatively few individuals eventually began to percolate down and be embraced by a broader spectrum of people. Hence, what was once only a minority opinion seems in time to have become the majority one. See Reinhart Koselleck, "*Historia Magistra Vitae*: The Dissolution of the Topos into the Perspective of a Modernized Historical Process," in *Futures Past: On the Semantics of Historical Time*, trans. Keith Tribe (Cambridge: MIT Press, 1985), 21–38, and David Lowenthal, *The Past Is a Foreign Country*, (Cambridge: Cambridge University Press, 1985), 232–33.

27. Reinhart Koselleck, "'Neuzeit': Remarks on the Semantics of the Modern Concept of Movement," in *Futures Past*, 231–66.

28. Many eighteenth-century philosophes who accepted this line of thinking nevertheless allowed for exceptions; the classical age of Greece and the Augustan Age of Rome, for example, were seen as two luminous moments shining out against an otherwise drab backdrop of myth and barbarism. But the philosophes pointed out that however great the Greeks and Romans may have been when measured by certain criteria, they still lacked the conveniences of everyday life, were at times bereft of "common humanity," tolerated slavery, and were, in comparison to the modern age, scientifically and technologically undistinguished.

29. The Marquis de Chastellux, in his *De la félicité publique* (1772), cited in Franklin L. Baumer, *Modern European Thought: Continuity and Change in Ideas, 1600–1950* (New York: Macmillan, 1977), 250 (translation slightly altered).

30. See my discussion of this development in "Remembering and Forgetting in the Modern City," *Social Epistemology* 4, no. 1 (1990): 3–22.

31. See M. Christine Boyer, *Dreaming the Rational City: The Myth of American City Planning* (Cambridge: MIT Press, 1983).

32. Comments made before the Society for the Protection of Ancient Buildings, cited in Charles Dellheim, *The Face of the Past* (Cambridge: Cambridge University Press, 1982), 91.

33. Freud, *Five Lectures*, 11:17.

34. Le Corbusier, *The City of Tomorrow* (Cambridge: MIT Press, 1971), 287–88.

35. See Gotthart Wunberg, "Mnemosyne. Literatur unter den Bedingungen der Moderne: ihre technik- und sozialgeschichtliche Begründung," in *Mnemosyne: Formen und Funktionen der kulturellen Erinnerung*, ed. Aleida Assmann and Dietrich Harth (Frankfurt: Fischer Taschenbuch Verlag, 1991), 91–93.

36. Jean Vallès, in *Le Nain jaune*, February 24, 1867, cited in Philippe Hoyau, "Heritage and the 'Conserver Society': The French Case," in *The Museum Time-Machine*, ed. Robert Lumley (New York: Routledge, 1988), 27.

37. Filippo Marinetti, "The Foundations of Futurism" (1909), in *Movements, Currents, Trends: Aspects of European Thought in the Nineteenth and Twentieth Centuries,* ed. Eugen Weber (Lexington, Mass.: D.C. Heath, 1992), 267–70.

38. See Tristan Tzara's 1918 manifesto "Dadaist Disgust," quoted in Helena Lewis, *The Politics of Surrealism* (New York: Paragon House, 1988), 5 (my italics). The citation from the Russian constructivists can be found in Manfredo Tafuri, *Theories and History of Architecture,* trans. Giorgio Verrecchia (New York: Harper and Row, 1980), 39.

39. Malcolm Bradbury and James McFarlane, "The Name and Nature of Modernism," in *Modernism: 1890–1930,* ed. Malcolm Bradbury and James McFarlane (New York: Penguin, 1978), 26.

40. Initially only a few individuals were involved in historic preservation before the 1850s, but by the early twentieth century interest in restoring the built environment of the past had gathered considerable steam. By the late twentieth century, historic preservation had risen, at least in many places in the Western world, to the status of a national policy.

41. See David Lowenthal, "Conclusion: Dilemmas of Preservation," in *Our Past before Us,* ed. David Lowenthal and Marcus Binney (London: Temple Smith, 1981), 216.

42. On these developments in the nineteenth century, see T. J. Jackson Lears, *No Place of Grace: Antimodernism and the Transformation of American Culture, 1880–1920* (New York: Pantheon, 1981), esp. 61–96, 142–81; Lowenthal, *The Past Is a Foreign Country,* 3–105, 148–82; Dellheim, *The Face of the Past;* Mark Girouard, *The Return to Camelot: Chivalry and the English Gentleman* (New Haven: Yale University Press, 1981); and Wolfgang Hardtwig, *Geschichtskultur und Wissenschaft* (Munich: Deutscher Taschenbuch Verlag, 1990), 224–29.

43. See Raoul de La Grassiere, *De la nostalgie et des instincts contraires comme facteurs psychologiques et sociaux* (Paris: M. Giard & E. Brière, 1911), 6, 14, 24, and Matsuda, *Memory of the Modern,* 46.

44. Cited in Leonard Krieger, *The Meaning of History* (Chicago: University of Chicago Press, 1977), 361.

45. Carl Becker, *Everyman His Own Historian* (New York: Crofts, 1935), 247–48.

46. Yerushalmi, *Zakhor,* 94.

47. Pierre Nora, "Between History and Memory: *Les Lieux de Mémoire,*" *Representations* 26 (1989): 8–9. It is worth noting here that this supposed opposition between memory and history was already staked out by Halbwachs in his *The Collective Memory* and has in effect simply been updated by Nora, Yerushalmi, Terdiman, and others in our own time. According to Halbwachs, there are on the one hand societies in which "living history" predominates and where *mémoire* consequently thrives (for example, premodern peasant societies where memory is carried forward mainly by means of rituals and oral traditions). And on the other hand there are societies such as those in the twentieth-century West in which written or formal *histoire* predominates, because the collective memory has been seriously weakened and people have been forced to rely chiefly on the historian for their general knowledge of the past. For Halbwachs, only the first amounts to true collective memory, while the second is not only something altogether different but something less important, since it gives us only "historical memory," not real collective memory. Halbwachs, *The Collective Memory,* 64, 78–87.

48. By the early 1990s it began to appear that class memories, especially working-class memories, had declined in importance at about the same rate that ethnic memories had increased in importance, not only in Western Europe and North America but in places such as the former Soviet Union or the former Yugoslavia. The reason for this shift in focus may simply have been that the institutions which were once prime carriers of class memories were greatly weakened, while those promoting ethnic memory in both its dangerous and harmless forms grew considerably stronger. However that may be, class memories have still only diminished, not disappeared altogether. For a discussion of the ways in which class memories persist, subtly and sometimes unconsciously, see especially Pierre Bourdieu, *Distinction: A Social Critique of the Judgement of Taste,* trans. Richard Nice (Cambridge: Harvard University Press, 1984).

49. On Warburg's concept of mnemonic energy, see Ernst Gombrich, *Aby Warburg: An Intellectual Biography* (Chicago: University of Chicago Press, 1986), 244.

50. Jean-François Lyotard, *Des dispositifs pulsionnels* (Paris: Christian Bourgeois Éditeur, 1980), 290, 303–4.

51. See Élie Théofilakis, *Modernes et Après? "Les Immatériaux"* (Paris: Éditions autrement, 1985), xi. Théofilakis contends that the achievements of the last several millennia have hardly advanced beyond the Stone Age when compared to what will be achieved in the next century or two.

52. Though deritualization can rightly be called the rule today, new media-driven rituals are replacing at least some of the older religious and political ones. In America, for instance, one could point to the ritual gatherings before the television set to watch annual beauty contests, Academy Awards celebrations, Superbowls, and the like. Arguably, these gatherings can be said to perform many of the same functions as previous rituals, binding people together, solidifying common values, and providing roughly an identical past to recall. Still, television does not seem to provide viewers with quite the same kind of "participation mystique" (Durkheim) that characterized earlier rituals. Though the electronic media do bring tens of millions of people together in apparent "shared moments," these moments are often experienced alone, or at best with a few friends, in the privacy of one's living room. By watching television, one is able to feel a vicarious unity with others not because one really is part of a fused collectivity, but simply because one is viewing the same program at the same time as everyone else and emotionally responding to it in similar ways.

53. Purportedly, a new museum is built every two weeks in Britain, and similar trends are reported elsewhere. In West Germany, 227 new museums were built in the 1960s, three hundred more in the 1970s, and about the same numbers in the 1980s. Alfred Frei and Walter Hochreiter, "Die neue Museumsboom—Kultur für alle?" *Neue Politische Literatur* 31 (1986): 385–97. For a further description of the so-called *Musealisierungsprozess,* see Hermann Lübbe's essay "Der Fortschritt und der Museum," in his *Die Aufdringlichkeit der Geschichte* (Graz: Verlag Styria, 1989), 13–18.

54. For a good discussion of today's museum tastes, see Raphael Samuel, *Theatres of Memory* (London: Verso, 1994), and Richard Prentice, *Tourism and Heritage Attractions* (London: Routledge, 1993), 77–118.

55. On some of the latest trends in contemporary museology, see Ivan Karp and Steven D. Levine, eds., *Exhibiting Cultures: The Poetics and Politics of Museum Display* (Washington, D.C.: Smithsonian Institution Press, 1991); John Rajchman, "The Post-

modern Museum," *Art in America* 73, no. 10 (1985): 111–17, 171; and Lumley, *Museum Time-Machine.*

56. On family reminiscing and social reminiscing in general, see Edward S. Casey, *Remembering: A Phenomenological Study* (Bloomington: Indiana University Press, 1987), 104–21.

57. Halbwachs, *On Collective Memory,* 54.

58. Ibid., 59, 68, 74, 83.

59. See James Fentress and Chris Wickham, *Social Memory* (Oxford: Blackwell, 1992), 112–13, and Françoise Zonabend, *The Enduring Memory: Time and History in a French Village,* trans. Anthony Forster (Manchester: Manchester University Press, 1980).

60. See Fredric Jameson, "The Cultural Logic of Late Capitalism," in his *Postmodernism* (Durham: Duke University Press, 1991), 1–54. It is difficult to say at this point in time whether postmodernism is (1) a reflective moment within a fading modernism, (2) an offshoot or extension of modernism that is nevertheless still deeply indebted to it, or (3) an entirely new "condition," radically different and separate from either modernism or modernity. In my view, the second of these three possibilities is probably closest to the mark.

61. Samuel, *Theatres of Memory,* 83.

62. Nora, "Between History and Memory," 7, and Sheldon Wolin, *The Presence of the Past: Essays on the State and the Constitution* (Baltimore: Johns Hopkins University Press, 1989), 33.

63. Halbwachs, *On Collective Memory,* 81–82.

Chapter Six: The Shapes of the Past

1. Le Goff, *History and Memory,* 59.

2. Halbwachs, *The Collective Memory,* 44.

3. The terms "emergent," "dominant," and "residual" are borrowed from Raymond Williams. See his *Marxism and Literature* (Oxford: Oxford University Press, 1977), 121–27.

4. See Bernard Guenée, *States and Rulers in Later Medieval Europe,* trans. Juliet Vale (Oxford: Blackwell, 1985), 4–6.

5. See David Cressy, "National Memory in Early Modern England," in *Commemorations: The Politics of National Identity,* ed. John R. Gillis (Princeton: Princeton University Press, 1994), 61–73, and *Bonfires and Bells: National Memory and the Protestant Calendar in Elizabethan and Stuart England* (Berkeley: University of California Press, 1989).

6. While the monarchies of the seventeenth and eighteenth centuries were pushing for political memory, the Catholic Church sought to advance its claims over religious memory, particularly in the rural areas of Europe. Reenergized by the Council of Trent, the Church strove with almost missionary zeal to impose on the peasantry the structures of Catholic thought and belief (including the proper way to interpret the historical past), which seemed to have lost much of their effectiveness since the late Middle Ages. On Catholic efforts toward a re-Christianizing of memory, see John Bossy, "The Counter-Reformation and the People of Catholic Europe," *Past and Present* 47 (1970): 51–70, and David A. Bell, "*Lingua Populi, Lingua Dei:* Language, Reli-

gion, and the Origins of French Revolutionary Nationalism," *American Historical Review* 100, no. 5 (1995): 403–37.

7. Talleyrand, commenting on the *fêtes* of the French Revolution, cited in Boyd Shafer, "When Patriotism Became Popular: A Study of the Festivals of Federation in France in 1790," *The Historian* 5, no. 2 (1943): 81.

8. For more detailed treatment of these developments, see Ozouf, *Festivals of the French Revolution,* and Mosse, *Nationalization of the Masses.* Also important are Thomas Nipperdey, "Nationalidee und Nationaldenkmal im 19. Jahrhundert," *Historische Zeitschrift* 206, no. 3 (1968): 529–85; Wolfgang Hardtwig, *Geschichtskultur und Wissenschaft,* 224–301; Volker Plagemann, "Bismarck-Denkmäler," in *Denkmäler in 19. Jahrhundert: Deutung und Kritik,* ed. Ernst Mittag and Volker Plagemann (Munich: Prestel-Verlag, 1972), 217–52; Eugen Weber, *Peasants into Frenchmen: The Modernization of Rural France, 1870–1914* (Stanford: Stanford University Press, 1976), 303–38; Charles Rearick, "Festivals in Modern France: The Experience of the Third Republic," *Journal of Contemporary History* 12, no. 3 (1977): 435–60; Steven Englund, "The Ghost of Nation Past," *Journal of Modern History* 64, no. 2 (1992): 299–320; and Eric Hobsbawm and Terence Ranger, eds., *The Invention of Tradition* (Cambridge: Cambridge University Press, 1988). I have also discussed some of these matters in my "Temporality and the Modern State," 53–82.

9. On American national memory, see Michael Kammen, *Mystic Chords of Memory: The Transformation of Tradition in American Culture* (New York: Vintage, 1993), 139–41, 263–64, 375, 444–47, 610–14, and John Bodnar, *Remaking America: Public Memory, Commemoration, and Patriotism in the Twentieth Century* (Princeton: Princeton University Press, 1992), 13–20, 35–38, 249–53. For a long time in America, most of the initiative for national remembering came from civic and patriotic organizations rather than from the federal government. It was only during and then more predominantly after World War I that the state began to take a more active hand in constructing monuments, building museums, and establishing national historical sites.

10. See Hamilton T. Burden, *The Nuremberg Party Rallies: 1923–1939* (New York: Praeger, 1967), and Klaus Vondung, *Magie und Manipulation: Ideologischer Kult und politische Religion des Nationalsozialismus* (Göttingen: Vandenhoeck and Ruprecht, 1971), 75–87. A good recent discussion of similar festivals of memory in Mussolini's Italy can be found in Emilio Gentile, *The Secularization of Politics in Fascist Italy,* trans. Keith Botsford (Cambridge: Harvard University Press, 1996).

11. Political memory in the Soviet Union developed somewhat differently than elsewhere. Because the October Revolution was seen by its defenders as bringing about a sharp break with an inglorious tsarist and bourgeois past, there was little reason to encourage historical consciousness, and as a result national memory was not much emphasized in the Soviet state between 1917 and the late 1930s. During World War II, however, and even more in the decades following the war, the situation was reversed as a politicized form of memory became increasingly relied upon to bolster a regime that in other respects was losing much of its social cement. Out of fear that the Soviet Union would be perceived by its own citizens as nothing more than a bureaucratic-administrative state, Stalin and his subordinates intentionally sought to elicit both warm and grandiose memories from within the Soviet popula-

tion in order to produce the emotional commitment thought necessary to make the state viable—and perhaps also to deflect attention away from the government's failure to satisfy everyday needs and expectations. The result was a massive production of monuments, memorials, political pageantries, "eternal flames," and the like from the beginning of the 1950s until the 1980s, all designed to strengthen, mainly by means of sentiment, the ties binding the Soviet population to the state. But even here, almost all state-sanctioned memory was focused on events that had taken place *since* 1917, the most important being the events of the Revolution itself, as well as the heroic achievements of the Great Patriotic War of 1941–45. Moreover, these official memories were naturally very selective, for they covered over at least an equal amount of historical forgetting, especially a forgetting of events such as the Moscow Purges or the Nazi-Soviet Pact of 1939, which were considered too politically incorrect to be recalled in any public venue.

Since the collapse of the Soviet Union in the early 1990s, indications are that most Soviet forms of memory are rapidly losing their hold on the population. Now, for example, it is not only the Revolution that is no longer deemed memorable in a good sense; except among the very old, even the Great Patriotic War seems to have lost much of the patriotic focus and emotional bite it had just a decade ago. On Soviet (and Russian) memory, see Catherine Merridale, "Death and Memory in Modern Russia," *History Workshop Journal* 42 (1996): 1–18; Nina Tumarkin, "Myth and Memory in Soviet Society," *Society* 24, no. 6 (1987): 69–72, and *The Living and the Dead: The Rise and Fall of the Cult of World War II in Russia* (New York: Basic Books, 1994); Michael Ignatieff, "Soviet War Memorials," *History Workshop Journal* 17 (1984): 157–63; Anne Duruflé-Lozinski, "URSS/Pologne: retour à Katyn," in *A l'Est, la mémoire retrouvée,* ed. Alain Brossat, Sonia Combe, Jean-Yves Potel, and Jean-Charles Szurek (Paris: Éditions la Découverte, 1990), 39–52; and Alain Brossat, "URSS: le cinquantiéme anniversaire du Pact germano-soviétique," in *A l'Est,* 53–77.

12. Stephen Heath, "Representing Television," in *Logics of Television: Essays in Cultural Criticism,* ed. Patricia Mellencamp (Bloomington: Indiana University Press, 1990), 274, 283.

13. See Henry Rousso, *The Vichy Syndrome: History and Memory in France since 1944,* trans. Arthur Goldhammer (Cambridge: Harvard University Press, 1991), and Gérard Namer, *La commémoration de France de 1945 à nos jours* (Paris: Éditions L'Harmattan, 1987).

14. Charles Péguy, *Un poète l'a dit* (Paris: Gallimard, 1953), 162–63, 175–76.

15. Anton Kaes, "History and Film: Public Memory in an Age of Electronic Dissemination," *History and Memory* 2, no. 1 (1990): 112.

16. See Aby Warburg's note on collective memory in his *Handelskammer* (1928), cited in Gombrich, *Aby Warburg,* 270–71.

17. Such defenders already see a resurgence of religious schemata in some Islamic countries and to a lesser extent in Israel as well. Many, it appears, would like to see the same take place in the secularized West. See Gilles Kepel, *The Revenge of God: The Resurgence of Islam, Christianity, and Judaism in the Modern World,* trans. Alan Braley (University Park: Pennsylvania State University Press, 1994).

18. Some contemporary observers have pointed out that in those cases where the mass media have not actually undermined statist frames of memory, they have taken

them over and reshaped them in a nonpolitical direction. The 1986 Statue of Liberty Centennial, for instance, was initially planned with a political message in mind, but the commemoration soon fell under the control of the entertainment industry, which turned it into a television extravaganza replete with twelve thousand performers including two hundred Elvis Presley impersonators, three hundred Jazzercize dancers, and an eight hundred–voice chorus performing on a twenty-tiered stage in front of five waterfalls. In France during the 1989 Bicentennial of the French Revolution, a parallel depoliticization occurred as the electronic media took over the representations of the Bicentennial, and in the process transformed the event into a media spectacle. The commercial advertiser and promoter Jean-Paul Goude, rather than a political figure, was given the task of "presenting" the Bicentennial to the general public. Being aware that over 700 million people around the world would be watching the ceremonies on television (compared to about 1 million viewing it live in Paris), Goude sought to make the Bicentennial a magnificently choreographed show business event of the first order. The event made only minimal references to the political memories it had been created to celebrate in the first place. On the Statue of Liberty Centennial, see Nicholaus Mills, "Culture in an Age of Money," *Dissent* 37 (1990): 11–17; on the French Bicentennial, see Steven L. Kaplan, *Farewell, Revolution: Disputed Legacies, France 1789/1989* (Ithaca, N.Y.: Cornell University Press, 1995).

19. See Theodore Zeldin, *An Intimate History of Humanity* (New York: Harper-Collins, 1994), 13–17, 50, 441–43.

20. This point was especially important for Habermas. In his view, there is always, in every polity, not only significant continuity between generations but also continuity in "forms of life" that persist through time. Once something comes into being in a nation's history, it does not and cannot suddenly vanish as if it had never happened. For Habermas, the Germany of the 1980s could not claim to have freed itself from the *Nazizeit*, even though that era was nearly fifty years in the past. "Our own life," he wrote, "is linked to the life context in which Auschwitz was possible not by contingent circumstances but intrinsically. Our form of life is connected with that of our parents and grandparents through a web of familial, local, political, and intellectual traditions that is difficult to disentangle—that is, through a historical milieu that made us what and who we are today. None of us can escape this milieu, because our identities, both as individuals and as Germans, are indissolubly interwoven with it." See Jürgen Habermas, "On the Public Use of History," in *The New Conservatism: Cultural Criticism and the Historians' Debate*, ed. and trans. Shierry Weber Nicholsen (Cambridge: MIT Press, 1989), 233. Most of the key documents from both sides of the *Historikerstreit* can be found in Rudolf Augstein, ed., *Historikerstreit. Die Dokumentation der Kontroverse um die Einzigartigkeit der nationalsozialistischen Judenvernichtung* (Munich: Piper-Verlag, 1987).

21. Habermas, "Public Use of History," 229.

22. See John Gross, "Knocking About the Ruins," in *The Future of the European Past*, ed. Hilton Kramer and Roger Kimball (Chicago: Ivan R. Dee, 1997), 70.

23. Bronislaw Baczko's *Les imaginaires sociaux: Mémoires et espoirs collectifs* (Paris: Payot, 1984) provides an excellent account of the resurgence of Polish memory in the 1980s.

24. Ibid., 192–96, 204–19. There can be no doubt that the "countermemories"

invoked in the Solidarity-sponsored commemorations during the tense months of 1980–81 were intentionally and unmistakenly anti-Russian (for example, the commemoration of the end of World War I [November 11, 1980], the celebration of the 150th anniversary of the Polish Insurrection of 1830, and the remembrance of the Second Partition of Poland in 1791 [May 3, 1981]). It was almost certainly the element of protest and resistance that made these and similar commemorations such popular public events.

25. Yerushalmi, *Zakhor*, 86.

26. See David G. Roskies, *Against the Apocalypse: Responses to Catastrophe in Modern Jewish Culture* (Cambridge: Harvard University Press, 1984); also Jack Kugelmass, ed., *Going Home: How Jews Invented Their Old Countries* (Evanston, Ill.: Northwestern University Press, 1994), and Kugelmass's essay "Mission to the Past: Poland in Contemporary Jewish Thought," in *Tense Past: Cultural Essays in Trauma and Memory*, ed. Paul Antze and Michael Lambek (New York: Routledge, 1996), 199–214.

27. Guy Debord, *Commentaires sur la société du spectacle* (Paris: Éditions Gérard Lebovici, 1988), 20. According to Debord, "that which the spectacle [that is, media culture] ceases to speak of for three days no longer exists."

Conclusion: Memory in Late Modernity

1. Eric Hobsbawm, *The Age of Extremes* (New York: Vintage, 1996), 16.

2. Martin Heidegger, *What Is Called Thinking?*, trans. F. D. Wieck and J. Glenn Gray (New York: Harper and Row, 1968), 30.

3. There is one important exception to this broad observation that deserves more commentary than I can give it here. It sometimes happens that there are brief flare-ups of interest in memory, even within an age that has apparently deemphasized memory. Such flare-ups, which usually take the form of yearnings for "the way things were," come about as a reaction to a surfeit of forgetfulness, that is, to a sense that the present is undergoing an evacuation of meaning that is too rapid or too total. These eruptions of social or cultural nostalgia never last very long, and they usually leave few traces. Not surprisingly, the media are often quick to respond to such bursts of interest in memory while they last, though when the nostalgic mood passes, so does the media attention.

4. Nietzsche, *Advantage and Disadvantage of History*, 8.

5. Schachtel, "Memory and Childhood Amnesia," 287.

6. This argument has been made by, among others, William Stern in his "Personalistik der Erinnerung," *Zeitschrift für Psychologie und Physiologie der Sinnesorgane* 118 (1930): 350–81; Friedrich Kümmel, *Über der Begriff der Zeit* (Tübingen: Niemeyer Verlag, 1962), 161–84; and Georges Gusdorf, *Mémoire et Personne* (Paris: Presses universitaires de France, 1951), 247–71.

7. I mean here that memory can help establish an obligation to take others and not just ourselves into consideration. The obverse case can be made that too much forgetting prepares the way for unethical behavior toward others—a point captured well by Mephistopheles' disingenuous remark to Faust: "Forget the past and it will be as if it never happened." If, as Mephistopheles is well aware, one can persuade oneself that what took place in the past "never happened" (the reference here is to Faust's

abandonment of Gretchen), one then has no responsibilities for anything that may have occurred previously. Instead, one can sink into the present and enjoy it with an untroubled conscience.

8. See Kierkegaard, *Either/Or*, 1:293–95 and 2:141–42.

9. Nietzsche, *Advantage and Disadvantage of History*, 10.

10. Immanuel Kant, "What Is Enlightenment?," in *The Enlightenment: A Comprehensive Anthology*, ed. Peter Gay (New York: Simon and Schuster, 1973), 384.

11. Nathaniel Hawthorne, *English Notebooks* (New York: Modern Language Association, 1941), 294.

12. Theodor W. Adorno, *Musikalische Schriften* 2, in *Gesammelte Schriften*, ed. Rolf Tiedemann (Frankfurt: Suhrkamp, 1978), 16:446.

13. The term "noncontemporaneous," or "noncontemporaneity" (*Ungleichzeitigkeit* in German) was used on a couple of occasions by Marx in the mid-nineteenth century, but it became conceptually more important only in the Germany of the 1920s and early 1930s, when the term was taken up and used for a variety of purposes by Karl Mannheim, Wilhelm Pinder, Ernst Bloch, Walter Benjamin, and Adorno himself.

14. See Max Horkheimer, *Die Sehnsucht nach dem ganz Anderen* (Hamburg: Furche, 1970).

15. Walter Benjamin, "Der Sammler," in Konvolut "H" of *Das Passagen-Werk:* in *Gesammelte Schriften*, V, 1, ed. Rolf Tiedemann (Frankfurt: Suhrkamp, 1991), 275.

16. Charles Baudelaire, *The Painter of Modern Life and Other Essays*, ed. and trans. Jonathan Mayne (London: Phaidon, 1964), 13.

17. See Rainer Maria Rilke, *Duino Elegies*, trans. J. B. Leishman and Stephen Spender (New York: W. W. Norton, 1963), especially the seventh and ninth elegies, 58–65, 72–77. Throughout his work, Rilke was mainly interested in what he called the *Dingwelt*, or "world of things," that had survived from the past; he was less interested in fragments of past practices, ideas, or beliefs that could likewise be said to have persisted from the past into the present.

18. This matter was made still worse for Rilke by the flooding into contemporary life of millions of new objects, such as recently manufactured commodities, which tended to crowd out venerable survivals from the past. The new commodities were of course the result of breakthroughs in capitalist production after 1900. Even though, for Rilke, these manufactured objects were by their very nature empty and inauthentic (because they lacked duration and consequently had "no stories to tell"), they nonetheless began to set the standard for what was or was not considered valuable in the modern world. In comparison to the plethora of new objects to be found nearly everywhere, the old ones left over from earlier decades seemed much shabbier and more destitute, and hence less worthy of esteem. Moreover, with such a mass of new things so ready at hand, it was no longer important that outlived objects be restored or refurbished. Now they could simply be forgotten.

19. It might be added here that, according to Rilke, the past not only needs us to complete it, but we need it to complete something in ourselves. If we pay no attention to the past to which we are in fact linked by hidden filiations we will fail to see something in us that needs to be developed. Proust expressed a similar idea in *Remembrance of Things Past*. When Marcel, riding in a carriage near Hudimesnil, sees three trees receding from him in the distance, he realizes that they are calling out for him

to fulfill something still unacknowledged in himself. As Proust put it, it is as if the trees were saying: "What you fail to learn from us today, you will never know. If you allow us to drop back into the hollow of this road from which we sought to raise ourselves up to you, a whole part of yourself which we were bringing to you will fall forever into the abyss." *Remembrance,* 1:545. For Rilke, the same held true with regard to the past; if one lets its appeals for recognition and fulfillment go unheeded, something in oneself will fall silent as well.

20. To be sure, for Hegel the "positive" aspects of the past are *aufgehoben,* that is, preserved and carried forward in a new synthesis. But that which is not judged to be positive is said to fall by the wayside, there to become historically insignificant. This vanquished material, which is canceled out without at the same time being lifted up and moved forward to a new level, is what Hegel considered the detritus of history. Generally speaking, this detritus did not much interest him. In his philosophy of history, for example, Hegel focused more on where the Worldspirit was headed—that is, toward a projected subject-object identity at some future point in time—than he did on the historical waste it had left behind.

21. See Jean Baudrillard, "Nécrospective autour de Martin Heidegger," *Libération,* January 27, 1988. An English translation titled "Hunting Nazis and Losing Reality" appeared in *New Statesman,* February 19, 1988, 16–17.

22. See Maurice Blanchot, *The Writing of the Disaster,* trans. Ann Smock (Lincoln: University of Nebraska Press, 1986), 42.

23. According to the German religious writer and critic Dorothee Sölle, honoring memory "requires behavior inimical to consumerism." See "Thou Shalt Have No Other Jeans before Me," in *Observations on "The Spiritual Situation of the Age,"* ed. Jürgen Habermas, trans. Andrew Buchwalter (Cambridge: MIT Press, 1984), 165.

24. Theodor W. Adorno, letter to Walter Benjamin, February 29, 1940; see T. W. Adorno, *Über Walter Benjamin* (Frankfurt: Suhrkamp, 1970), 159.

25. Nietzsche, *Advantage and Disadvantage of History,* 22.

26. The phrase is Walter Benjamin's. See his "Zentralpark," in *Gesammelte Schriften,* I, 2, ed. Rolf Tiedemann and Hermann Schweppenhäuser (Frankfurt: Suhrkamp, 1991), 666.

27. According to Heidegger, memory (*memor* in Latin) originally meant being "mindful" of something or, more strongly, being "devoted" to or "abiding with" it. See Heidegger, *What Is Called Thinking?,* 11, 140; also J. Glenn Gray, "Heidegger on Remembering and Remembering Heidegger," *Man and World* 10 (1977): 65–66.

28. See Alexander Gonzales and Philip G. Zimbardo, "Time in Perspective," *Psychology Today* 19, no. 3 (1985): 21–26.

Bibliography

Adorno, Theodor W. *Musikalische Schriften* 2. In *Gesammelte Schriften,* vol. 16, edited by Rolf Tiedemann. Frankfurt: Suhrkamp, 1978.

———. *Über Walter Benjamin.* Frankfurt: Suhrkamp, 1970.

———. "Was bedeutet: Aufarbeitung der Vergangenheit." In *Erziehung zur Mündigkeit: Vorträge und Gespräche mit Helmut Becker, 1959–1969,* edited by Gerd Kadelbach. Frankfurt: Suhrkamp, 1970.

Amato, Joseph A. II. *Guilt and Gratitude: A Study of the Origins of Contemporary Conscience.* Westport, Conn.: Greenwood, 1982.

Anderson, Harold H. *Creativity and Its Cultivation.* New York: Harper and Row, 1959.

Apostolidès, Jean-Marie. *Le roi-machine: Spectacles et politique au temps de Louis XIV.* Paris: Éditions de Minuit, 1981.

Aquinas, St. Thomas. *Summa Theologica.* 2 vols. Translated by the Fathers of the English Dominican Province and revised by Daniel J. Sullivan. Great Books of the Western World Series. Chicago: Encyclopaedia Britannica, 1952.

Arendt, Hannah. *Willing.* Vol. 2 of *The Life of the Mind.* New York: Harcourt Brace Jovanovich, 1978.

Aristotle. *De Memoria et Reminiscentia.* In *Aristotle on Memory,* edited by Richard Sorabji. Providence: Brown University Press, 1972.

———. *Nicomachean Ethics.* Translated by David Ross and revised by J. L. Ackrill and J. O. Urmson. New York: Oxford University Press, 1980.

Arréat, Lucien. *Mémoire et imagination.* Paris: Félix Alcan, 1904.

Assmann, Aleida, and Dietrich Harth, eds. *Mnemosyne. Formen und Funktionen der kulturellen Erinnerung.* Frankfurt: Fischer Taschenbuch Verlag, 1991.

Assmann, Jan. "Collective Memory and Cultural Identity." *New German Critique* 65 (1995): 125–33.

Assmann, Jan, and Tonio Hölscher, eds. *Kultur und Gedächtnis.* Frankfurt: Suhrkamp, 1988.

Augstein, Rudolf, ed. *Historikerstreit. Die Dokumentation der Kontroverse um die Einzigartigkeit der nationalsozialistischen Judenvernichtung.* Munich: Piper-Verlag, 1987.

Augustine, St. *Confessions.* Translated by Henry Chadwick. Oxford: Oxford University Press, 1991.

Baczko, Bronislaw. *Les imaginaires sociaux: Mémoires et espoirs collectifs.* Paris: Payot, 1984.

Bartlett, Frederic. *Remembering: A Study in Experimental and Social Psychology.* Cambridge: Cambridge University Press, 1964.

Baudelaire, Charles. *The Painter of Modern Life and Other Essays.* Translated and edited by Jonathan Mayne. London: Phaidon, 1964.

Baudrillard, Jean. "Hunting Nazis and Losing Reality." *New Statesman,* February 19, 1988, 16–17.

Baumer, Franklin J. *Modern European Thought: Continuity and Change in Ideas, 1600–1950.* New York: MacMillan, 1977.

Beaume, Collette. *The Birth of an Ideology: Myths and Symbols in Late Medieval France.* Translated by Susan Ross Huston. Berkeley: University of California Press, 1991.

Becker, Carl. *Everyman His Own Historian.* New York: Crofts, 1935.

Bell, David A. "*Lingua Populi, Lingua Dei:* Language, Religion, and the Origins of French Revolutionary Nationalism." *American Historical Review* 100, no. 5 (1995): 403–37.

Benjamin, Walter. *Illuminations.* Translated by Harry Zohn. New York: Schocken, 1969.

——. "Aus einer kleinen Rede über Proust." In *Gesammelte Schriften,* vol. 2, pt. 3. Edited by Rolf Tiedemann and Hermann Schweppenhäuser. Frankfurt: Suhrkamp, 1977.

——. "Der Sammler." In *Gesammelte Schriften,* vol. 5, pt. 1. Edited by Rolf Tiedemann. Frankfurt: Suhrkamp, 1991.

——. "Zentralpark." In *Gesammelte Schriften,* vol. 1, pt. 2. Edited by Rolf Tiedemann and Hermann Schweppenhäuser. Frankfurt: Suhrkamp, 1991.

Bergson, Henri. *Matter and Memory.* Translated by Nancy Margaret Paul and W. Scott Palmer. London: Allen & Unwin, 1911.

——. *Two Sources of Morality and Religion.* Translated by R. Ashley Audra and Cloudesley Brereton. New York: Doubleday, 1935.

Bersani, Leo. *A Future for Astyanax: Character and Desire in Literature.* Boston: Little, Brown, 1976.

Bertrand, Pierre. *L'oubli: Révolution ou mort de l'histoire.* Paris: Presses Universitaires de France, 1975.

Binswanger, Ludwig. "The Case of Ellen West." Translated by Werner M. Mendel and Joseph Lyons. In *Existence: A New Dimension in Psychiatry and Psychology.* Edited by Rollo May, Ernest Angel, and Henri F. Ellenberger. New York: Simon and Schuster, 1958.

Blanchot, Maurice. *The Writing of the Disaster.* Translated by Ann Smock. Lincoln: University of Nebraska Press, 1986.

Bloch, Marc. *Feudal Society.* 2 vols. Translated by L. A. Manyon. London: Routledge and Kegan Paul, 1965.

Blondel, Charles. *Introduction à la psychologie collective.* Paris: Armand Colin, 1928.

Bloom, Harold. *The Anxiety of Influence: A Theory of Poetry.* New York: Oxford University Press, 1973.

Bodnar, John. *Remaking America: Public Memory, Commemoration, and Patriotism in the Twentieth Century.* Princeton: Princeton University Press, 1992.

Boer, P. A. H. de. *Gedenken und Gedächtnis in der Welt des Alten Testaments.* Stuttgart: W. Kohlhammer Verlag, 1962.

Boss, Menard. *Psychoanalysis and Daseinanalysis.* Translated by Ludwig B. Lefebvre. New York: Basic Books, 1963.

Bossy, John. "The Counter-Reformation and the People of Catholic Europe." *Past and Present* 47 (1970): 51–70.

Bourdieu, Pierre. *Distinction: A Social Critique of the Judgement of Taste.* Translated by Richard Nice. Cambridge: Harvard University Press, 1984.

Boyer, M. Christine. *Dreaming the Rational City: The Myth of American City Planning.* Cambridge: MIT Press, 1983.

Bradbury, Malcolm, and James McFarlane, eds. *Modernism: 1890–1930.* New York: Penguin, 1978.

Brossat, Alain, Sonia Combe, Jean-Yves Potel, and Jean-Charles Szurek, eds. *A l'Est, la mémoire retrouvée.* Paris: Éditions la Découverte, 1990.

Brown, Norman O. *Life against Death: The Psychoanalytic Meaning of History.* Middletown, Conn.: Wesleyan University Press, 1959.

Burden, Hamilton T. *The Nuremberg Party Rallies: 1929–1939.* New York: Praeger, 1967.

Carruthers, Mary. *The Book of Memory: A Study of Memory in Medieval Culture.* New York: Cambridge University Press, 1990.

Casey, Edward S. *Remembering: A Phenomenological Study.* Bloomington: Indiana University Press, 1987.

Childs, Brevand S. *Memory and Tradition in Ancient Israel.* London: SCM Press, 1962.

Cicero. *De inventione.* Translated and edited by H. M. Hubbell. Loeb Classical Library Series. Cambridge: Harvard University Press, 1949.

Clanchy, M. T. *From Memory to Written Record: England 1066–1307.* Oxford: Oxford University Press, 1993.

——. "Remembering the Past and the Good Old Law." *History* 55, no. 184 (1970): 165–76.

Coleman, Janet. *Ancient and Medieval Memories: Studies in the Reconstruction of the Past.* Cambridge: Cambridge University Press, 1992.

Congar, Yves. *The Meaning of Tradition.* Translated by A. N. Woodrow. New York: Hawthorn, 1964.

Connerton, Paul. *How Societies Remember.* Cambridge: Cambridge University Press, 1989.

Cottle, Thomas J. *Perceiving Time.* New York: Wiley, 1976.

Cressy, David. *Bonfires and Bells: National Memory and the Protestant Calendar in Elizabethan and Stuart England.* Berkeley: University of California Press, 1989.

——. "National Memory in Early Modern England." In *Commemorations: The Politics of National Identity,* edited by John R. Gillis. Princeton: Princeton University Press, 1994.

Crossett, John. "Love in the Western Hierarchy." In *The Concept of Order,* edited by Paul G. Kurtz. Seattle: University of Washington Press, 1968.

Dante (Alighieri). *Purgatory.* Part 2 of *The Divine Comedy.* Translated by Mark Musa. New York: Penguin, 1985.

——. *Vita Nuova.* Translated by Mark Musa. New Brunswick, N.J.: Rutgers University Press, 1957.

Debord, Guy. *Commentaires sur la société du spectacle.* Paris: Éditions Gérard Lebovici, 1988.

Dellheim, Charles. *The Face of the Past.* Cambridge: Cambridge University Press, 1982.

Descartes, René. *Discourse on Method and Meditations.* Translated by Laurence J. Lafleur. Indianapolis: Bobbs-Merrill, 1960.

Duby, Georges. "French Genealogical Literature: The Eleventh and Twelfth Centuries." In *The Chivalrous Society,* translated by Cynthia Postan. Berkeley: University of California Press, 1977.

———. "Memories with No Historians." *Yale French Studies* 59 (1980): 7–16.

Dugas, Ludovic. *La mémoire et l'oubli.* Paris: Flammarion, 1919.

———. "Sur la fausse mémoire." *Revue philosophique de la France et l'Étranger* 37 (1894): 34–45.

Dunbabin, Jean. "Discovering a Past for the French Aristocracy." In *The Perception of the Past in Twelfth-Century Europe,* edited by Paul Magdalino. London: Hambledon, 1992.

Durkheim, Émile. *The Division of Labor in Society.* Translated by George Simpson. New York: Free Press, 1964.

Duruflé-Lozinski, Anne. "URSS/Pologne: retour à Katyn." In *A l'Est, la mémoire retrouvée,* edited by Alain Brossat, Sonia Combe, Jean-Yves Potel, and Jean-Charles Szurek. Paris: Éditions la Découverte, 1990.

Duvignaud, Jean. "La fête civique." In *Histoire des spectacles,* edited by Guy Dumur. Paris: Gallimard, 1965.

Ebbinghaus, Hermann. *Memory: A Contribution to Experimental Psychology.* Translated by Henry A. Ruger and Clara E. Bussenius. New York: Columbia University Press, 1913.

Edelman, Gerald M. *Neural Darwinism: The Theory of Neuronal Group Selection.* New York: Basic Books, 1987.

———. *The Remembered Present: A Biological Theory of Consciousness.* New York: Basic Books, 1989.

Eichthal, Eugène d'. *Du role de la mémoire dans nos conceptions métaphysiques, esthétiques, passionnelles, actives.* Paris: Félix Alcan, 1920.

Eliade, Mircea. *Myth and Reality.* Translated by Willard R. Trask. New York: Harper and Row, 1963.

Elkine, D. "De l'influence du groupe sur les fonctions de la mémoire." *Journal de Psychologie* 24 (1927): 827–30.

Englund, Steven. "The Ghost of Nation Past." *Journal of Modern History* 64, no. 2 (1992): 299–320.

Erikson, Erik. *Childhood and Society.* New York: W. W. Norton, 1963.

———. *Identity: Youth and Crisis.* New York: W. W. Norton, 1968.

Fentress, James, and Chris Wickham. *Social Memory.* Oxford: Blackwell, 1992.

Frank, Lawrence. "Time Perspectives." *Journal of Social Philosophy* 4, no. 4 (1939): 293–312.

Frei, Alfred G., and Walter Hochreiter. "Die neue Museumsboom—Kultur für alle?" *Neue Politische Literatur* 31 (1986): 385–97.

Freud, Sigmund. *The Complete Letters of Sigmund Freud to Wilhelm Fliess, 1877–1904.* Translated and edited by Jeffrey Moussaieff Masson. Cambridge: Harvard University Press, 1985.

———. *Five Lectures on Psychoanalysis.* In vol. 11 of *Standard Edition,* translated and edited by James Strachey. London: Hogarth Press, 1957.

———. "Mourning and Melancholia." In vol. 14 of *Standard Edition,* translated and edited by James Strachey. London: Hogarth Press, 1957.

———. *The Psychopathology of Everyday Life.* In *The Basic Writings of Sigmund Freud,* translated and edited by A. A. Brill. New York: Modern Library, 1938.

———. "Remembering, Repeating, and Working-Through." In vol. 12 of *Standard Edition,* translated and edited by James Strachey. London: Hogarth Press, 1958.

Freud, Sigmund, and Josef Breuer. *Studies in Hysteria.* In vol. 2 of *Standard Edition,* translated and edited by James Strachey. London: Hogarth Press, 1955.

Galinsky, Karl. *Classical and Modern Interactions.* Austin: University of Texas Press, 1992.

Geary, Patrick J. *Living with the Dead in the Middle Ages.* Ithaca, N.Y.: Cornell University Press, 1994.

———. *Phantoms of Remembrance: Memory and Oblivion at the End of the First Millennium.* Princeton: Princeton University Press, 1994.

Genicot, Leopold. "La noblesse au Moyen Age dans l'ancienne 'France.'" *Annales: Economies, sociétés, civilisations* 17, no. 1 (1962): 1–22.

Gentile, Emilio. *The Secularization of Politics in Fascist Italy.* Translated by Keith Botsford. Cambridge: Harvard University Press, 1996.

Gergen, Kenneth J. "Multiple Identity: The Healthy, Happy Human Being Wears Many Masks." *Psychology Today* 5, no. 12 (1972): 31–35, 64–66.

———. *The Saturated Self: Dilemmas of Identity in Contemporary Life.* New York: Basic Books, 1991.

Gibbon, Edward. *The Decline and Fall of the Roman Empire.* 2 vols. New York: Modern Library, 1932.

Giddens, Anthony. *Modernity and Self-Identity: Self and Society in the Late Modern Age.* Stanford: Stanford University Press, 1992.

Giesey, Ralph. *Cérémonial et puissance souvraine: France XVe–XVIIe siècle.* Paris: Armand Colin, 1987.

Girouard, Mark. *The Return to Camelot: Chivalry and the English Gentleman.* New Haven: Yale University Press, 1981.

Glover, John A., Royce R. Ronning, and Cecil R. Reynolds, eds. *Handbook of Creativity.* New York: Plenum Press, 1989.

Goethe, Johann Wolfgang von. *Goethes Gespräche.* Edited by Flodoard Freiherr von Biedermann. Leipzig: F. W. v. Biedermann, 1910.

Gombrich, Ernst. *Aby Warburg: An Intellectual Biography.* Chicago: University of Chicago Press, 1986.

Gonzales, Alexander, and Philip G. Zimbardo. "Time in Perspective." *Psychology Today* 19, no. 3 (1985): 21–26.

Gray, J. Glenn. "Heidegger on Remembering and Remembering Heidegger." *Man and World* 10 (1977): 62–78.

Groningen, B. A. van. *In the Grip of the Past: Essays on an Aspect of Greek Thought.* Leiden: E. J. Brill, 1953.

Gross, David. *The Past in Ruins: Tradition and the Critique of Modernity.* Amherst: University of Massachusetts Press, 1992.

——. "Remembering and Forgetting in the Modern City." *Social Epistemology* 4, no. 1 (1990): 3–22.

——. "Temporality and the Modern State." *Theory and Society* 14, (1985): 53–82.

Gross, John. "Knocking about the Ruins." In *The Future of the European Past*, edited by Hilton Kramer and Roger Kimball. Chicago: Ivan R. Dee, 1997.

Groys, Boris. *Über das Neue: Versuch einer Kulturökonomie.* Munich: Carl Hanser Verlag, 1992.

Guenée, Bernard. *States and Rulers in Later Medieval Europe.* Translated by Juliet Vale. Oxford: Oxford University Press, 1985.

Guenée, Bernard, and Françoise Lehoux. *Les entrées royales françaises de 1328 à 1515.* Paris: Éditions du Centre National de la Recherche Scientifique, 1968.

Gui, Bernardo. "The Life of St. Thomas Aquinas." In *Biographical Documents for the Life of St. Thomas Aquinas,* edited by Kenelm Foster. Oxford: Blackfriars, 1949.

Guillon, Albert. *Les maladies de la mémoire: Essai sur les hypermnésies.* Paris: Libraire J.-B. Bailliére & Fils, 1897.

Gurevitch, A. J. *Categories of Medieval Culture.* Translated by G. L. Campbell. London: Routledge and Kegan Paul, 1985.

Gusdorf, Georges. *Mémoire et Personne.* Paris: Presses universitaires de France, 1951.

Gutting, Gary, ed. *Paridigms and Revolutions: Appraisals and Applications of Thomas Kuhn's Philosophy of Science.* Notre Dame, Ind.: Notre Dame University Press, 1980.

Habermas, Jürgen. "On the Public Use of History." In *The New Conservatism: Cultural Criticism and the Historians' Debate,* translated and edited by Shierry Weber Nicholsen. Cambridge: MIT Press, 1989.

Hacking, Ian. "Memory Sciences, Memory Politics." In *Tense Past: Cultural Essays in Trauma and Memory,* edited by Paul Antze and Michael Lambek. New York: Routledge, 1996.

Halbwachs, Maurice. *The Collective Memory.* Translated by Francis J. Ditter, Jr. and Vida Yazdi Ditter. New York: Harper and Row, 1980.

——. *On Collective Memory.* Edited and translated by Lewis A. Coser. Chicago: University of Chicago Press, 1992.

Hammerich, L. L. "Horrenda Primordia: Zur *Germania* c. 39." *Germanisch-Romanische Monatsschrift* 33 (1952): 228–33.

Hardtwig, Wolfgang. *Geschichtskultur und Wissenschaft.* Munich: Deutscher Taschenbuch Verlag, 1990.

Harpham, Geoffrey Galt. *The Ascetic Imperative in Culture and Criticism.* Chicago: University of Chicago Press, 1987.

Harris, William V. *Ancient Literacy.* Cambridge: Harvard University Press, 1989.

Hartman, Geoffrey H., ed. *Holocaust Remembrance: The Shapes of Memory.* Oxford: Blackwell, 1994.

Hartmann, W. "'Modernus' und 'Antiquus': Zur Verbreitung und Bedeutung dieser Bezeichnungen in der wissenschaftlichen Literatur vom 9. bis zum 12. Jahrhundert." In *Antiqui et Moderni: Traditionsbewusstsein und Fortschriftsbewusstsein im Späten Mittelalter,* edited by A. Zimmermann. Berlin: Walter de Gruyter, 1974.

Havelock, Eric. *Preface to Plato.* Cambridge: Harvard University Press, 1963.

Hawthorne, Nathaniel. *English Notebooks.* New York: Modern Language Association, 1941.

Heath, Stephen. "Representing Television." In *Logics of Television: Essays in Cultural Criticism,* edited by Patricia Mellencamp. Bloomington: Indiana University Press, 1990.

Hebert, A. G. "Memory." In *A Theological Handbook of the Bible,* edited by Alan Richardson. London: Macmillan, 1950.

Heidegger, Martin. *What Is Called Thinking?* Translated by F. D. Wieck and J. Glenn Gray. New York: Harper and Row, 1968.

Hillman, James. *Archetypal Psychology.* Dallas: Spring Publications, 1968.

———. *Re-Visioning Psychology.* New York: Harper and Row, 1977.

Hindus, Milton. *The Proustian Vision.* Carbondale: Southern Illinois University Press, 1967.

Hobsbawm, Eric. *The Age of Extremes.* New York: Vintage, 1996.

Hofer, Johannes. "Medical Dissertation on Nostalgia." Translated by Carolyn K. Anspach. *Bulletin of the History of Medicine* 2 (1934): 376–91.

Homer. *The Odyssey.* Translated by Richard Lattimore. New York: HarperCollins, 1991.

Horkheimer, Max. *Die Sehnsucht nach dem ganz Anderen.* Hamburg: Furche, 1970.

Hoyau, Jean. "Heritage and the 'Conserver Society': The French Case." In *The Museum Time-Machine,* edited by Robert Lumley. New York: Routledge, 1988.

Huyssen, Andreas. *Twilight Memories: Making Time in a Culture of Amnesia.* New York: Routledge, 1995.

Ignatieff, Michael. "Soviet War Memorials." *History Workshop Journal* 17 (1984): 157–63.

Irwin-Zarecka, Iwona. *Frames of Remembrance: The Dynamics of Collective Memory.* New Brunswick, N.J.: Transaction Books, 1997.

James, William. *The Principles of Psychology.* 2 vols. New York: Henry Holt, 1890.

Jameson, Frederic. *Postmodernism, or The Cultural Logic of Late Capitalism.* Durham, N.C.: Duke University Press, 1991.

Janet, Pierre. *L'évolution de la mémoire et la notion du temps.* Paris: A. Chahine, 1928.

Jennings, Bruce. "Tradition and the Politics of Remembering." *Georgia Review* 36, no. 1 (1982): 167–82.

Judt, Tony. "The Past in Another Country: Myth and Memory in Postwar Europe." *Daedelus* 121, no. 4 (1992): 83–118.

Jung, Carl Gustav. *Psychological Reflections.* Edited by Jolande Jacobi. New York: Harper and Row, 1961.

Kaes, Anton. "History and Film: Public Memory in an Age of Electronic Dissemination." *History and Memory* 2, no. 1 (1990): 111–29.

Kammen, Michael. *In the Past Lane: Historical Perspectives on American Culture.* New York: Oxford University Press, 1997.

———. *Mystic Chords of Memory: The Transformation of Tradition in American Culture.* New York: Vintage, 1993.

Kant, Immanuel. "What Is Enlightenment?" In *The Enlightenment: A Comprehensive Anthology,* edited by Peter Gay. New York: Simon and Schuster, 1973.

Kaplan, Steven L. *Farewell, Revolution: Disputed Legacies, France 1789/1989.* Ithaca, N.Y.: Cornell University Press, 1995.

Karp, Ivan, and Steven D. Levine, eds. *Exhibiting Cultures: The Poetics and Politics of Museum Display.* Washington, D.C.: Smithsonian Institute Press, 1991.

Kaufmann, David. "Thanks for the Memory: Bloch, Benjamin, and the Philosophy of History." *Yale Journal of Criticism* 6, no. 1 (1993): 143–62.

Kepel, Gilles. *The Revenge of God: The Resurgence of Islam, Christianity, and Judaism in the Modern World.* Translated by Alan Braley. University Park: Pennsylvania State University Press, 1994.

Kierkegaard, Søren. *Either/Or.* 2 vols. Translated by Howard H. Hong and Edna H. Hong. Princeton: Princeton University Press, 1987.

King, John Owen III. *The Iron of Melancholy.* Middletown, Conn.: Wesleyan University Press, 1983.

Klein, Melanie. *The Writings of Melanie Klein.* 4 vols. Edited by R. E. Money-Kyrle. New York: Free Press, 1964–75.

Koselleck, Reinhart. *Futures Past: On the Semantics of Historical Time.* Translated by Keith Tribe. Cambridge: MIT Press, 1985.

Kraepelin, Emil. "Über Erinnerungsfälschungen." *Archiv für Psychiatrie* 17 (1887): 830–43; and 18 (1888): 199–239, 395–436..

Krell, David Farrell. *Of Memory, Reminiscence, and Writing.* Bloomington: Indiana University Press, 1990.

Krieger, Leonard. *The Meaning of History.* Chicago: University of Chicago Press, 1977.

Kubler, George. *The Shape of Time: Remarks on the History of Things.* New Haven: Yale University Press, 1962.

Kugelmass, Jack. "Mission to the Past: Poland in Contemporary Jewish Thought." In *Tense Past: Cultural Essays in Trauma and Memory,* edited by Paul Antze and Michael Lambek. New York: Routledge, 1996.

——, ed. *Going Home: How Jews Invented Their Old Country.* Evanston, Ill.: Northwestern University Press, 1994.

Kuhn, Thomas S. *The Structure of Scientific Revolutions.* Chicago: University of Chicago Press, 1962.

Kümmel, Friedrich. *Über der Begriff der Zeit.* Tübingen: Niemeyer Verlag, 1962.

La Grassiere, Raoul de. *De la nostalgie et des instincts contraire comme facteurs psychologiques et sociaux.* Paris: M. Giard & E. Brière, 1911.

Langer, Lawrence. *Holocaust Testimonies: The Ruins of Memory.* New Haven: Yale University Press, 1991.

Lasson, Adolf. *Das Gedächtnis.* Berlin: R. Gaertners Verlagsbuchhandlung, 1894.

Lavelle, Louis. *The Dilemma of Narcissus.* Translated by W. T. Gairdner. London: Allen & Unwin, 1973.

Lears, T. J. Jackson. *No Place of Grace: Antimodernism and the Transformation of American Culture, 1880–1920.* New York: Pantheon, 1981.

Le Corbusier. *The City of Tomorrow.* Translated by Frederick Etchells. Cambridge: MIT Press, 1971.

Le Goff, Jacques. *History and Memory.* Translated by Steven Rendall and Elizabeth Claman. New York: Columbia University Press, 1992.

Lewis, Helena. *The Politics of Surrealism.* New York: Paragon House, 1988.

Lewis, R. W. B. *The American Adam: Innocence, Tragedy, and Tradition in the Nineteenth Century.* Chicago: University of Chicago Press, 1955.

Leys, Ruth. "Traumatic Cures: Shell Shock, Janet, and the Question of Memory." In

Tense Past: Cultural Essays in Trauma and Memory, edited by Paul Antze and Michael Lambek. New York: Routledge, 1996.

Leyser, Karl. "The German Aristocracy from the Ninth to the Early Twelfth Century." *Past and Present* 41 (1968): 25–53.

Lifton, Robert J. *The Protean Self: Human Resilience in an Age of Fragmentation.* New York: Basic Books, 1993.

Lincoln, Bruce. *Death, War, and Sacrifice: Studies in Ideology and Practice.* Chicago: University of Chicago Press, 1991.

Lowenthal, David, and Marcus Binney, eds. *Our Past before Us.* London: Temple Smith, 1981.

Lowenthal, David. *The Past Is a Foreign Country.* Cambridge: Cambridge University Press, 1985.

——. *Possessed by the Past: The Heritage Crusade and the Spoils of History.* New York: Free Press, 1996.

Lübbe, Hermann. *Die Aufdringlichkeit der Geschichte.* Graz, Vienna, Cologne: Verlag Styria, 1989.

Lumley, Robert, ed. *The Museum Time-Machine.* New York: Routledge, 1988.

Lyotard, Jean-François. *Des dispositifs pulsionnels.* Paris: Christian Bourgeois Éditeur, 1980.

Martindale, Jane. "The French Aristocracy in the Early Middle Ages: A Reappraisal." *Past and Present* 75 (1977): 5–45.

Maslow, Abraham. "The Creative Attitude." In *Explorations in Creativity,* edited by R. L. Mooney and Taher A. Razik. New York: Harper and Row, 1967.

Matsuda, Matt K. *The Memory of the Modern.* New York: Oxford University Press, 1996.

McCole, John. *Walter Benjamin and the Antinomies of Tradition.* Ithaca, N.Y.: Cornell University Press, 1993.

Merleau-Ponty, Maurice. *The Structure of Behavior.* Translated by Alden L. Fisher. Boston: Beacon Press, 1963.

Merridale, Catherine. "Death and Memory in Modern Russia." *History Workshop Journal* 42 (1996): 1–18.

Miller, David LeRoy. *The New Polytheism: Rebirth of the Gods and Goddesses.* Dallas: Spring Publications, 1981.

Mills, Nicholaus. "Culture in an Age of Money." *Dissent* 37 (1990): 11–17.

Minkowski, Eugène. *Lived Time.* Translated by Nancy Metzel. Evanston, Ill.: Northwestern University Press, 1970.

Mongin, Olivier. "Une mémoire sans histoire? Vers une autre relation à l'histoire." *Esprit* 190 (1993): 102–13.

Montaigne, Michel de. "On Liars." In *Essays,* translated by J. M. Cohen. Baltimore: Penguin, 1961.

Morris, Herbert. *On Guilt and Innocence: Essays in Legal Philosophy and Moral Psychology.* Berkeley: University of California Press, 1976.

Mosse, George L. *The Nationalization of the Masses: Political Symbolism and Mass Movements in Germany from the Napoleonic Wars to the Third Reich.* New York: Howard Fertig, 1975.

Namer, Gérard. *La commémoration en France de 1945 à nos jours.* Paris: Éditions L'Harmattan, 1987.

Natopoulos, J. A. "Mnemosyne in Oral Tradition." *Transactions and Proceedings of the American Philological Association* 69 (1938): 465–93.

Neisser, Ulric, and Eugene Winograd, eds. *Remembering Reconsidered: Ecological and Traditional Approaches to the Study of Memory.* Cambridge: Cambridge University Press, 1988.

Nietzsche, Friedrich. *On the Advantage and Disadvantage of History for Life.* Translated by Peter Preuss. Indianapolis, Ind.: Hackett, 1980.

——. *On the Genealogy of Morals.* Translated by Walter Kaufmann. New York: Vintage, 1969.

——. *The Portable Nietzsche.* Edited and translated by Walter Kaufmann. New York: Viking, 1962.

——. *The Will to Power.* Translated by Walter Kaufmann and R. J. Hollingdale and edited by Walter Kaufmann. New York: Vintage, 1968.

Nipperdey, Thomas. "Nationalidee und Nationaldenkmal im 19. Jahrhundert." *Historische Zeitschrift* 206, no. 3 (1968): 529–85.

Nogué, J. "Le problème de la mémoire historique de la société sur la réminiscence." *Revue Philosophique de la France et l'Étranger* 99 (1925): 389–424.

Nora, Pierre. "Between Memory and History: *Les Lieux de Mémoire.*" *Representations* 26 (1989): 7–25.

——, ed. *Realms of Memory: The Construction of the French Past.* Vol. 1. Translated by Arthur Goldhammer and edited by Lawrence D. Kritzman. New York: Columbia University Press, 1996.

Ochse, R. *Before the Gates of Excellence: The Determinants of Creative Genius.* Cambridge: Cambridge University Press, 1990.

Oexle, Otto Gerhard. "Liturgische Memoria und historische Erinnerung. Zur Frage nach dem Gruppenbewusstsein und dem Wissen der eigenen Geschichte in der mittelalterlichen Gilden." In *Tradition als historische Kraft: Interdisziplinäre Forschungen zur Geschichte des früheren Mittelalters,* edited by Norbert Kamp and Joachim Wollasch. Berlin: Walter de Gruyter, 1982.

——. "Memoria und Memorialbild." In *Memoria: Der geschichtliche Zeugniswert des liturgischen Gedenkens im Mittelalter,* edited by Karl Schmid and Joachim Wollasch. Munich: Wilhelm Fink Verlag, 1984.

——. "Memoria und Memorialüberlieferung im frühen Mittelalter." *Frühmittelalterliche Studien* 10 (1976): 70–95.

——, ed. *Memoria als Kultur.* Göttingen: Vandenhoeck and Ruprecht, 1995.

Ogilvy, James. *Many-Dimensional Man.* New York: Oxford University Press, 1977.

Ozouf, Mona. *Festivals and the French Revolution.* Translated by Alan Sheridan. Cambridge: Harvard University Press, 1988.

Pascal, Blaise. *Pensées.* Edited by Philippe Selliers. Paris: Mercure de France, 1976.

Paulhan, Frédéric. *La fonction de la mémoire et la souvenir affectif.* Paris: Félix Alcan, 1904.

Peck, M. Scott. *The Road Less Traveled.* New York: Simon and Schuster, 1978.

Péguy, Charles. *Un poète l'a dit.* Paris: Gallimard, 1953.

Pick, A. "Zur Causistik der Erinnerungsfälschungen." *Archiv für Psychiatrie* 6 (1876): 568–74.

Piéron, Henri. *L'évolution de la mémoire.* Paris: Flammarion, 1910.

Plagemann, Volker. "Bismarck-Denkmäler." In *Denkmäler in 19. Jahrhundert: Deutung und Kritik,* edited by Ernst Mittag and Volker Plagemann. Munich: Prestel-Verlag, 1972.

Plato. *The Collected Dialogues of Plato.* Edited by Edith Hamilton and Huntington Cairns. Princeton: Princeton University Press, 1973.

Plotinus. *The Enneads.* Translated by Stephen MacKenna. London: Faber and Faber, 1962.

Poulet, Georges. *Studies in Human Time.* Translated by Elliott Coleman. New York: Harper and Row, 1959.

Prentice, Richard. *Tourism and Heritage Attractions.* London: Routledge, 1993.

Proust, Marcel. *Pastiches et mélanges.* Paris: Éditions de la Nouvelle Revue Français, 1919.

——. *Remembrance of Things Past.* 2 vols. Translated by C. K. Scott Moncrieff and Frederick A. Blossom. New York: Random House, 1934.

Rajchman, John. "The Postmodern Museum." *Art in America* 73, no. 10 (1985): 110–17, 171.

Ranschburg, Paul. *Das kranke Gedächtnis.* Leipzig: J. A. Barth Verlag, 1911.

Rauch, Angelika. "The Broken Vessel of Tradition." *Representations* 53 (1996): 74–96.

Rawitz, Bernhard. "Über das Vergessen." *Archiv für systematische Philosophie* 20 (1914): 265–89.

Rearick, Charles. "Festivals in Modern France: The Experience of the Third Republic." *Journal of Contemporary History* 12, no. 3 (1977): 435–60.

Ribot, Théodule. *Diseases of Memory.* Translated by William Huntington Smith. New York: D. Appleton, 1890.

Rilke, Rainer Maria. *Duino Elegies.* Translated by J. B. Leishman and Stephen Spender. New York: W. W. Norton, 1963.

Robinson, Judith. "Valéry's View of Mental Creation." *Yale French Studies* 44 (1970): 3–18.

Rogers, Carl R. *On Becoming a Person: A Therapist's View of Psychotherapy.* Boston: Houghton Mifflin, 1961.

——. *A Way of Being.* Boston: Houghton Mifflin, 1980.

Rosenfield, Israel. *The Invention of Memory: A New View of the Brain.* New York: Basic Books, 1988.

Roskies, David G. *Against the Apocalypse: Responses to Catastrophe in Modern Jewish Culture.* Cambridge: Harvard University Press, 1984.

Roth, Michael S. "Hysterical Remembering." *Modernism/modernity* 3, no. 2 (1996): 1–30.

——. "Remembering Forgetting: *Maladies de la Mémoire* in Nineteenth-Century France." *Representations* 26 (1989): 49–68.

Rousso, Henry. *The Vichy Syndrome: History and Memory in France since 1944.* Translated by Arthur Goldhammer. Cambridge: Harvard University Press, 1991.

Samuel, Raphael. *Theatres of Memory.* London: Verso, 1994.

Schachtel, Ernest G. *Metamorphosis: On the Development of Affect, Perception, Attention, and Memory*. New York: Basic Books, 1959.

Scheler, Max. "The Meaning of Suffering." In *Max Scheler, 1874–1929: Centennial Essays*, edited by Manfred S. Frings. The Hague: Nijhoff, 1974.

———. *Ressentiment*. Translated by Lewis B. Coser and William W. Holdheim. Milwaukee, Wisc.: Marquette University Press, 1994.

Schwer, Wilhelm. *Stand und Ständeordnung im Weltbild des Mittelalters*. Paderhorn: Schöningh Verlag, 1934.

Scullard, H. H. *Festivals and Ceremonies of the Roman Republic*. Ithaca, N.Y.: Cornell University Press, 1981.

Shafer, Boyd. "When Patriotism Became Popular: A Study of the Festivals of Federation in France in 1790." *The Historian* 5, no. 2 (1943): 77–96.

Shattuck, Roger. *The Innocent Eye: On Modern Literature and the Arts*. New York: Farrar, Straus and Giroux, 1984.

Simmel, Georg. "Faithfulness and Gratitude." In *The Sociology of Georg Simmel*, translated and edited by Kurt H. Wolff. New York: Free Press, 1950.

Simondon, Michelle. *La mémoire et l'oubli dans la pensée grecque jusqu'à la fin du Ve siècle avant J.-C.* Paris: Société d'Édition "Les Belles Lettres," 1982.

Skinner, B. F. *Beyond Freedom and Dignity*. New York: Knopf, 1971.

Sölle, Dorothee. "Thou Shalt Have No Other Jeans before Me." In *Observations on "The Spiritual Situation of the Age*," edited by Jürgen Habermas and translated by Andrew Buchwalter. Cambridge: MIT Press, 1984.

Sophocles. *Antigone*. In *The Three Theban Plays*, translated by Robert Fagles. New York: Penguin, 1984.

Stambolian, George. *Marcel Proust and the Creative Encounter*. Chicago: University of Chicago Press, 1972.

Stern, William. "Personalistik der Erinnerung." *Zeitschrift für Psychologie und Physiologie der Sinnesorgane* 118 (1930): 350–81.

Sternberg, Robert J., ed. *The Nature of Creativity: Contemporary Psychological Perspectives*. Cambridge: Cambridge University Press, 1988.

Strong, Ray. *Art and Power: Renaissance Festivals, 1450–1650*. Berkeley: University of California Press, 1984.

Tacitus. *The Agricola and the Germania*. Translated by H. Mattingly and revised by S. A. Handford. London: Penguin, 1970.

Tafuri, Manfredo. *Theories and History of Architecture*. Translated by Giorgio Verrecchia. New York: Harper and Row, 1980.

Tatarkiewicz, Władysław. "Creativity: History of the Concept." *Dialectics and Humanism* 4, no. 3 (1977): 48–65.

Terdiman, Richard. "Deconstructing Memory: On Representing the Past and Theorizing Culture in France since the Revolution." *diacritics* 15, no. 4 (1985): 13–36.

———. *Present Past: Modernity and the Memory Crisis*. Ithaca, N.Y.: Cornell University Press, 1993.

Thelen, David. "Memory in American History." *Journal of American History* 75, no. 4 (1989): 1119–29.

Théofilakis, Élie. *Modernes et Après? "Les Immatériaux*." Paris: Éditions autrement, 1985.

Thompson, Diane Oenning. *The Brothers Karamazov and the Poetics of Memory.* Cambridge: Cambridge University Press, 1991.

Todorov, Tzvetan. *Les abus de la mémoire.* Paris: Arléa, 1995.

Tumarkin, Nina. *The Living and the Dead: The Rise and Fall of the Cult of World War II in Russia.* New York: Basic Books, 1994.

——. "Myth and Memory in Soviet Society." *Society* 24, no. 6 (1987): 69–72.

Turkle, Sherry. *Life on the Screen: Identity in the Age of the Internet.* New York: Simon and Schuster, 1995.

Vernant, Jean Pierre. *Myth and Thought among the Greeks.* London: Routledge and Kegan Paul, 1983.

Vondung, Klaus. *Magie und Manipulation: Ideologischer Kult und politische Religion des Nationalsozialismus.* Göttingen: Vanderboeck and Ruprecht, 1971.

Watson, John B. *Behavior: An Introduction to Comparative Psychology.* New York: Henry Holt, 1914.

Weber, Eugen, ed. *Movements, Currents, Trends: Aspects of European Thought in the Nineteenth and Twentieth Centuries.* Lexington, Mass.: D.C. Heath, 1992.

——. *Peasants into Frenchmen: The Modernization of Rural France, 1870–1914.* Stanford: Stanford University Press, 1976.

Whitney, Charles. *Francis Bacon and Modernity.* New Haven: Yale University Press, 1986.

Wille, Ludwig. *Über die psycho-physiologischen und pathologischen Beziehung des Gedächtnisses.* Basel: F. Reinhardt Verlag, 1901.

Williams, Raymond. *Marxism and Literature.* Oxford: Oxford University Press, 1977.

Wittkower, Rudolf, and Margot Wittkower. *Born under Saturn.* New York: Random House, 1963.

Wohlfarth, Irving. "On the Messianic Structure of Walter Benjamin's Last Reflections." *Glyph* 3 (1978): 148–212.

Wolff, Kurt. *Surrender and Catch.* Boston: D. Reidel, 1976.

Wolin, Sheldon. *The Presence of the Past: Essays on the State and the Constitution.* Baltimore: Johns Hopkins University Press, 1989.

Wunberg, Gotthart. "Mnemosyne. Literatur unter den Bedingungen der Moderne: ihre technik- und sozialgeschichtliche Begründung." In *Mnemosyne: Formen und Funktionen der kulturellen Erinnerung,* edited by Aleida Assmann and Dietrich Harth. Frankfurt: Fischer Taschenbuch Verlag, 1991.

Yates, Frances A. *The Art of Memory.* Chicago: University of Chicago Press, 1966.

Yerushalmi, Yosef Hayim. *Zakhor: Jewish History and Jewish Memory.* New York: Schocken, 1989.

Zeldin, Theodore. *An Intimate History of Humanity.* New York: HarperCollins, 1994.

Zonabend, Françoise. *The Enduring Memory: Time and History in a French Village.* Translated by Anthony Forster. Manchester: Manchester University Press, 1980.

Index

Adorno, Theodor Wiesengrund, 127, 141, 151, 160, 178
The Advancement of Learning (Bacon), 98
Aeneas, 16–17
Aeneid (Virgil), 16
Africanus, Julius, 101
Albertus Magnus, Saint, 157
anamnesis, 29, 51, 92, 138. *See also* Plato
Anthony, Saint, 29
Antigone, 15–16
Aquinas, Saint Thomas, 27, 28, 157
archetypes (Jung), 78, 165–66
Aristotle, 3, 28, 34
Augustine, Saint, 17–18, 64, 140
Auschwitz, 129, 176

Bacon, Francis, 98
Bartlett, Frederic, 83, 84
Baudelaire, Charles, 144–48
Baudrillard, Jean, 149
Beatrice (Portinari), 18–19, 156
Becker, Carl, 106, 107
Behaviorism, 158
Benedict, Saint, 52
Benjamin, Walter, 34, 40, 45–47, 48, 50, 144, 178; on *Erlebnis* vs. *Erfahrung,* 46–47
Bergson, Henri, 35, 40, 42–50; on "independent recollections," 42–45; on "motor mechanisms," 42–43; on "pure memory," 43; on "voluntary recollections," 44–45
Binswanger, Ludwig, 23

Bloch, Ernst, 178
Bloch, Marc, 95
Blondel, Charles, 81
Britain, memory in, 108
The Brothers Karamazov (Dostoevsky), 164
Brown, Norman O., 163
Burke, Edmund, 13

Les cadres sociaux de la mémoire (Halbwachs), 81, 112
Calypso, 14
capitalism, 30, 99, 118, 169–70, 178
Carruthers, Mary, 51
Catholic Church, 95, 117, 119, 123, 173
Cervantes, Miguel de, 98
Chastellux, Marquis de, 101–2
Cicero, 157
Circe, 156
Coleridge, Samuel Taylor, 58
Condorcet, Marquis de, 102
Confessions (Augustine), 17–18, 64, 140
conscience collective (Durkheim), 78, 165
constructivism (Russian), 104
Council of Trent, 173
Courtney, Leonard, 102
Covenant (Jewish), 89–91
Creon, 15–16
criticism, social, 141, 148–53; types of, 150
Critique of Judgment (Kant), 58

dadaism, 104
Daniel, 101
Dante (Alighieri), 18–19, 156

Data of Ethics (Spencer), 34
Debord, Guy, 132, 177
The Decline and Fall of the Roman Empire (Gibbon), 56
Descartes, René, 98, 99
Dido, 16–17
Discourse on Method, 98
The Divine Comedy (Dante), 19
Dostoevsky, Fyodor, 164
Duby, Georges, 79
Duino Elegies (Rilke), 146–47
Dürer, Albrecht, 159
Durkheim, Émile, 78, 84, 116, 165, 172

Ebbinghaus, Hermann, 13, 31, 81
Either/Or (Kierkegaard), 152
Eliade, Mircea, 55, 88
Enneads (Plotinus), 51
Erikson, Erik, 64–65
L'evolution de la mémoire (Piéron)
exempla, 94–95
Existentialism, 137

"false memory syndrome," 32, 157
Fêtes de la Féderation, 121
Ficino, Marsilio, 37
Five Lectures on Psycho-Analysis (Freud), 40
forgetter, characteristics of as a type, 23–24, 27–30, 39, 66–69, 74, 135
forgetting: benefits of, 15–16, 31–34, 35, 36, 39, 40–42, 51–55, 65–69, 97–104, 134, 135, 138, 139, 140–41, 149, 152; and concept of self, 2–3, 35–36, 54–55, 63–69, 72–74, 135, 164–65; and creativity, 55–59, 70–71, 162; drawbacks of, 13, 16–17, 51, 55, 87–97, 135, 138, 141–53, 177; and experience of the present, 54, 57, 70, 140; and freedom, 3, 53, 65–69, 135; and happiness, 54, 55, 59–63, 71–72, 163
France, memory in, 108, 124
Francis of Assisi, Saint, 29
Frankfurt School, 160
French Revolution Bicentennial (1989), 176
Freud, Sigmund, 32, 35, 40–42, 47, 49, 50, 59, 60, 103, 138, 160, 162

Gergen, Kenneth, 138
Germany, memory in, 108, 128–30, 176
Gibbon, Edward, 56
gnosticism, 51
Goethe, Johann Wolfgang von, 63, 73
Goude, Jean-Paul, 176
Gourmont, Remy de, 57
The Great Instauration (Bacon), 99
Great Patriotic War (USSR), 175
Gregory I, Pope, 52
Groningen, B. A. van, 92
Gui, Bernardo, 29
Guillon, Albert, 158
Gunpowder Plot (1605), 120

Habermas, Jürgen, 129, 176
habit. *See* memory: and habit
Halbwachs, Maurice, 81–84, 112–13, 115, 123, 167, 171
Haussmann, Baron Georges Eugène, 145
Heath, Stephen, 123
Hegel, Georg Wilhelm Friedrich, 26, 71, 149, 179
Heidegger, Martin, 127, 135, 160
Heimweh (homesickness), 20–21
Helmholtz, Hermann, 31
Hesiod, 100
Hillman, James, 68–69
historical consciousness, 106–7
historic preservation, 105, 171
Historikerstreit (Historian's dispute), 128–30
Hobsbawm, Eric, 134
Hofer, Johannes, 20–21
Holocaust, 60–62, 109
Holocaust Testimonies (Langer), 61, 109
Homer, 14, 100
Horkheimer, Max, 142
hysteria, 40–41

imagination, 30, 32, 57–58
Industrial Revolution, 102

Jäckel, Eberhard, 129
Jahweh, 89–91, 150
James, William, 32, 34, 158
Jameson, Frederic, 113

Janet, Pierre, 31, 81, 162
Jung, Carl Gustav, 78, 84, 116, 165–66

Kant, Immanuel, 58, 140
Kierkegaard, Søren, 71, 139, 152–53
Kosovo Polje, Battle of (1389), 124–25

La Grassiere, Roaul de, 106
Langer, Lawrence L., 61
late modernity, definition of, 155
Lavelle, Louis, 54
Lebensphilosophie, 33
Le Corbusier (pseud. Charles Édouard
    Jeanneret), 103
Le Goff, Jacques, 116
Lifton, Robert J., 67–68, 138
Lived Time (Minkowski), 38
Lowenthal, David, 105
Luther, Martin, 97
Lyotard, Jean-François, 109, 114
Lyrical Ballads (Wordsworth), 56

Machiavelli, Niccolò, 94
Mannheim, Karl, 178
Marcuse, Herbert, 122, 160
Marinetti, Filippo, 104
Marx, Karl, 53, 99, 178
mass media. *See* memory: and mass
    media.
Matter and Memory (Bergson), 42, 43,
    45
Maudsley, Henry, 31
melancholia, 37–38, 40
Melanchton, 159
mémorial (Pascal), 20
memory: accuracy of, 3–5, 11, 31–34, 155;
    in ancient Greece, 27–30, 55–56, 91–93;
    in archaic period, 1–2, 55, 79, 87–89,
    166, 168; assault on, 3, 31–39, 52, 97–
    104, 110–14; benefits of, 1–2, 12–13, 41–
    42, 72, 87–97, 104–6, 135–38, 139, 141–
    53, 164; and character, 2, 27–28, 64–65;
    and Christianity, 26–30, 95–97, 117,
    119, 126, 157, 173; and concept of self,
    2–3, 12–13, 17–18, 21–22, 49, 63–69, 72–
    74, 140, 164–65, 178–79; constructed
    nature of, 3–4, 32, 155, 157; content of,
    3–4, 11, 22, 25, 29–30, 46, 77; and cre-
    ativity, 29–30, 47, 50, 55–59, 69–71,
    140, 141, 143–48, 160, 161, 162; and the
    dead, 2, 15, 26, 89, 93, 157, 168; disor-
    ders of, 32–42, 44; drawbacks of, 4–5,
    31, 32–34, 38–39, 52–55, 97–104, 135,
    137–38, 151–52; and ethics, 26–27, 43,
    177; excesses of, 5, 23–24; in families,
    82, 112–13; forces undermining, 30–
    34, 97–104, 109, 110–14, 134, 147; and
    habit, 2–3, 12, 27–30, 34–36, 42–43, 53,
    135, 158, 160; and happiness, 42, 59–63,
    71–72, 79; and history, 106–7, 171; of
    ideals, 18–20, 29; and images, 3–4, 43,
    56, 58; Jewish, 60–62, 89–91, 109, 131,
    149, 168; and mass media, 73, 109, 118–
    19, 122–28, 131–32; and Middle Ages,
    19, 26–30, 56, 79, 95–97, 117, 119, 157,
    163; in the modern city, 102–3, 144–46;
    in museums, 110–12, 172; and nostal-
    gia, 105–6, 170, 177; pain caused by,
    59–63, 71–72, 79, 137–38, 162, 163; per-
    sistence today, 107–9; and piety, 26,
    30, 93, 157; and popular culture, 118,
    122–26, 127–28, 129, 132, 134; and post-
    modernism, 113–14; and prudence,
    27, 157; and Roman world, 26–27, 56,
    93–95, 157, 168; scientific study of, 13,
    31–34; and social criticism, 141, 148–
    53; social uses of, 1–2, 77–81, 87–97,
    104–6, 116–17, 166–67, 174–75; and the
    state, 117, 119–22; storage of, 3–4, 155,
    162; "truth value" of, 149–53; types of,
    11–22
Mephistopheles, 177–78
Minkowski, Eugène, 38
Mirabeau, Comte de, 39
Mnemosyne, 30, 56, 92
le mode rétro, 108, 114
modernism, 63, 104, 113–14
Mommsen, Hans, 129
monasticism, 52, 163
Mondrian, Piet, 104
Montaigne, Michel de, 98
Moscow Purges, 175
Müller, Georg Elias, 81
museums. *See* memory: in museums

National Socialism, 121, 129, 149, 167, 176
Nazi-Soviet Pact (1939), 175
Nietzsche, Friedrich, 6, 38, 39, 54, 63, 73–74, 79, 133, 135, 139, 151, 165
Nolte, Ernst, 128, 129
noncontemporaneity, 141–53
Nora, Pierre, 107, 114

Odysseus, 14–15, 16, 21, 156
Odyssey, 14
Old Testament, 90, 150
On the Advantage and Disadvantage of History for Life (Nietzsche), 6, 73–74, 135

Pascal, Blaise, 19–20
Peck, M. Scott, 163
Péguy, Charles, 126, 150
Piéron, Henri, 58
piety (*pietas*). *See* memory: and piety
Pinder, Wilhelm, 178
Plato, 3, 29, 51, 58, 92, 138. See also *anamnesis*
Plotinus, 51
Poland, memory in, 130–31, 177
postmodernism, 63, 66, 108, 113–14, 155, 165, 173
Poulet, Georges, 50
Principles of Psychology (James), 34, 158
progress, theory of, 101–2, 170
Proust, Marcel, 21–22, 35–36, 40, 47–50, 67, 140, 160, 163, 178–79; on contents of memory, 47–50; on "intermittent selves," 67; on "involuntary memories," 35–36, 47–50, 163; on memory and creativity, 47, 49–50; on "voluntary memories," 47, 48
prudence (*prudentia*). *See* memory: and prudence
Pythagoras, 28

Quixote, Don, 31, 98, 101

Ranke, Leopold von, 106
Raphael, 159
rationalism, 99
Reformation, 96–97, 117

remember, characteristics of as a type, 23–24, 25–30
Remembering: A Study in Experimental and Social Psychology (Bartlett), 83
Remembrance of Things Past (Proust), 21–22, 47, 48, 140, 160, 178–79
Renaissance, 37, 96–97
resentment, 38–39
Ribot, Théodule, 31, 33, 158
Rilke, Rainer Maria, 146–48, 178–79
Rimbaud, Arthur, 67–68, 163
rituals, 1, 109, 119, 166, 172
Rogers, Carl, 66
Romanticism, 27, 37, 58, 105
Russian Revolution (1917), 174–75

Schachtel, Ernest, 83–84, 136–37
Scheler, Max, 38
schemata (memory frames), 4, 80–86, 115, 116–32, 133, 136, 167; religious, 117–20, 122, 124, 126, 127, 131; political, 117–22, 124–25, 126, 128–30, 175–76; and mass media, 118–19, 122–32, 175–76
Schulze, Hagen, 128
Serbia, memory in, 124–25
Seurat, Georges, 57
Simmel, Georg, 72
Sölle, Dorothee, 179
Sophocles, 15
Soviet Union, memory in, 122, 126, 174–75
Spanish Armada, 120
Spencer, Herbert, 34
Stalin, Josef, 174–75
Statue of Liberty Centennial (1986), 176
Studies in Hysteria (Freud and Breuer), 41
Stürmer, Michael, 128, 129

Tacitus, 87
Talleyrand, Prince Charles Maurice, 120
television, 122–27, 131, 172
tradition, 1, 53, 77, 93, 96, 127, 142, 143, 150
Treatise on the Mass (Luther), 97
Turkle, Sherry, 164–65

United States, memory in, 83, 108, 121, 152, 174, 176

Vallès, Jules, 104
Vasari, Giorgio, 159
Vernant, Jean Pierre, 92
Virgil, 16–17
vitalism, 33
Vita Nuova (Dante), 19

Warburg, Aby, 108
Watson, John B., 158
West, Ellen, case study of (Binswanger), 23
Wolin, Sheldon, 114
Wordsworth, William, 56
Wundt, Wilhelm, 81

Yerushalmi, Yosef, 107